REINVENTING
THE CFO

REINVENTING THE CFO

HOW FINANCIAL MANAGERS CAN TRANSFORM THEIR ROLES AND ADD GREATER VALUE

JEREMY HOPE

HARVARD BUSINESS SCHOOL PRESS

Boston, Massachusetts

No part of this publication may be reproduced, stored in or introduced into
a retrieval system, or transmitted, in any form, or by any means (electronic,
mechanical, photocopying, recording, or otherwise), without the prior
permission of the publisher. Requests for permission should be directed to
permissions@hbsp.harvard.edu, or mailed to Permissions, Harvard Business
School Publishing, 60 Harvard Way, Boston, Massachusetts 02163.

978-1-59139-945-2 (ISBN 13)

Library of Congress Cataloging-in-Publication Data
    Hope, Jeremy.
    Reinventing the CFO : how financial managers can transform their roles
and add greater value / Jeremy Hope.
        p.   cm.
    ISBN 1-59139-945-9
    1. Chief financial officers. 2. Corporations—Finance. I. Title.
    HG4027.35.H67 2006
    658.15—dc22

                                                          2005030853

The paper used in this publication meets the minimum requirements of the
American National Standard for Information Sciences—Permanence of Paper
for Printed Library Materials, ANSI Z39.48-1992.

*This book is dedicated
to Dot, Ben, Vicky,
and Oliver.*

CONTENTS

PREFACE

Since cofounding the Beyond Budgeting Round Table (BBRT) in 1997 with colleagues Robin Fraser and Peter Bunce, I have visited many organizations that have successfully broken free from the annual performance trap set by fixed targets and annual budgets. Many of these organizations have seen a step change in performance as their managers learn to manage the business rather than the numbers. In 2003 Robin and I completed a book entitled *Beyond Budgeting* that included twelve principles that have since guided the actions of many organizations in their attempts to adopt this management model. These principles were primarily based on the philosophy of Dr. Jan Wallander and the management model he built at Swedish bank Svenska Handelsbanken in the 1970s.

Since we started the BBRT, many member companies have come and gone. Some were just curious, some made useful changes around the edges of their performance management systems, and some are on their way to adopting the whole set of beyond budgeting principles and radically changing their performance management systems and culture. Organizations such as American Express, Schneider Electric, Scottish Enterprise, Telecom New Zealand, UBS, Unilever, and the World Bank have all, to some degree or another, benefited from this knowledge and experience. These are organizations that joined our group and learned, for example, that just implanting a rolling forecast or a balanced scorecard into the existing budget-driven system would not, on its own, be sufficient. The old and the new processes need to join together in a seamless and coherent way.

While these messages resonate with business leaders, many CFOs have preferred to stick with what they know. But it wasn't until I talked to many of them that I fully realized the extent of their problems. They are overwhelmed with detail and complexity and constantly buffeted by external regulatory changes. They have had little time or energy to focus on improving their performance management systems. It is no wonder that many of them have used the latest offerings from IT vendors to tighten the coils of central control. That's one reason I wrote this book. I wanted to set out a vision for the CFO that would enable the finance team to take the initiative and not only build more adaptive systems with fewer targets and performance contracts, but also rescue managers from excessive detail, complexity, and micromanagement and enable them to focus on improving performance.

This book also addresses many questions about the performance of the finance operation that have been asked recently. "How do we lighten the workload and focus on the key issues?" "How do we help managers to respond more rapidly?" "How do we constantly match resources to the best investment opportunities?" "How do we improve performance measurement?" "How do we manage risk across the whole organization?" and "How do we become a world-class finance operation?" are some of the questions that CFOs are struggling with. The book also offers CFOs a more comprehensive guide to new thinking and practice across the whole spectrum of performance management.

The new vision for the CFO presented in this book does not follow conventional wisdom. It does not place management tools and IT systems at the center of performance improvement. Instead, its focus is on simplifying processes and making managers more accountable for business improvement. The aim is to give managers more time and freedom to make carefully crafted decisions. Finance managers are partners in that process, always on hand to provide the essential performance insights (while maintaining an independent view) that turn those decisions from average to excellent.

This book would not have been possible without the help and support of many people. These include colleagues at the Beyond Budgeting Round Table. My thanks go to Robin Fraser, Peter Bunce, Steve Player, and Niels Pflaeging. Other colleagues within the BBRT community have also given their support, and I would like to particularly thank Matthew Leitch and Chuck Horngren.

I've also been fortunate to interview a number of finance leaders who have transformed their finance operations. Their insights are the building blocks of this book. My sincere thanks go to: Marko Bogoievski, CFO, Telecom New Zealand; Gary Critten-den, CFO, American Express (United States); Lennart Francke, CFO, Svenska Handelsbanken (Sweden); Ken Lever, CFO, Tomkins PLC (United Kingdom); Tom Manley, CFO, Cognos Inc. (Canada); Steve Morlidge, Finance Change Leader, Unilever PLC (United Kingdom); Thierry Moulonguet, CFO, Renault (France); Jim Parke, CFO, GE Capital (United States); Carl Tsang, ex-CFO, Slim·Fast (United States); Glenn Uminger, General Manager, Toyota North America (United States); John Wilton, CFO, World Bank (United States); and Tom Woods, CFO, Canadian Imperial Bank of Commerce (Canada).

I would also like to thank Jacque Murphy at Harvard Business School Press. Without her constant support and guidance my ideas would not have been translated into this book.

I hope that the outcome of this book will be a less strident CFO who, along with the finance team he or she leads, adds real value to the organization not by chasing the shadows of shareholder value but by helping managers to adapt to change, providing insights into performance improvement, and accepting nothing less than the highest ethical standards.

—Jeremy Hope
Baildon, England
August 2005

INTRODUCTION

In the post-capitalist society it is safe to assume that anyone with any knowledge will have to acquire new knowledge every four or five years or else become obsolete.

—Peter F. Drucker, *Post-Capitalist Society*

TOO MANY CFOS have failed to heed Drucker's advice and keep their knowledge up-to-date. They remain prisoners of dysfunctional systems and mental models that were developed for a role that is fast becoming obsolete. Many spent their formative years working in accounting departments and had little contact with other people inside the organization. They focused on recording transactions, managing budgets, getting the accounts out on time, and preparing tax returns. They weren't expected to be part of the team running the business. And many operating people didn't seek their advice. CFOs were seen as unhelpful, always demanding answers to trivial questions about budget variances or expense claims. Now they are expected to be business generalists, risk management experts, and business intelligence sources. They are expected to provide instant replies to just about any question that the CEO asks about business performance. And they are expected to meet these new challenges with lower costs, which of course usually means fewer people.

CFOs are feeling these added pressures and leaving their jobs in droves. In a recent article in the *New York Times* entitled "Where Have All the Chief Financial Officers Gone?" one CFO encapsulated the feelings of many of his colleagues: "I got tired of spending years defending strategies I knew were flawed, of working with values that weren't my own, of being responsible to chief executives and boards that were under huge pressure to perform."[1] In the three years to November 2004, 225 CFOs of the *Fortune* 500 left their jobs.[2] This disaffection has also spread to their finance colleagues (a 2004 survey found that 34 percent of financial executives planned a career change in the next two years).[3] They are often working extended hours and weekends to keep up (the average working week in 2004 was fifty-three hours, compared with forty-nine hours two years earlier).[4] Sixty-two percent of finance executives indicated that they were under "great" or "very great" pressure at work, and 68 percent said they were under more pressure than two years earlier.[5] Sixty-three percent said that the strain was affecting their health. Around 40 percent blame regulatory rules and staff cuts for their newly dismal working lives.[6]

While finance jobs have been cut the workload has remained the same and, in some cases, has intensified. One of the problems is that new technology has complicated rather than simplified finance practices. Managers are overwhelmed with irrelevant data and spurious measures. Though most have invested in enterprise resource planning (ERP) systems—companywide (integrated) accounting and management information systems that handle all related transactions from taking a customer's order to collecting the cash— many have simply automated inefficient and ineffective processes. The potential gains have been lost. The truth is that the CFO's resources are stretched to breaking point. The finance function has been benchmarked to death in recent years (the average cost compared with revenue has halved over the past ten years). Two-thirds of their shrunken departments are fighting to keep their transaction processing systems afloat while implementing new systems.

Despite this doom and gloom picture, there are many shining examples of CFOs who have made a real difference to the success of their organizations. These CFOs (some of whom we will meet in this book) have built highly competent teams that satisfy the needs of their management colleagues in a consistent and uncomplicated way. While they are recognized as integral members of the strategic management team, they maintain a strong, independent view and oversee effective internal controls and risk management systems. But, perhaps above all, they have time to spend with their people and with important stakeholders, including nonexecutive directors and investment analysts.

Why the CFO Is Under Pressure

Before we can talk about "reinventing the CFO" and "transforming finance" we need to better understand the pressures bearing down on the CFO. They come from two directions. One is from extensive changes in the external environment such as the rise of new competitive success factors, a new regulatory environment, and the increasing demands from shareholders. The other is from the changing needs of hard-pressed managers inside the business, especially the demand for better information and support to cope with the challenges of a more competitive marketplace and changing customer needs.

The External Pressures

Until the 1980s, the world of the CFO hadn't changed much for decades. Success was seen in terms of balance sheets bristling with buildings, plant, inventories, and receivables underpinned by income statements showing a healthy return on capital. The annual planning process dictated what was made and sold and informed people what they had to achieve by when. It was assumed that knowledge was accumulated at, and best deployed from, the center. But this view of corporate success was to change radically as the balance of power shifted from producers to consumers and from aging directors to young talented managers. Ex-CEO of General Electric Jack Welch neatly encapsulated this changing climate when he said, "we had constructed over the years a management apparatus that was right for its time, the toast of the business schools. Divisions, strategic business units, groups, sectors, all were designed to make meticulous, calculated decisions and move them smoothly forward and upward. This system produced highly polished work. It was right for the 1970s, a growing handicap in the 1980s, and it would have been a ticket to the boneyard in the 1990s.[7] The boneyard is indeed where many stellar performers of the 1970s and 1980s found their resting place as they failed to adapt. Of the original thirty-six "excellent" companies listed in Peters and Waterman's 1982 book *In Search of Excellence*, only two (Wal-Mart and IBM) remained in the *Forbes* top 100 companies in 2002 based on similar criteria.[8]

NEW SUCCESS DRIVERS. Many CFOs now realize that business success is no longer driven by physical assets and financial capital but by intellectual assets and human capital. Whereas in the industrial age the primary constraints on growth were access to capital and distribution channels, the primary constraints in the information age are talented people and information systems. To succeed in today's marketplace, organizations need to respond rapidly to new threats and opportunities, attract and keep talented people, produce innovative products and strategies, continuously improve operational excellence, and attract and keep the right customers. The implications for performance management systems are far-reaching. CFOs need to rethink their planning, resource allocation and performance measurement systems to enable managers to focus on these new success drivers. Planning what to make and sell twelve to eighteen months in advance just doesn't make any sense when markets are changing rapidly and customers can switch loyalties at the click of a mouse. Managers need to know where they are right now (not seven days after the end of the month) and what the next six to twelve months looks like so that they can influence those outcomes. These are challenging demands for most CFOs.

A NEW REGULATORY ENVIRONMENT. In recent years a wave of corporate governance scandals has shaken the self-confident world of finance to its core. Like a financial tsunami, the wave first hit U.S. companies such as Enron, WorldCom, and Tyco; devastated global accounting firm Arthur Andersen; and spread around the world to damage a range of companies from Parmalat in Italy and HIH in Australia to Vivendi in France and Ahold in Holland. These problems have driven governments and regulators worldwide to act. The best known example is the Sarbanes-Oxley (SOX) legislation in the United States. It mandates that both CEOs and CFOs must personally certify quarterly and annual financial statements as well as take responsibility for their accuracy. It has forced CFOs to tighten their internal controls and reporting procedures to the point of recording and documenting just about every transaction and communication. And it demands that directors must disclose any material changes in their financial conditions or operations on a "rapid and current" basis (i.e., within two working days). These regulations have absorbed huge amounts of time and cost and invariably deflected the resources of the finance team from the pressing needs of business managers (though in most of my CFO interviews the view was that much of the SOX work was necessary).

Another regulatory burden has been the upsurge in standards/ pronouncements issued by accounting standards bodies. In particular, the switch from national to international financial reporting standards has absorbed the time of some of the brightest finance managers. Some of this is taken up by difficult consultations with (often unsympathetic) external investors as CFOs attempt to explain why the new rules have decimated reported profits but left the business fundamentals unchanged. Their message to investors is to look at cash flow instead of earnings per share, but in most cases it falls on deaf ears.

MORE DEMANDING SHAREHOLDERS. Shareholders used to be a fairly passive bunch, rarely turning up at annual meetings and almost never initiating motions. But shareholder activism has arrived with a vengeance. Not only are investors demanding more information about current and future performance but they are also more prepared to challenge board proposals at annual meetings. According to the Investor Responsibility Research Center, shareholders filed some 1,126 proposals with U.S. corporations in 2004 compared with around 800 in 2002. Finance executives are dismayed by this new wave of investor radicalism. In a recent survey, 53 percent indicated that they are spending more time with shareholders than ever before, yet only 11 percent believe that adopting these shareholder activists' recommendations will improve their ability to create value for those investors.[9] CFOs today need to be skilled communicators, especially when it comes to discussing the meaning of strategies and accounting results with analysts, investors, and financial journalists.

The Internal Pressures

A number of CEOs and their boardroom colleagues have been asking awkward questions about what finance does and how it adds value. Some are even asking, "While we need accounting do we really need accountants?" "Can't we buy in these services like cleaning or catering?" Replies such as "We are needed to prepare accounts," "We've always had a strong finance function," or "There are two hundred of us, so we must be adding value" are no longer sufficient answers.

CFOs have not taken these stinging criticisms lying down. Their aspirations for change were expressed in the 1997 book *CFO: Architect of the Corporation's Future*, written by the Price Waterhouse Finance and Cost Management Team. It used survey evidence to suggest that over the next three years, the costs of finance would be substantially reduced and that decision support would move from 10 percent to around 50 percent of the work of the finance operation.[10] Looking at these predictions with the benefit of considerable hindsight confirms that their first prediction has come true. Finance costs have reduced from around 3 percent of revenue to around 1 percent for average companies. But their second prediction has been a long way wide of the mark. In fact, decision support as a percentage of finance's work has hardly changed at all (it's still around 11 percent for average companies).

While most boards are happy enough that finance costs have been reduced, the rest of the organization is less than overwhelmed by the poor level of support it receives. The evidence of poor performance is extensive; indeed, finance has been subjected to more surveys and benchmarking studies than most functions over the past five years. Finance journals and consultants do regular surveys of the finance operation. While these surveys are not always as rigorous as they might be, they are so numerous and their results so similar that they paint a credible and consistent picture of poor performance. They show that there is too much detail and complexity, not enough time for decision support, inadequate forecasting capability, too little understanding of how to reduce costs, too many measures, and a lack of risk management expertise.

TOO MUCH DETAIL AND COMPLEXITY. The technology "bandwidth" is widening every year, and the resulting data flow throughout the organization is overwhelming managers' ability to make sense of it. Of 158 corporate executives surveyed in late 2003, half said that the amount of information available to their businesses had doubled or tripled since the previous year.[11] "Can't see the forest for the trees," "swamped with information," and "drowning in detail and thirsting for knowledge" are all regularly heard comments. And the problem has got worse since the introduction of Sarbanes-Oxley, which demands that organizations keep just about every document (including e-mails) that flows through the organization every day. According to one expert, between 10 and 30 percent of recorded data is inaccurate, inconsistent, incorrectly formatted, or entered in the wrong field, so one can only imagine what the storage and retrieval problems will be.[12]

The average large organization wrestles with ten different ledger systems, twelve different budgeting systems, and thirteen different reporting systems—in comparison, best-practice companies have standardized on a single platform.[13] And within these systems there are far too many accounts. One large U.K. company had over five thousand general ledger accounts, but when it analyzed the data flow it found that only 250 accounts had more than two entries in a year. The trouble is that each account is a building block in the budgeting and reporting system with consequences for further analysis and management workload. Part of the reason for this level of detail is that local managers don't want to be caught out if and when they are asked detailed questions. Too many boardroom members demand answers to trivial questions about, for example, why this quarter's telephone account was higher than budget when they should be more concerned with where the organization is heading and whether managers are taking the right actions to execute its strategies.

One of the key drivers of detail and complexity is the annual planning and budgeting process. For the typical company, this takes up to nine months, with four months spent on strategy and another five months spent on financial planning and budgeting.[14] A senior manager at a global carrier explained the problem: "At 475 pages and 3.5 kilograms in weight, our budgeting manual is a major cause of deforestation! There are thousands of budget centers and it takes nine months to put together, soaking up around 20 percent of management time (we estimate the annual cost at around €30 million to €35 million). It all amounts to a huge distortion of people's behavior and a complete waste of everyone's time."

There is a pervasive belief that greater detail leads to greater accuracy—the average company's plan has 372 line items.[15] This doesn't make sense. Finding and focusing on the right performance drivers (and there are only a few of them) is far more important than spending weeks and months preparing detailed budgets and forecasts. Mistaken assumptions at the bottom of the budgeting or forecasting pyramid can grow exponentially as they affect other assumptions higher up. The best finance functions spend 44 percent of their planning time on forecasting and action planning, compared with only 20 percent in average companies.[16] Detailed and complex planning and budgeting systems make it difficult for finance professionals and operating managers to focus on the key issues.

NOT ENOUGH TIME FOR DECISION SUPPORT. While the finance function has shrunk under the pressures of benchmarking, few CFOs have realized their aim of transferring resources from transaction processing (e.g.., accounts payable/receivable, travel and expense, fixed assets, credit, collections, customer billing, general accounting, external reporting, project accounting, cost accounting, cash management, tax accounting/reporting, and payroll) to decision support (e.g., cost analysis, business performance analysis, new business/pricing analysis, and strategic planning support).[17] Average finance operations spend 66 percent of their time on transaction processing and only 11 percent on decision support (compare this with 50 percent and 20 percent, respectively, for leading-edge finance operations).[18] And analysts at average companies spend 51 percent of their time just searching for data for standard reports, against just 13 percent of the time of analysts at world-class companies.[19] It is hardly surprising that only 37 percent of senior executives believe that their own finance department does a good job of decision support (54 percent said it was average and 9 percent said it was poor).[20] Part of the problem is that finance keeps adding new measures and reports without taking anything away. And analysis codes and reports remain in the system long after anyone can remember why they were needed in the first place.

One way to reduce routine work and create more time for decision support is through the effective use of technology. But finance has not taken advantage of this opportunity. Only 2 percent of systems are fully integrated and 69 percent partly integrated; 29 percent are not integrated at all (i.e., they are made up of multiple-legacy systems).[21] This means that a lot of time is spent rekeying in data. "You've got people customizing and formatting spreadsheets for the majority of the day rather than providing insights into business performance," notes Cody Chenault, finance practice leader at the Hackett Group.[22]

INADEQUATE FORECASTING CAPABILITY. Many CFOs are trying to focus less on annual budgeting and more on regular forecasting. But it takes an average of fifteen days to develop a forecast. At one global company there were seventy-five levels of review and consolidation; consequently, it took a huge amount of time and effort to produce a forecast. Such was the detail involved that it took one business unit alone 585 people days over eight weeks to produce a forecast that was immediately out-of-date. Not only do forecasts take too long, but their quality also leaves a lot to be desired.[23] According to a 2004 survey, only 21 percent of executives said that finance was any good at preparing forecasts (25 percent said they were hopeless).[24] The forecasting system is also too limited in outlook. In most cases, forecasts are geared to keeping on track to meet the target numbers rather than inform-ing strategic reviews that go beyond the next fiscal year-end.[25] Consolidated forecasts take too long and often involve too many spreadsheets with variable methodologies and algorithms.

TOO LITTLE UNDERSTANDING OF HOW TO REDUCE COSTS. Leading-edge companies have lower costs than their rivals. They spend less on finance than their average counterparts (0.56 percent versus 1.06 percent of revenue); they spend less on human re-sources per employee ($1,008 versus $2,299); and they spend less on information technology (IT) per user ($391 versus $661).[26] Some of the reasons are structural; for example, flattening the hierarchy and moving transaction processing to shared services units (or outsourcing it to a third party). Others are based on process improvements, making more effective use of technology and removing the "budget protection" mentality. Cost budgets have a lot to answer for. They set a ceiling for spending but they also set a floor below which no self-respecting manager will allow his or her resources to fall without a fight. They will justify every expense line item and make every argument as to why their busi-ness will suffer if resources are cut. And to support their claims, they will spend every cent whether justified or not. CFOs need to be more aware of the hidden costs inside their organizations—poor quality, unnecessary work, misaligned (or unnecessary in-centives), absenteeism, staff turnover, errors and rework within the transaction processing system, wrong acquisitions, and many more—that don't appear on budgets or profit and loss accounts.

TOO MANY MEASURES. The number of measures keeps growing. Companies report an average of 132 metrics to senior management every month (83 financial and 49 operational).[27] This is more than six times the number recommended by Kaplan and Norton for a balanced scorecard.[28] This measurement mania has been one of the primary factors why the majority of balanced scorecard implementations fail to realize their potential.[29] The average management report is not only far too long and complex (usually including thousands of data points) but managers typically use only a fraction of the information.[30] This complexity slows down month-end reporting and makes organizational change a nightmare for the finance department. For the average company, monthly close times *rose* from an average of 5.2 days in 2003 to 5.5 days in 2004. It takes a further six days to provide monthly reports—that's eleven days after the month-end.[31]

Managers are lost in a fog of measurement. Few measures provide useful information about what's happening now and where the business is heading—for the average company, 85 percent of measures are internal and 75 percent are based on lagging indicators.[32] Even fewer lead to action and change behavior—57 percent of companies still report all budget variances.[33] Another problem is that most measures focus on what can be easily measured (e.g., functions or activities) rather than what *should* be measured (e.g., customer value). An effective measure should help managers to understand and improve performance and to this extent should be an integral part of the work they do. Few measures pass this test. The real casualty is learning and improvement.

LACK OF RISK MANAGEMENT EXPERTISE. Only 19 percent of executives believe that their finance colleagues do a good job of managing risk.[34] Too much reliance is placed on keeping within budget guidelines and not enough support is focused on how risk and uncertainty affect decision making. Inappropriate stretch targets reinforced by financial incentives are often the cause of excessive levels of risk taking and unethical behavior as managers strive and strain to meet them. A divisional director whose compensation is loaded with short-term profit incentives is more likely to accept a high-risk opportunity with a payback within the fiscal year. A purchasing manager given a target of reducing costs is likely to order in bulk or pay suppliers late but has no responsibility for the poor quality of the products bought, the costs of high inventories, or the deteriorating relationships with suppliers. A pensions sales-person will sell those products that provide her with the highest commissions rather than those that fit the client's needs. These behavioral problems are not caused by mischievous managers, nor are they isolated examples. They are *systemic*. That's why the CFO needs to transform the whole system.

A New Vision for the CFO

I've spent the past twelve years talking to finance managers about how to improve their performance. With my colleagues at the Beyond Budgeting Round Table, I have spoken to hundreds of managers and written dozens of case studies about a wide range of organizations and across a variety of industries and countries. I have little doubt that there is a striking correlation between ex-cellent financial management practices and wider organizational performance—in a recent survey of European companies the top-ranking CFO and CEO came from the same company in fourteen out of thirty-one industry sectors.[35]

Part of the reason is the link between performance management processes and management behavior. Whenever I see management processes that are designed to control performance through a plethora of targets, budgets, incentives, and measures, I see bureau-cratic systems, uninspired leaders, and frustrated managers who are not trusted to make decisions. This usually points to an organ-ization with a poor-to-average long-term growth record. Con-versely, whenever I see management processes that are designed to

FIGURE I-1

Two visions for improving the finance operation

Vision A	Vision B
• Increase targets, measures, and controls	• Reduce targets, measures, and controls
• Improve financial and accounting expertise	• Improve business analysis skills
• Tighten top-down planning and control	• Enable local managers to respond to events
• Manage costs through tighter budgets	• Eliminate costs that add no value
• Measure to tighten accountability	• Measure to learn and improve
• Manage risk through better procedures	• Manage risk by raising competences

support local decision making within a framework of clear principles and values, and with measures designed to support learning and improvement, I see a lean head office with few directives, inspired leaders, and energetic managers who are trusted to make decisions based on continuously improving their performance. These organizations are usually at or near the top of their peer groups.

I also attend many conferences for finance executives and listen to their visions of improvement (invariably reinforced by consultants and IT vendors). These often include using the increasing power of IT systems to tighten top-down financial control (Vision A in figure I-1). IT vendors play to the audience by emphasizing fast drill-down capabilities and detailed analysis. Their systems can tell you how many blue pens were bought in the Mauritania office in the third week of February this year compared with last year. And their planning systems allow you to key in the desired profit figure and tell you how much of product A or B you need to make and sell.

It is a vision of control by detailed analysis and measurement, usually against a predetermined target or budget (one practitioner, the U.K. National Health Service, sets around 750 targets, of which 450 were added in one year alone!). It is rooted in the age-old (but dismal) economic theory that people are driven by self-interest and respond only to the "carrot-and-stick" style of management. It is a vision of cost reduction through economies of scale, either through acquisition and rationalization or through frequent reorganization. And it is a vision of "fixing" identified problems (e.g., using key performance indicators (KPIs) to fix the "measurement" problem or a rolling forecast to fix the "forecasting" problem) rather than seeing the whole interdependent performance management system itself as the problem. This vision comes from a mind-set that sees business performance improvement through the lens of managing results through accounting numbers. W. Edwards Deming once said that while we need good results, "management by results is not the way to get good results. It is action on outcome, as if the outcome came from a special cause. It is important to work on the causes of results—i.e., on the system."[36] Those who manage by results focus on the bottom-line target and consider that achieving financial goals justifies short-term actions. The result, alas, is usually more complexity, more work (and higher cost), and the wrong behavior.

Unlike Vision A, Vision B (see figure I-1) is not about more contracts and controls. Nor is it about quick-fix solutions. It is about applying a number of clear and simple principles and practices that lead to the liberation of both the finance team and their management colleagues. It is rooted not in self-interest but greater trust and cooperation. It means simplifying everything finance does and freeing them to provide effective decision support and performance insights that really help managers to improve their results. Instead of using crude targets to drive performance results, the CFO believes that a better and more sustainable approach is to relentlessly focus managers on improving processes that, in turn, will lead to increasing levels of customer value and higher levels of profitability than peers. This approach encourages managers to eliminate costs that add no value, use measures to improve their work, and make sensible risk-adjusted decisions. Managers are accountable with hindsight for their results compared with peers, prior years, and benchmarks. Words such as *clarity, simplicity, transparency,* and *accountability* best describe this vision. This is how finance becomes a valued and trusted business partner.

This book explains how Vision B has been implemented at a number of leading organizations around the world. The CFO can be its champion and, in some cases, even its leader. Gary Crittenden, CFO of American Express, articulated this vision when he said that, "an ideal finance function spends very little time on reconciliations and a minimal amount of time reporting on what has happened. Instead, a great organization spends the majority of its time trying to anticipate what's going to happen in the future, making sure the company's resources are allocated to the most important opportunities that it has, and to ensuring that the company operates with tight controls and great processes."[37]

In the seven chapters that follow, we will look a number of key issues that the CFO and the finance team must deal with to travel along this road successfully and transform the finance operation.

- *Chapter 1—The CFO as Freedom Fighter.* The first task for the CFO is to liberate both finance and business managers from huge amounts of detail and the proliferation of complex systems that increase their workload and deny them time for reflection and analysis. This means purging their systems, measures, and reports and eradicating work that adds little value (e.g., detailed planning processes, redundant systems, and irrelevant reports). It also means being more wary of implementing new tools and IT systems that soak up valuable time and money but fail to provide reasonable value. Creating space and time for higher-value work is the crucial step that turns transformation rhetoric into practical reality.

- *Chapter 2—The CFO as Analyst and Adviser.* Breaking free from detail and complexity creates time for finance to provide the information that managers need to make effective decisions. But that alone is insufficient to build a credible finance team that will be seen by managers as a trusted and valued business partner. The CFO must also work hard to attract and keep the best people and build the right team: people who know the business, can achieve high-levels of analytical skills, and are able to contribute improvement ideas. They will also be able to communicate effectively and work in teams. They will become teachers and mentors as they spread financial knowledge and decision-making capabilities across the organization. They will also use technology to eliminate low-value work, improve controls, and deliver information in a timely way. In this way the finance team can earn its place at the strategy table by delivering value-adding services and performance improvement insights. A strong, independent view on investment decisions will also add to their credibility.

- *Chapter 3—The CFO as the Architect of Adaptive Management.* Managers will feel truly liberated only if the CFO can release them from the chains of the detailed annual planning cycle and replace targets and budgets with more effective steering mechanisms, including continuous planning reviews and rolling forecasts, that enable managers to sense and respond more rapidly to unpredictable events and to changing markets and customers. The CFO must also be prepared to devolve some planning and decision-making scope and authority to frontline teams, otherwise the benefits of faster response will be lost. But controls are not compromised; in fact they are strengthened as managers use fast actuals, key performance indicators, rolling forecasts, and trend analysis to influence future events rather than dwell on past results. Target-setting and performance evaluation systems also need to be changed. Measures of relative improvement against peers and prior periods replace annual targets as the primary approach to performance appraisal. This enables managers to focus on managing reality rather than the plan.

- *Chapter 4—The CFO as Warrior Against Waste.* With more time to add value, the CFO and the finance team are able to focus on eliminating huge swathes of costs that have remained unchallenged for years. The aim should be to flatten the hierarchy, centralize and standardize transaction processing, and ensure that all projects are necessary and add value. The CFO must also learn and apply the lessons from lean thinking, a concept elegantly summarized by Tai-ichi Ohno, architect of the Toyota Production System: "All we are doing is looking at the time line from the moment the customer gives us an order to the point when we collect the cash. And we are reducing that time line by removing the non-value-added wastes."[38] Eradicating non-value-adding work from all processes has the potential to cut costs while improving cycle times and customer service. Such cost reductions will make the organization more flexible and competitive. But some of this work will need the support of other key people including the board.

- *Chapter 5—The CFO as Master of Measurement.* The CFO needs to bring measurement back under control and provide clear guidance about its meaning. Managers at every level only need six or seven measures. Measures should relate to purpose and strategy and be used to enable local managers to learn and improve. They should not be linked to targets, otherwise managers will change their behavior, taking actions to meet those targets instead of more value creating alternatives. At the higher level, senior managers see patterns and trends and need intervene at local levels only if these show abnormalities that warrant detailed explanations.

- *Chapter 6—The CFO as Regulator of Risk.* The CFO needs to provide an effective framework for good governance and risk management. This can be done by using multiple levers of control that support corporate governance controls, internal controls, strategic controls, and feedback controls. The pressure points that encourage excessive risk taking need to be identified and dealt with. Risk management also moves from a narrow focus on individual units and projects to a wider focus on the whole enterprise and the project portfolio so that the right balance of risk can be effectively managed. Managers should be encouraged to approach future uncertainty with an open mind rather than see risk management as just another hurdle to overcome to get their investment proposals accepted. The CFO must insist that risk management is everyone's responsibility, not just the province of specialists.

- *Chapter 7—The CFO as Champion of Change.* In this final chapter we will look at how a number of CFOs have transformed their finance operations, examining how they started, what vision or goals they set for themselves, how they got buy-in from key people, and how they implemented the changes. It will include a number of case examples, including American Express, Tomkins, and the World Bank.

The Transformation Journey

The transformation road is a tough one to follow because it challenges many of the finance team's accepted practices and systems. These problems must be recognized and the difficulties faced before the journey can begin. A good place to start is by understanding what transformation really means. The formula $D \times V \times F > R$ describes the task well (D = dissatisfaction, V = vision, F = first steps, and R = resistance to change). It tells us that dissatisfaction, no matter how deep, is not enough on its own. There must also be a compelling vision of how the new organization will look and feel when we get there. But even these two together require a third partner—a clear understanding of the first steps along the journey to build credibility and thus take key people with you. All three must be in evidence and in sufficient strength to overcome the resistance to change.

An increasing number of organizations are building first-class finance operations that support a management culture of learning and improvement. Though not an exhaustive list, here are some that stand out (in alphabetical order).

- *Ahlsell:* A $1 billion Swedish distributor that is consistently at the top of its peer group in terms of profitability. It has acquired twenty-three companies over the past eight years.

Each one immediately becomes part of its unique performance management model. Fixed targets disappear. Business units are placed in league tables (they are usually shocked to find how poor their relative performance is). Each unit is accountable for its profitability and can make its own decisions. There is a constant dialogue with central support. Quarterly rolling forecasts are prepared by each team and quickly consolidated at head office. Performance management systems support self-regulation rather than central control.

- *American Express:* A $29 billion U.S. financial services company that has improved to such an extent over recent years that it now has the highest price/earnings ratio in its peer group. It has introduced a streamlined planning process with an emphasis on driver-based rolling forecasts. It no longer allocates resources months in advance. It looks at its forecasts every month and decides its funding priorities from a list of applications from business units. The result is less gaming of resource requirements, more accountability for funds and better alignment with strategy. The company has also reduced costs dramatically by moving from many data centers to only a few low cost shared services centers.

- *Cognos:* An $800 million Canadian software company that is one of the software industry's fastest growing and most profitable companies. It is a world leader in corporate performance management (CPM) and business intelligence systems that enable continuous planning, forecasting, reporting, and control. In recent years it has upgraded its internal systems and now provides business intelligence and real-time performance information to many users, thus improving its compliance and control systems dramatically.

- *GE Capital:* A U.S.-based company with assets of approximately $600 billion that serves consumers and businesses in forty-seven countries around the world. It has a reputation for being one of the best finance functions in America and has often been called the "jewel" in the GE crown. The way it develops finance talent is exceptional and many graduates of its development program go on to become stars in the wider General Electric group and beyond.

- *Svenska Handelsbanken:* A $2 billion universal Swedish bank with ten thousand employees and six hundred profit centers, Handelsbanken is one of the most cost-efficient and profitable banks in the world. It transformed its performance management systems over thirty years ago. It produces fast and reliable numbers with no fixed performance contracts to distort behavior. Each region and branch are compared with their peers in monthly league tables based on a few simple metrics. Information is fast and open. Branches can produce income statements online and deconstruct them by customer.

- *Telecom New Zealand:* An innovative telecommunications company that provides a full range of Internet, data, voice, mobile, and fixed-line calling services to customers in New Zealand and Australia. With revenues of around NZ$5.2 billion (70 percent in New Zealand and 30 percent in Australia) the company has overhauled its performance management systems in recent years; this has contributed to its exceptional performance. In the past few years its share price has outperformed its rivals to a significant degree.

- *Tomkins:* This $5 billion Anglo-American multiproducts company has a hundred separate units reporting directly into a small head office. Units now report with the aid of "flash" rolling forecasts on the fourth working day *prior* to the month-end, together with eighteen-month quarterly rolling forecasts. This puts the board in control. There are no fixed contracts; teams are rewarded based on their improvement over prior years. Units have more autonomy and more accountability. Forecasts are now the primary management tool and are separated from performance measurement. Gaming behavior has evaporated and the willingness to disclose problems has improved. In the past few years, Tomkins's shares have outperformed the index by 25 percent.

- *Unilever:* An Anglo-Dutch organization with sales of €43 billion and 234,000 employees that is one of the world's leading suppliers of fast-moving consumer goods. For the past few years it has been transforming its finance operation, including reforming the target-setting and performance evaluation process. Though it's still early days, the signs are that these changes are supporting a companywide transformation in performance.

- *The World Bank:* Provides loans, policy advice, technical assistance, and knowledge sharing services to low- and middle-income countries to reduce poverty. While the bank invests around $20 billion p.a. in developing countries, it also spends around $1.9 billion p.a. on operating expenses and has always operated with a traditional budget. But in recent years the finance team has been challenging how this process works, and concluded that it takes too long, costs too much, and adds too little value. So the team has introduced a more strategic, cost-effective process underpinned by quarterly performance reviews. The new project is known as "budget reform."

This book will explain how CFOs and their finance teams can remove many of the major barriers that otherwise prevent the transition to a more *adaptive, lean,* and *ethical* organization. It is a challenging road to follow, and I am not promising an easy ride. All I can say is that the prize on offer is well worth the effort.

A CHECKLIST FOR THE CFO

- ☐ If you and your finance team are regularly working overtime and weekends (usually unpaid!), don't you owe it to yourself and your team to do something about it? Start today!

☐ Ask yourself what's causing this overtime and stress. Are your efforts at improvement making the organization less or more complex? Are you trying to cope with too much detail? Are you implementing too many systems? Have you cut jobs but left the workload the same (or actually increased it)?

☐ Look at the finance operation in the mirror and make an honest assessment of its performance compared with best practice organizations. How good are you at planning, budgeting, forecasting, reporting, and risk management? Conduct an opinion survey among both finance and business managers.

☐ Talk to board members and operating managers and ask them whether they are getting the information they need when they need it. What more do you have to do?

☐ Do you know your critical success factors? And are they aligned with your strategies, measures, goals, and actions? If not, this could be a major cause of the wrong actions and behavior. If they are, communicate them to all stakeholders (including investors).

☐ What is your vision for improving the finance operation? If it is Vision A (more top-down targets and controls) then think again. You are probably tinkering at the edges and not tackling the real (systemic) problems. What's worse, you are probably stifling ambition and innovation.

☐ Set your course for Vision B. This will take you in a different direction—toward an adaptive, lean, and ethical organization. It is not just more uplifting, but it will also enable finance to have a huge impact on the performance of the whole organization.

CHAPTER ONE

THE CFO AS FREEDOM FIGHTER

*Most everyone in the industrialized world can get their
hands on a silo full of data and stimulus in a matter of
minutes. The challenge is to get the most relevant, meaningful,
contextualized information so that we can turn that into
useful knowledge and wisdom.*

—David Shenk

FINANCE MANAGERS are trained to handle lots of raw data and make sense of it. But these data streams are overflowing and flooding the channels of information and knowledge. Context and meaning are being lost in a fog of detail and complexity. General ledgers and budgets are being over-loaded with unnecessary levels of detailed analysis. Finance is cre-ating more measures and reports that are overwhelming managers' abilities to absorb and react to key messages. And precious thinking and planning time is being sacrificed to "management by remote control" as senior executives use more powerful IT systems to drill down to increasing levels of detail and demand instant answers to irrelevant questions.

I have seen major ERP vendors advertising a vision of a management cockpit where head office staffers can use banks of computer screens showing red, amber, and green traffic lights to control the performance of every business unit and operating team against predetermined targets and plans. This is clearly an excessive, even counterproductive, use of IT capabilities. But I'm not arguing against centralized information systems; there is an important distinction to be made here, and we shouldn't dismiss out of hand the vision of using IT systems to provide greater detail. On the contrary, senior managers need a centralized information system (including one group general ledger) to monitor performance, but they should be focusing on the bigger picture of patterns and trends rather than detailed variances at the unit level. As long as the trend lines are heading in the right direction, managers should not intervene or even demand explanations about short-term blips.

But that is not how many CFOs see the opportunities that more powerful IT systems now provide; their improvement vision is toward *more* centralization of planning, decision making, and control. This is the approach taken by the U.K. Treasury. While ministers espouse increased decentralization, they are at the same time unleashing powerful centralizing forces by expanding the number of targets that, among others, health care, education, and police department managers must meet. One target in the police service is to improve crime-detection rates. In their efforts to meet this target, some U.K. police forces record domestic incidents (husband and wife assaults) as two incidents (i.e., each on the other) so that when they are solved there are two positive results instead of one, which of course helps to skew the numbers in a helpful way. Contrary to its intention, this vision of "accountability through targets" fails to stretch and drive improvement. Instead it stifles ambition and innovation and focuses managers on meeting minimum standards rather than improving systems.

The CFO needs to call a halt to this insane data-induced micromanagement. Of course data and documents need to be recorded somewhere in the system and should be accessible when needed (Sarbanes-Oxley now requires this) but that is different from allowing them to clog up the arteries of general ledgers, budgets, and reporting systems. It is up to the CFO to lead a crusade for less detail and complexity and the creation of more time for reflection and analysis. He must start to trust people with information and decisions. It sometimes comes as a shock that if information is transparent—that is, all managers have access to organization-wide information at the same time, not just access to "need to know" as dictated by some central authority—people at the front line will reach the same decisions as those at the top. This reduces the need for detailed top-down controls. The result is faster execution and lower cost. This approach also releases the most powerful control system an organization can have—fast, open, and transparent information systems.

But winning the battle against complexity doesn't happen without a fight. The CFO has to overcome the resistance of a number of people with vested interests in preserving the status quo. These are often people whose skill is in spinning, fudging, and manipulating information so that higher-level managers see and hear only a customized (and usually sanitized) version of the truth. These people will likely include some of the CFO's own finance colleagues who, in some cases, believe that their jobs are at risk.

This chapter will examine these challenges. It will suggest that the CFO should:

- Rescue managers from information overload

- Simplify systems and reports

- Focus on truth and transparency

- Avoid unnecessary tools and systems

Rescue Managers from Information Overload

The average *Fortune* 500 worker sends and receives 178 messages per day; the average American businessperson spends one to two hours per workday dealing with communications, plus another one to two hours outside of normal work time.[1] With this information "overhead" it is understandable that the average manager has little time left for thinking, analyzing, and planning. Author David Shenk thinks that "we need information and contact but we're now in a situation where the challenge is not so much to get hold of it as it is to be discriminate about what we expose ourselves to."[2] Another author, Gerry McGovern, believes a "macho" element that sprang from Silicon Valley has fuelled the demand for information. "People were seen as smarter if they handled a greater number of calls, or e-mails, or more productive if they worked eighteen-hour days and never took holidays," he notes. But he goes on to say that managers might be making better decisions if they were just making a few.[3]

The increase in the *volume* of data and the *capability* to handle that data is a major change for senior management, including the CFO. In the past CFOs were somewhat protected from what went on simply because the capacity to keep them informed was limited. So with much greater volume and capability, what happens? The CFO's in-trays and e-mail folders become overloaded; even if they have the intellectual capacity to make good use of this information, they physically don't have the time to process it. It is little wonder that many CFOs suffer from attention deficit disorder. They are unable to make sense of the world, always reacting and then reacting again. And lack of control generates stress.

Separate the Signals from the Noise

Steve Morlidge, finance change leader at Unilever, sees another problem. "The majority of the information is internally generated," he notes. "The amount of data we can extract from the outside world, because it is difficult to collect, hasn't increased by anything like the same amount, so this information gets squeezed out. This means that CFOs are overwhelmed with internal detail and haven't time to address the key external opportunities and threats that can make or break the business."[4] Morlidge believes that what managers need is a way of filtering out what's significant from what isn't. Most people hear the constant stream of information as noise—often just random variations within the internal system. But they need to understand that the noise they're hearing may be a signal to someone else. So there needs to be a way of filtering the information so that everyone gets clear and consistent signals. One way of achieving this is through statistical process control, a technique that can help managers to filter data so that they only act when they should. There are two types of variation in any system or process: those that stem from common causes—faults in the system that can be identified and eliminated (e.g., error rates or poor information systems)—and those arising from special causes—one-off or fleeting events that appear like spikes in a time-series graph. If instead of seeing accounting variances in "this month" or "year-to-date" columns, managers monitored trends and abnormalities over time—in other words, relied on statistical process control techniques—they would be in a better position to react to signals rather than wasting their time having to explain noise.

Devolve Decision Making

Another powerful way of filtering is through the *devolution* of planning, forecasting, and decision making. If senior managers empower people lower down the organization to make the right decisions and act on them, then these people can filter out a lot of data that would otherwise end up on the CFO's desk. So it's a way of buffering the CFO, and other senior managers, from detail they don't need to know. They don't need to get involved in the details of what a local unit does; rather they just need to monitor the whole unit and react if they see patterns and trends change in a way that triggers an alert on the senior-management radar screen.

This leads to fewer people handling data and therefore less scope for error and misreporting. Devolution is not a strategic choice. It is an essential change in the creation of an adaptive, lean, and ethical organization.

This is what happens at Danish petrochemicals company Borealis. Business unit managers are accountable for continuously improving performance over time and against industry benchmarks. There is no micromanagement from the center. Each unit controls its own costs within directional boundaries (in the mid-1990s the directional trend of fixed costs was set at a significant reduction). Senior managers see patterns and trends rather than detailed variances. Only if the trend lines go out of bounds does the corporate center demand detailed explanations. This approach addresses the key questions that senior managers want answering, such as "Are costs under control?" and "Are they moving in the right direction?"

DEVOLUTION VERSUS DECENTRALIZATION. We must pay attention to the difference between *devolution* and *decentralization.* Many companies have, of course, decentralized their operations. In many cases, this simply means creating lower levels of *centralized decision making,* for example, at the divisional or large-business-unit level. Division chiefs can get very upset if lower-level units surprise them with either good or bad results. This invariably leads to conformance rather than initiative.

The challenge is to release the chains of regimented control and enable local management teams to maximize performance, often through the pursuit of innovative strategies. The word I prefer to describe this change is *devolution*—an unfamiliar word to many managers. It means the transfer of power from the center to front-line managers, vesting in them the authority to use their intuition and initiative to achieve results within agreed boundaries but *without being constrained by some specific contract or target.* It is about enabling and encouraging responsive yet coordinated actions, not dictating and directing them. The relationship between the U.S. Congress and individual state authorities is a good example of devolution in practice.

While numerous studies show that devolution brings significant benefits, it is also a minefield of misconceptions and contradictions. Harvard professor Chris Argyris has spent a lifetime studying it and, like other observers, wonders why there has been little growth over the past thirty years. He notes that while managers love devolution in theory, it is the command-and-control model that they know and trust. And employees also think it is great as long as they are not held personally accountable. But, according to Argyris, the real reason empowerment is like the emperor's clothes ("we praise it loudly in public and ask ourselves privately why we can't see it") is that there are two kinds of commitment. First there is the *extrinsic* commitment that derives from external demands. This is the typical performance contract that must be achieved. Then there is the *intrinsic* commitment that comes from within individuals. This is derived from their participation in some plan or goal and leads to people taking risks and accepting responsibility for their actions.[5]

The problem is that many leaders preach empowerment and *internal commitment,* but at the same time all goals, plans, and reward and recognition systems send clear messages of *external commitment.* Thus there is a massive collision of cultures with only one winner—the power of top-down measures will always be the primary determinant of behavior in a culture that values meeting fixed targets.

Manage by Exception

Management by exception is hardly a new idea but its application has been overlooked as the bandwidth of data has expanded over recent years. It is based on a simple operating principle. Trust people to act within values and policies and punish them if they abuse that trust, generally with the ultimate sanction—losing their jobs. But many organizations are reluctant to do this. Take employee expense claims. Employees are often treated like criminals when it comes to their expense accounts; there is a pervasive view that people are going to cheat. Judging by recent revelations in the Tyco and Hollinger cases, in which CEOs spent hundreds of thousands of dollars of company funds on personal items, it is easy to understand why companies feel the need to vet expenses carefully. But handling and approving expense submissions in detail is a time-consuming and costly exercise and one that is annoying for employees who are waiting for the company to reimburse the expenses they've incurred on its behalf.

Organizations that manage by exception do not design their systems to catch the 1 percent of people who will abuse any system. They allow employees to submit expenses online and then reimburse them automatically straight into their bank accounts. But a selective number of expense submissions are chosen at random and investigated thoroughly. Anyone caught cheating faces dismissal. Online processing reduces handling costs dramatically as there is little checking and keying into the general ledger to be done.

This type of random sampling should be designed to give senior managers the reassurance they need. And the same principle can apply to internal management control. At Handelsbanken, senior managers go to every branch every year and instead of following an agenda determined by the management of the branch, the meeting is an unstructured conversation about present and future performance, the environment, and risks. That's also what an effective internal audit team should do. Suppliers, for example, can be certified as having passed quality tests and then monitored periodically. Trust is a reciprocal deal. But the first move has to come from senior management. Random sampling can then follow. It is one of the most simple, powerful, and inexpensive control mechanisms available.

Simplify Systems and Reports

While the devolution of decision making and management by exception offer the CFO an effective way to manage increasing levels of data, there are other actions that can be taken to reduce the workload, especially in the area of transaction processing. Over two-thirds of the work of the average finance department remains locked into transaction processing and other routine work, much of it prone to error. Take the case of one sales and accounts receivable department in the U.K. division of an American computer manufacturer reckoned to be one of the best-managed firms in its sector. A study showed that 43 percent of sales quotations were wrong, 76 percent of deliveries were incorrect, and 45 percent of orders were incorrectly processed. For the sales region as a whole, 35 pence in every pound was spent on wasted work.

To create space and time to add greater value, the CFO needs to reduce the time spent on this type of work. There is much that can be done including simplifying transaction processing, budgeting, general ledger work, and reporting.

Simplify Transaction Processing

According to the Hackett Group, leading organizations have reduced routine transaction processing work by 16 percent and cut costs by around 50 percent. Management spans of control have also increased from a ratio of 1:7 in average companies to the 1:15 to 1:20 range in world-class organizations.[6] Some organizations have outsourced their transaction processing. BP, for example, has outsourced its entire accounting and finance function to IBM. Service centers in Tulsa, Lisbon, and Bangalore handle accounts payable, accounts receivable, and financial reporting. This approach (if done well) not only separates transaction processing from mainstream finance but it also transfers many of the burdens now imposed on data management and recording by the Sarbanes-Oxley legislation to the outstanding contractor.

Most organizations, however, have not yet gone that far though there is a move toward the centralization of back-office functions within a few data centers. American Express, for example, has moved from forty-six data centers to just two shared services centers. Most of its normal accounting, reporting, and transaction processing is now done in Phoenix, Arizona (United States), and Delhi (India). Notes CFO Gary Crittenden, "This move was critical to saving a thousand heads and $100 million per annum. Previously a lot of work was being done in individual markets around the world with a few controllers and a few accounting people here and there, well away from the corporate head office. That was quite scary. But now it's all housed in a well-controlled environment with high-quality standards and practices. We just needed to make sure that the communications were clear between the shared services centers and the markets. This really was a big early win for finance." According to Crittenden, there are four main advantages. "First, there are considerable cost savings. Second, it is easier to make improvements (you can more easily set common standards). Third, it facilitates a more visible career path for back-office employees. And fourth, by having multiple centers, it serves as a hedge against the disruption of the back office."[7] These shared services centers have also created more reliable, standardized information for use in the company's business planning efforts.

Other functions can also be centralized and standardized. Human resources and information technology are two primary candidates. In fragmented organizations, error rates in benefits administration are two-and-a-half times higher, payroll costs are three times higher, and the costs per paycheck are 98 percent higher than in firms that have centralized these processes. IT costs are similarly reduced—the cost of application development is reduced by 41 percent.[8] Another area in which centralization can have a profound impact is procurement. By automating the procurement cycle from requisition to purchase order processing to ordering and shipping, companies can realize huge cost reductions through faster cycle times and better accuracy.

One company that has automated its transaction processing is Intel, a $26 billion semiconductor company. Take accounts payable. Intel's motto in 2003 was "key no more in 2004." With over four thousand suppliers registered to do Web-based invoicing, the finance function is making good progress toward becoming a "100 percent e-corporation." VP for planning and finance Leslie Culbertson predicts that the benefits of "hands-free AP" will include more accurate data, reduced throughput time, reduced cost-per-transaction, and less human involvement in the process. Intel conducted a pilot of its web-invoicing project in April 2001 and completed full implementation in May 2002 (although new suppliers are coming on stream all the time). In late 2003, the system was processing sixteen thousand transactions a month.[9]

Ken Lever, Tomkins's CFO, has all his business finance teams looking at ways to simplify processes, including accounts payable, accounts receivable, and invoice processing. Notes Lever: "The idea is to take the non-value-added activities out of those processes. This includes some simple things like reducing the number of times that people handle documents. If we could get our administrative processes to the same level of efficiency as our manufacturing processes we'd probably see a huge reduction in costs and a big increase in efficiency. In most administrative processes you will typically find that only 15 to 20 percent of transactions get from point A to point B without being held up or without some other problem that needs to be solved."[10]

An increasing focus on Web-enabled technology is undoubtedly the future for transaction processing work. The fewer the manual hand-offs the less likelihood there is for errors and rework and the lower the costs will be. However, the CFO will also recognize that the level of human interaction with suppliers and customers (both internal and external) needs to be of the highest quality.

Simplify (or Even Abandon) the Budgeting Process

Another process that absorbs huge amounts of low-value work is planning and budgeting. One global best-practices study concluded that finance staff still spent 79 percent of their planning time on lower-value-added activities such as gathering and processing data and only 21 percent of their time analyzing and interpreting the numbers.[11] There is too much detail in most budgeting systems, and this leads to high error rates and a longer completion cycle. Some organizations, including American Express, GE Capital, and Toyota, have something they call a budget, but its toxic effects have been neutralized. Most have moved to shorter *rolling* planning cycles (usually quarterly) and now treat the budget as the four quarterly plans that fall within the fiscal year.

Other organizations, Handelsbanken, Ahlsell, Tomkins, and the World Bank among them, have taken more radical steps and abandoned the annual budget completely. One CFO lifted a huge weight off the shoulders of the finance department by refusing to do another annual budget. The impact on the workload of the finance team was a revelation. For the first time that anyone could remember there was no overtime working through January to March, not only saving thousands of pounds but also alleviating considerable stress from such an intense work schedule. Moreover, between October 1999 and April 2000 (the first year of the new system), the management team also had to implement a reorganization of the business (a task that would have entailed multiple budget recompilations), a new KPI-based reporting system, a new accounting system that reduced the monthly closing period from eight to four days, and finally complete the year-end accounts. All this work was completed with no extra staff and with no overtime. Instead of detailed budgeting, some CFOs now do much more "light-touch" forecasting, thus saving huge amounts of work. Borealis reckoned the saving was 95 percent of the time spent on budgeting.

Cutting out the budget will on its own free up huge amounts of capacity within the finance operation that can be used to provide more value-adding work. It will also improve the image of finance across the organization as managers like nothing better than a change initiative that means *less* work. How organizations can manage without budgets will be explained in chapter 3.

Simplify the General Ledger

According to David Axson, cofounder of the Hackett Group, the general ledger chart of accounts may contain five to ten times the number of accounts actually needed to fulfill the basic requirements to close the accounting books.[12] One of the problems is the allocation of shared costs. I heard of one bank department that was involved in an argument that lasted for months over whether it should carry a computer charge or if the charge should be allocated to other departments. In the end a senior executive had to get involved. The saga took months of time for no benefit at all (except to the department's costs), but the cost to the bank was huge. Some CFOs have simplified their general ledgers. They now contain only high-level accounts that are relevant for analysis and reporting purposes. If senior executives demand more detail on a particular account, someone goes to find it.

Rupert Taylor, finance change leader at U.K. bank Barclays PLC, has reduced finance costs by approximately £30 million and pared its headcount from 1,650 to 1,150. There is now less time spent gathering and processing data, and more time spent on analysis and business advisory services. Taylor began by integrating all the finance systems into a common ERP platform, including what had been thirty-seven different general ledger systems. "That wasn't just about cost savings," explains Taylor. "Much of the business case also centered on having a single version of the truth; improving the control environment; consolidating into a shared services center our accounts payable, general ledger and management reporting operations; and strengthening our supply chain management to make sure we get not just proper deals with our suppliers but also that we pay to terms. We're very pleased with what we've been able to accomplish."[13]

In their book *Practical Lean Accounting*, Brian Maskell and Bruce Baggaley suggest that lean principles can equally apply to the finance department itself. Accounts payable, accounts receivable, general ledger, month-end closing, and internal control are all candidates for the application of lean principles. Just focusing on the general ledger and month-end close, the authors' views are quite radical. First, they suggest that all general ledger accounts below the organizational level of the value stream should be eliminated. In lean manufacturing organizations like Toyota, the general ledger is organized around large value streams such as product lines and product families. Thus all the transactions related to a value stream are posted to that account. The average cost of a vehicle is simply the accumulated total cost divided by the number of units produced. Secondly, they suggest that all end-of-period accruals and allocations should also be eliminated and that the company should move to a cash basis of accounting.[14]

Lean thinking can transform transaction processing. Take accounts payable. In one large U.S. auto company, the accounts payable department employed over five hundred people. In an effort to reduce costs, managers targeted reductions of 20 percent. That looked like a stretch target until they realized that one of their smaller rivals handled the same operation with just four people! Even allowing for the difference in scale, the contrast was amazing. When managers analyzed their existing systems, they realized the full extent of the problem. Documents were moving around for checking and approval at a rapid rate, and many employees spent their time matching orders to goods received notes, and matching goods received notes to purchase invoices. In fact, for each document there were fourteen checks involved, which in turn involved a high percentage of mismatches, reconciliation problems, and letters and calls to suppliers, and generally resulted in slow approval procedures, unpredictable payment schedules, and unhappy suppliers.

Its lean competitor didn't have these problems. For a start, it had dispensed with the need for purchase invoices. When a purchase order was issued it is simply recorded on an online database. When the goods arrived, the goods received note would be matched against this database record and if it was in order the goods were accepted and an automatic (electronic) payment was generated; if it was incorrect, the goods would be rejected and returned to the supplier. No other alternative course of action would be possible. In other words, this company had eliminated the need for checking, reconciling, chasing, matching, posting, and summarizing that causes most of the work of transaction processing. And of course its costs were a fraction of those of its larger rival.

Simplify Reporting Systems

Finance tends to dictate the reporting agenda and this is primarily focused on accounting cycles rather than strategic demands.

Ninety-two percent of reports are based on calendar reporting cycles and only 8 percent are available on demand.[15] The number of reports seems to grow year after year. I heard in one large organization that they produced around 750 reports every month, whereas only a fraction was reckoned to be of value. According to one source, companies often find that 50 percent of reports can be eliminated, and 20 to 50 percent of what remains can be consolidated. Many of those consolidated reports can be automated and a smaller number of people can generate what remains.[16] A few CFOs have conducted their own value analysis and without consulting potential users have just stopped producing large numbers of reports and then waited for the complaining phone calls and e-mails to arrive. But they seldom came. Sony Pictures Entertainment is adopting such an approach. According to Irwin Jacobson, the company's VP and controller of the Studio Services division, "We're constantly pushing back to corporate to see if the things that they're requesting are: one, truly needed; two, being looked at; three, are useful; and four, could be done in a different way altogether."[17]

The best finance functions focus on removing unnecessary reports and liberating operating people from the burdens of unnecessary meetings. Some CFOs now produce only a few (important) reports as standard and enable local managers to access the data warehouse on a do-it-yourself basis. But, most importantly, their senior people have learned not to demand answers to dumb questions. Removing variance reports is another way to achieve this. At one global organization, board members failed to notice for a whole year that budget variances were no longer included in the monthly management accounts! The board now focuses on what's important and how the business can be improved. Knowledge and insight are the key words.

Architect of the Toyota Production System, Taiichi Ohno, had an aversion to accounting controls. He is alleged to have said that the Toyota Production System succeeded only because Mr. Toyoda kept the cost accountants out of his hair.[18] Handelsbanken periodically examines all its reports for relevance. In one year, for example, the bank reviewed many of its reporting procedures resulting in a reduction of 30 percent in memos and 40 percent in computer reports.

A CFO at a U.K. brewery challenged the relevance of a number of reports. During the course of factory meetings to discuss changes to the budgeting system she kept hearing about a "green book." This turned out to be a report prepared for the factory manager every week that compared actual to standard efficiencies. Every weekend he would take it home, study it, and on Monday morning he would have a go at a number of people for poor performance. Everyone knew the drill. So employees would play all sorts of games to improve the numbers in the green book. If the Thursday night figures were better than Friday's, then those were the ones they would enter. No one else used the green book, and the CFO worked out that it cost a fortune to prepare ($120,000 p.a.).

A number of CFOs have established "hit squads" to decimate detail and redundant reports. Earl Shanks, CFO at NCR, says the company used to handle twelve hundred customized reports generated by the finance organization. A standardization project has reduced this number to just over one hundred.[19] Ralph Nicoletti, CFO at Kraft Foods, created a "work elimination team" to simplify the processes of all finance staffers in the wake of the Kraft-Nabisco merger. One four-person squad, for example, analyzed the "gymnastics the organization has to go through to prepare monthly updates and estimates." After intensive analysis, the team pared these updates to just seven pages, supplemented by three more of system generated data with key messages distilled down to the areas of greatest importance.[20]

Focus on Truth and Transparency

One reason why some finance functions demand excessive levels of detail is that they need to validate the numbers produced by business units. Most cost numbers, for example, are constructed from smaller pieces of data and are subject to the definitions and interpretations of the person compiling them and the purpose for which they are being prepared. The same data that creates a loss using conventional accounting practices can be used to create a profit under different conventions such as economic value added or activity-based management. Another area of obfuscation is cost allocations—in one large U.S. bank, for example, around 60 percent of budgeting time was spent on cost allocations and transfer pricing. The answer is to demand full transparency with only one "version of the truth" circulating within the organization at any one time. This is rarely the case. Some companies have one set of books for cost accounting, another for management accounting, another for financial accounting, and yet another for reporting to tax and regulatory authorities.

If Sarbanes-Oxley had been in force prior to the Enron fiasco, it is unlikely that the fraud would have been stopped. Enron checked off all the boxes. But what the organization didn't have was transparent information. Many CFOs believe that information should only reach those people authorized to see it. "The risks of having a completely open system would be too great," they say. "Anyhow, how can we trust people with sensitive information? It would reach our competitors in no time at all." In contrast, Bill Gates, chairman of Microsoft, is one who believes that leaders would be better advised to stop trying to control information and open it up to broader scrutiny: "The value of having everybody get the complete picture and trusting each person with it far outweighs the risk involved."[21]

Lennart Francke, CFO of Handelsbanken, believes that one of his most obvious operational responsibilities is to keep the internal accounting system in line with the external one. And, as he admits, it's a continuous struggle:

> There are always forces in an organization that want you to use different types of incentives to stress one promotion or another. For example, many people believe that if you want to have more credit card business, then you should build in a specific incentive to increase branch managers' efforts. I would always stand back and say we just don't

do that. We put the right costs and the right revenues on our card business just as we do for our other products. This means that what internal managers see on their profit and loss accounts is exactly the same as would appear on the external accounts. We are very wary about internal profit taking. It can create a lot of disputes and focus our attention on making internal profits instead of those that come from real paying customers.[22]

Avoid Unnecessary Tools and Systems

The CFO is on every consultant's list as potential buyer of the latest performance management system and toolset. Most of these tools are based on sound theory but suffer from poor practice. And many, having absorbed huge amounts of management time and expense, are abandoned as the consultants move out and the internal project champions move on. Some of this poor implementation experience is caused by abject change management (typically imposing systems on people rather than seeking their views and support), but many of these systems should never have been taken on in the first place. Abortive efforts to implement systems and tools are a major source of management frustration, added complexity, and wasted time. CFOs should be on their guard.

Let's look at just one of the most popular strategy tools around today: the balanced scorecard. The balanced scorecard rose to fame in the mid-1990s as a better way to manage strategy (see discussion in the introduction). Like most of the other tools and models that we've seen in the past ten or fifteen years, the philosophy behind the scorecard is neat. Who would argue that organizations shouldn't be "strategy-focused"? The real problems are in its implementation. Despite the pleadings of its originators, Kaplan and Norton, the vast majority of scorecards are "KPI scorecards" used as top-down control systems. This is also how the software industry has interpreted them. The telltale signs are the "target actual variance" reporting systems with different-colored "traffic lights" to tell us whether indicators are going up or down. These types of implementation rarely add much value, nor do they last long. Notes John McMahan, senior business adviser at the Hackett Group: "Most companies get very little value out of balanced scorecards because they haven't followed the basic rules that make them effective."[23]

Effective scorecard applications are those that put local teams in charge. When they looked at successful users, Kaplan and Norton began to realize how important devolving strategy to frontline people was noting that these users "created open reporting, making the performance results available to everyone in the organization." Building on the principle that "strategy is everyone's job" they empowered "everyone" by giving each employee the knowledge needed to do his or her job.[24]

The problem is that the selection and implementation of most tools and systems fall into the Vision A category—they are aimed at improving top-down control and making existing (often dysfunctional) systems work more efficiently. That's why most quality improvement systems usually end up making managers check off list items rather than fundamentally improve their systems. In 2003, Toyota recalled 79 percent fewer vehicles in the United States than Ford and 92 percent fewer than Chrysler.[25] Isn't that a staggering statistic? So, if Toyota is so good at quality, why does it not have any quality departments? The answer is that it keeps things simple and uses very few "tools" of any kind. Its primary concern is to build quality into its systems rather than inspect for it.

Many organizations are currently investing in another tool— customer relationship management (CRM) systems. The belief is that there is real value in a rigorous tracking system and the ability of everyone to "see" the status of each customer transaction. But the success rate of CRM systems has been patchy, to say the least. One U.K. report noted that 70 percent bring *negative* results.[26] Implementing these systems can make problems worse by focusing on recording, scanning, queuing, batching, counting, routing, and archiving (each process is prone to error and rework) instead of rethinking the system from the customer's perspective.

What's more, these systems need constant maintenance (which absorbs time and cost) but whether they add any value and improve the experience of the customer is doubtful.

As the following case illustrates, streamlining process flows is often the best solution. A U.K. local council service responsible for assessing and paying housing benefits transformed itself from the worst in the country to one of the best in the space of a few months, with no extra resources and not a CRM system in sight. A year before the change the council was in the dreadful position of having 7,700 claims waiting to be processed, twenty times the norm. The department was taking more than six months to pay a claim. Only around one-third of letters, phone calls, and visits concerned new claims. All the rest were waste: demand resulting from a previous failure. Only 3 percent of clients had their claim settled in one visit to the office; most came in at least three times; some up to ten. When scanning documents, the system was designed to sort them three times and check them eight times. It was no wonder the council couldn't deal with the backlog.

The council started to tackle the problem by understanding what customers wanted and doing only work that improved their service experience. Next, it made sure that work went out 100 percent perfect, taking whatever time was needed and drawing on all necessary resources. Finally, it managed customers through to the end of the process, keeping them informed of progress. The key to improvement was getting "clean" information into the system (the real bottleneck was not assessing claims, the presumed culprit, but getting clean information in the first place). So the council formulated a bargain: if claimants provided all the right documents it promised to deal with the claim immediately, or within days if it had to be referred elsewhere. The group implemented measures to tell staff how well they were achieving things that mattered to customers, not how well they were achieving official specifications. After a three-week pilot it was clear that redesigning the system into a single flow allowed staff to cope with claims in days, if not hours. Live claims came down to three hundred, and staff were coming to terms with unaccustomed gifts of flowers and cake instead of brickbats. Morale and quality were up, and extra capacity had been delivered to the front line at no extra cost.

Lean organizations like Toyota and Handelsbanken approach new systems by first trying to understand the problem, work out one or a number of potential ways to solve it, then (and only then) examine whether an IT solution can create additional value and benefits. Toyota is wary of heavy spending on IT, even though it spends billions on robotics. It continues to use many systems that were developed years previously. They are upgraded only when there is a burning reason and the benefits are clear to see. Plant managers believe more in the "go and see" approach rather than relying on computer-based information. As one manager in the parts department explained, "From the warehouse person's perspective, sitting and looking into a computer screen doesn't tell you everything you need to know. You have to have a feel for the size of the parts and the real situation in the warehouse. The computer recommends an inventory level to the procurement analyst, but it can't tell him if the inventory will make life tough for the person on the warehouse floor because there isn't enough space to store it."[27] As Toyota people would say, "We do not make information systems, we make cars. Show me the process of making cars and how the information system supports that."

Author David Shenk advocates "skeptical thought" about the use of new tools and systems: "Don't use new technologies blindly," he notes. "Don't use them just for the fun of it. Think about how all of your tools encourage certain behaviors and discourage other behaviors and make sensible judgments about whether you like those tendencies or need to be alert against their shaping your life in a way you're not happy about."[28]

Cutting Bureaucracy, Simplifying Systems, and Decentralizing Decision Making at Svenska Handelsbanken

When Robin Fraser and I wrote our first report on Handelsbanken we submitted it to Chairman Dr. Jan Wallander, who first complimented us on a well-documented analysis of how the organization worked. But he then said that we'd made an important error—in the final paragraph we had written that "this was the most advanced management model we had ever seen." He suggested that we strike out the word "advanced" and replace it with the word "simple." Then we began to realize what he meant. Organizations used to be smaller, more intimate places where people trusted each other to do what was in the best interests of the business. But over the decades, as increasing bureaucracy has made such intimacy impossible, layers of controls have evolved to make people comply with rigid rules and regulations, and these have gradually become more and more intrusive. Examples include directives from head office on everything from travel allowances to how much can be spent on the Christmas party, and the budget is tailor-made for the corporate controller to query every penny that differs from the agreed plan. "Simplicity and speed" go together in the same way as "budgets and controls," yet they reflect fundamentally different philosophies of how a business should be managed in the new economy.

Handelsbanken's underlying philosophy is that well-trained highly capable employees vested with personal authority and able to act quickly and decisively at a local level lead to satisfied, loyal, and profitable customers. This, in turn, brings sustainable long-term profitability and increasing shareholder value. In management parlance it represents a radical cultural shift from centralized control to frontline entrepreneurship, supported by careful employee selection, continuous development, and the resources and support of a large, mature organization. Such words as trust, integrity, responsibility, and commitment spring easily to mind. This is how Wallander, architect of the Handelsbanken management model, described the changes he made when he cut bureaucracy, simplified systems, and decentralized decision making in the early 1970s:

> [Central] departments were forbidden to send out any more memos to the branch offices apart from those that were necessary for the daily work and reports to authorities. All activities connected with setting up a budget or

following up a previous one were closed down. There were altogether 110 committees and working groups at the head office that were engaged in various development projects. These groups were told to stop their work at once and the secretaries were asked to submit a report on not more than one page describing what the work had resulted in so far. Several hundred people were working on a radically new data system. The work was stopped. Similarly, the department concerned with long-term planning and the formulation of visions and strategies was told to stop its work. At the time Handelsbanken was one of Sweden's largest advertisers. There was a marketing department of forty people at the head office that prepared the major advertising campaigns and extensive advertising activities at the central and local levels. This work was stopped, and after a while the number of employees in that department fell from forty to one.[29]

The force that now drives managerial performance is not some individual target that brings rich personal rewards. It is a much higher motivating force that appeals to that most basic of human needs—being valued by your peers for your contribution to the collective goal. At Handelsbanken, all performance measures and rewards are geared to beating the competition, both inside the bank (e.g., branch to branch comparisons) and outside the bank (e.g., bank to bank comparisons). And there is a long-term group profit sharing scheme that encourages branches to compete with each other (though not for customers) and share knowledge and best practices.

The paradox for most observers is that decentralization leads to more effective control. With only three management levels there is not much room for fudging and spinning the numbers. There is much greater transparency. Controls are no longer based on the rear view mirror of budgets; they are based on knowing what is happening today. So successful transparency depends entirely on a fast (online), open (everyone gets the same information at the same time), and comprehensive (all user needs are supported) information system. And senior managers don't use the system to micromanage frontline operations. They monitor and observe patterns of transaction volumes, customer gains and losses, customer profits, branch profits, cost patterns, productivity, and much more. If the regional controller sees branch profit trends heading in the wrong direction, the regional manager will make a suggestive call to the branch. That's all that happens—it is then up to the branch whether or not to take action. It is an acknowledgement that the real art of management is to spot the exceptional pattern or the unusual event and deal with it before it becomes a real problem, and otherwise leave well alone. The lesson is to use knowledge sensibly (e.g., spotting macro trends and managing risk across the group) to support and develop people rather than control them.

Current CFO Lennart Francke has grown up with the bank and is a devout believer in its management approach. He explains how he constantly fights to maintain and, where possible, improve this model:

> We always try to keep things as simple as possible. I'll give you an example. One of the important things that we do in my department is to provide top management with a monthly report that does not contain any, let's say, result figures. But it does contain relevant information on how our different business lines are performing from a gross revenue point of view. It also tells them about business volumes and volumes in different sections. We prepare that report here in my department. And I look at myself as the editor of the report, which gives me the mandate to not only put new things into it but actually to take away information that I judge to be less important. So we are actually trying and also succeeding in keeping the volume of the report down to a constant level.
>
> I am also acutely aware that we need to be constantly on our guard against new systems that are unnecessary and that increase complexity. For example, we are skeptical about new systems like the balanced scorecard that

appear on the scene from time to time. We have a management control system that hasn't fundamentally changed for thirty-five years. And it has lived through tremendous changes in the market and the business environment. We've been through a severe financial crisis, we've been through deregulation and we've seen the business cycle move up and down five or six times since we started running the bank according to our decentralized model. I think that proves that we have a system that has been tested in every possible way and come through with flying colors. This tells us that we don't need to keep track of all the new trends in business strategy or management control systems. When the balanced scorecard came along we could see that there were, and there still are, parts of that concept that we have already been using for quite some time. For example, we've always been clearly focused on meeting our goal (to be the best bank in our peer group) and we have aligned our measures and actions with that goal. The power of new technology is certainly making it easier to centralize. Some organizations use this power to take decisions away from front line people. This goes against everything that we believe in. If you don't resist these developments you will be a prisoner of these systems.[30]

Management books and journals are replete with success stories that support one management model or another, but how many can point to companies that have consistently beaten their rivals for over thirty years without having a dominant market position or some other special factors? Looking back on the performance generated by Wallander's vision at Handelsbanken, the benefits are evident everywhere. Returns to shareholders have been outstanding (33 percent higher than its nearest rival). Its Moody's rating (Aa1) is the third-highest in Europe. Talented graduates want to join Handelsbanken more than any other financial services company—not because it offers the highest salaries and benefits, but because young managers are expected to "run their own business" within a radically decentralized structure. Employee turnover is extremely low (around 3 percent), reflecting high levels of satisfaction (redundancies are unknown).

Using the two key measures of costs-to-total assets and cost-to-income, Handelsbanken is by far the most cost-efficient bank in Europe. It achieved a cost-to-income ratio of 45 percent in 2004, compared with over 60 percent for most international banks. One reason is that costs are constantly challenged rather than protected by the budgeting system; another is that bad debts are exceptionally low, largely due to its policy of devolving credit responsibility to frontline people. It is perhaps because branches "own" their customers (no matter where transactions take place), make fast decisions, and provide customized solutions that Handelsbanken has the lowest number of complaints in its sector and consistently tops the customer satisfaction charts in Sweden. One survey showed that 38 percent of Swedes would change to Handelsbanken if they were to change banks, compared with only 11 percent who would change to another bank. Great emphasis is placed on personal responsibility, especially when dealing with customers. Half the Handelsbanken staff has lending authority. This means that customers receive a fast response. Knowledge of customer needs and the ability to tailor products is another crucial element in the customer satisfaction process.

Maintaining a Simple, Devolved Management Model at Guardian Industries

Just in case you think that this type of management model can flourish only in high-trust environments such as Scandinavia, Guardian Industries provides a shining example of how it works just as well in North America (and in a manufacturing setting!). And the results are the same. Guardian Industries manufactures float glass products for the commercial, automotive, and construction industries. It is one of the world's largest float glass manufacturers, with a turnover of $5 billion, nineteen thousand employees, and operations in fifty countries. It operates in highly volatile and competitive markets in which huge sums are spent on automation. Though it was a public company for fifteen years (in the 1960s and 1970s), Guardian is now a private company owned by William Davidson, one of America's richest people.

As with Handelsbanken, Guardian's highly decentralized management model is the key. The company's success is attributable to a strong corporate culture that promotes personal responsibility, mutual trust, and continuous improvement. Key components include an adaptive planning process, a deep sense of responsibility throughout its workforce, and a recognition and rewards system based on an employee's worth rather than his or her job title. Along with his passionate dislike of bureaucracy and budgets, Davidson feels that managing Guardian like a family will foster creativity and establish a culture of team responsibility. Davidson never wants to hear people say, "we're from the corporate center" as though it is a sign of authority.

Despite its size, Guardian operates with clean, simple lines of management and very few levels of authority. Its employees follow Davidson's philosophy that bureaucracy stifles creativity and discourages action. Examples of this cultural mind-set are seen in the eradication of formal mission statements, organizational charts, corporate policy manuals, and all the baggage of bureaucracy, including top-down target setting and budgeting. In the Guardian culture, people are judged by results, not good intentions. This approach has enabled the company to sustain continuous growth and profits over forty-five years.

––––––––––––

To break free from generally accepted practices and systems takes belief and courage. But the CFO should be encouraged by the numbers of organizations that are making these changes. Many are getting the message about information overload and fewer are being seduced by all embracing panaceas and IT systems. They will also find a change in the perception of the finance team's role. The clear message sent to managers throughout the organization is one that says that the CFO and the finance team are reducing the non-value-adding work that frustrates all managers. And they are raising their game and building their capability (and credibility) as analysts and advisers. They are now in a position to be welcomed into the business development team as trusted and valued partners.

A CHECKLIST FOR THE CFO

☐ Lead a crusade against more complexity. Make your aim *clarity, simplicity, transparency,* and *accountability.*

☐ Aim for a unified, integrated group general ledger but reject more micromanagement. Manage data at the appropriate level in the organization. Focus senior management and the board on the bigger performance picture.

☐ Separate the signals from the noise. See activities and financial data as patterns and trends and deal with abnormalities. Ignore normal fluctuations.

☐ Provide clear principles, boundaries, and guidelines so that managers can manage their own data and make their own decisions.

☐ Manage by exception and trust people to do what they should do properly (e.g., complete expense forms), but be extremely tough on deliberate abuses of this trust (use random sampling to deter abuses).

☐ Identify the root causes of low-value work and eliminate them. Be brutal with the number of general ledger accounts—it has a knock-on effect up the measurement and reporting chain.

☐ Centralize and standardize routine work such as payroll, benefits administration, some software development, and procurement. Streamline transaction processing by improving systems integration, reducing detailed analysis, or (where appropriate) separating its management from mainstream finance (for example, by establishing one or two highly efficient shared services centers). If this is too difficult, then consider outsourcing.

☐ Eradicate budgeting detail and complexity. More detail doesn't lead to more accuracy. In fact, it is more likely to have the opposite effect. Less planning leads to fewer reports. Consider abandoning budgeting altogether (see chapter 3).

☐ Cut back on measurement to the point where only six or seven measures are used at every level.

☐ Root out redundant reports. You have probably twice as many reports as you need, and they are more expensive to produce than you think. Just stop producing them and see what happens.

☐ Use only "one truth" as far as the numbers are concerned.

☐ Be skeptical about investing in additional IT systems and improvement projects. Start with examining existing systems, looking outside-in and from end-to-end. Understand how work flows and identify how the system can be improved. Only then consider whether IT will provide a value-adding solution.

CHAPTER TWO

THE CFO AS ANALYST AND ADVISER

In our culture, the CFO has always been a part of the business team and, in some cases, grown into leading that team.

—Jim Parke, CFO, GE Capital

S URVEYS SHOW THAT most CFOs want to upgrade their role from accounting specialists to strategic or business partners. But this aspiration has remained exactly that—an *aspiration*. The gap between rhetoric and reality has remained uncomfortably large and reasonably consistent for the past ten years. Few CFOs have actually made the change primarily because they have neither the time nor the necessary capabilities within the current finance team. But for those who have, the rewards have been tangible. They have become trusted and indispensable members of the business development team, people who can add real value through incisive analysis and experienced interpretation of historic and emerging knowledge. The perception of their roles is also changed. They are seen as business generalists first and accountants second. As one finance manager turned business partner at global carrier UPS put it, "our business is delivering packages, not debits and credits."[1]

Not every CFO shares this vision. Some believe that the finance role should first and foremost be about effective stewardship and scorekeeping rather than business advice and score making. Despite these reservations, over the past fifty years the balance of these roles has been moving inexorably toward the latter activities. This doesn't mean that CFOs can take their eye off the compliance and control ball. Sarbanes-Oxley has been a sharp reminder of the importance of these duties. But neither can the CFO and the finance team use this as an excuse to revert to a bean-counting and controlling role that enables them to avoid eye contact with front line managers faced with increasingly difficult decisions.

What do business partners do that accountants don't? Of course, their accounting expertise is taken for granted. But they are involved in many more tasks such as strategic planning, forecasting, resource management, project management, process improvement, decision support, operational effectiveness, and risk management. Many physically relocate to operations away from the finance center and become an integral part of the decision-making team. This means continuous involvement, not just checking or validating decisions that have effectively been made. Another change is that they no longer just provide the information that operations people request. They bring all their knowledge and experience to bear on planning options and key decisions. Their approach to investment proposals and other project-based decisions is constructive skepticism rather than outright cynicism. They challenge their colleagues, sometimes to the point of disagreement. And they take strong positions that are immovable if they believe that ethical lines are being crossed.

Finance experts turned analysts and advisers have another selling point. They are generally seen as independent members of the team with no vested interests in decision outcomes. Whereas marketing people are focused on market share and production people on volume and quality output, finance people are just interested in making the right decision. And if the risks are too great for the potential returns, they will say so.

However, there are a number of important steps that the CFO and the finance team need to take to be in a position to act as trusted and valued business partners. Thus the CFO needs to:

- Strike the right balance between control and decision support

- Build a high performance team

- Use technology to deliver high quality information

- Provide effective decision support

Strike the Right Balance Between Control and Decision Support

Some CFOs feel uncomfortable with becoming business partners first and controllers second. They believe their role is to be independent and objective and not be too involved in decision making. At French oil company Total, CFO Robert Castaigne defines his role as "cautionary counterweight" to CEO Thierry Desmarest, whose bold acquisition and investment strategy over the past decade has transformed Total into the world's fourth-biggest oil company. Whereas Desmarest is always optimistic, Castaigne feels that his duty is to be a bit of a doomsayer to ensure that things don't go wrong.[2] Others see their primary roles as analysts and advisers, with compliance and control being farmed out to specialist internal teams or even outsourced completely. Perhaps a new finance model is emerging (see figure 2-1). In this model the central finance operation becomes a small specialist team setting standards and best practices and supervising the work of finance managers in (a) the "accounting and control" team and (b) the "decision support" teams within the lines of business.

This is the model chosen by General Electric. Since its first investment in 1997, GE Capital has been building its finance capabilities

FIGURE 2-1

An emerging model for the finance role

in India (the operation is known as GE Capital International Services, or Gecis). Following a number of acquisitions in the 1990s, by the early 2000s GE Capital decided to reduce costs by around a billion dollars per year. According to CFO Jim Parke,

> We focused on two lines of attack. One was to consolidate our systems and take a lot of the manual activities out. The other was to consolidate as much activity as we could in India and we grew the GE Capital International Services business to a total of seventeen thousand people (eleven thousand in financial services). We've just sold 60 percent of it to some financial buyers because we thought they could do a better job growing the business with external customers. We love the capability that it brought us because it combined perfectly with the whole push on controllership. They could put control mechanisms in (even if it was manual for a while) that we had a difficult time doing

in the United States or Europe. They also adapted to Six Sigma better than anybody else in the world. The intellectual capital in India is incredible. This might seem odd to some people but we don't think of them as outsourcing contractors. We think of them as our people in India doing this activity for us, and we take that same responsibility—if it's not getting done right it's because we aren't doing it right.[3]

Gecis now manages 450 processes (split into centers of excellence) categorized by industry or function. As well as handling all transaction processing, the finance and accounting center of excellence, comprising 250 employees (average age, twenty-seven), crunches the relevant data to provide analysis and reports on a whole range of issues from inventory returns to the use of cash and productivity improvement. Perhaps this is a glimpse of the future of finance—just a few people in head office being served by highly effective teams in service centers who perform not only basic accounting work but also provide a complete service including data analysis and reporting. At the analytics center of excellence, the seven hundred statisticians, MBAs, and PhDs on the team serve as quasi–vice presidents of their GE business clients. They create models from which market strategies are made and conduct due diligence for GE's targeted acquisitions.[4]

Charging GE businesses at arm's-length prices has enabled Gecis to make $404 million in revenues in 2004. All told, says VN Tyagarajan, head of global business development, GE units saved 35 to 40 percent on cost alone. He estimates another 40 percent is saved when a client relationship reaches three years, because by then the benefits of Gecis's drive for process improvement start to kick in. This is where CEO Pramod Bhasin thinks the future of outsourcing lies. "Too much of what is happening today is still what one of my customers calls 'My mess for less,'" he says. "They're just moving the work, and you're just executing the work. Not enough is being done around process expertise and domain knowledge." Improving the process that's outsourced, he argues, can deliver savings equivalent to the labor arbitrage benefits."[5]

Build a High-performance Team

It is highly unlikely that finance managers will be invited to join the business development team unless they have relevant knowledge and are capable of pulling their weight. But more than two-thirds of CFOs feel they need to do more to motivate people and invest in the capabilities of their staff. Another problem is the skills of CFOs themselves. Even though they consider this to be the most important enabler of a high-quality finance organization, they recognize that they are poor at coaching and development (only 22 percent rated themselves highly at these skill sets).[6] And finally there is little doubt that credible expertise in analysis and advice is the passport to becoming a valued business partner. At average companies only 58 percent of analysts have operating knowledge, against 100 percent of analysts at leading organizations.[7] "Not surprisingly," according to David Axson, "analysts working for best-practice organizations are held in higher regard by operating management with over 90 percent considered to be business partners."[8]

But to get to this position, finance needs competent people to interpret the flow of information and support operating managers at every level. Jonathan Chadwick, Cisco Systems' VP for finance and planning, put it this way: "What we need to be able to do is actually to provide the business with intelligence that can provide a different perspective or different decision points or opportunities to our business people."[9] Kent Potter, CFO of Chevron Phillips, a $6 billion chemicals joint venture between Chevron Texaco and Phillips Petroleum, also believes that this is the critical step toward transforming the finance operation. "Ultimately", he said. "the 10 percent or so of the companies in America that have really transformed their finance departments have done it by changing people."[10] CFOs need to recruit the right people and then develop their skills. But this is a challenge that many CFOs struggle to meet. In fact, finding and keeping capable and committed people is now one of the biggest problems facing the CFO.

Recruit the Right People

The CFO's problems begin with the recruitment process. Too many finance people are recruited on the basis of fit with the job rather than fit with the culture. Unfortunately, the majority of finance managers are not well endowed with analytical and communication skills. The key to Southwest Airlines' responsibility culture is that it hires the right people—those that have the right attitude. As Chairman Herb Kelleher has said, "If you don't have a good attitude, we don't want you, no matter how skilled you are. We can change skill level through training. We can't change attitude."[11]

Finance professionals must also be adaptive. In many industries, the business changes rapidly but the finance staff doesn't adapt quickly enough. It is a real handicap if a person is competent at only one job. It also leads to instability if key people leave the organization, and it is time-consuming and expensive—if new people are required, it takes on average forty days to find a replacement and costs over $50,000 to replace a mid- to high-level finance employee.[12] Most employees change jobs every three years, which can leave the finance department in a constant state of flux.[13] Blake Barnet, CFO of Yan Can restaurants, a unit of Yum! (which also owns Pizza Hut and Taco Bell) says his goal is to hire fewer, but better, employees. His main criteria are that they be bright, be able to learn about the various aspects of the business quickly, and be relationship builders. "The need is greater for this kind of person today", says Barnet. "Previously, you had people who were strictly finance, but now you need both depth and breadth."[14]

In some cases, the finance team is already supremely competent; they just need some disciplines and principles to guide them. This is what Thierry Moulonguet, ex-CFO of Nissan (and current CFO of Renault) found when he embarked with CEO Carlos Ghosn on the Nissan Revival Plan following the Renault acquisition in 1999. As Moulonguet explains, "this was a paradox and it was the same right across Nissan. The people were very competent and capable. We didn't hire one extra person [in finance]. I just came with one or two French colleagues. We worked with the finance teams all around the world. There was a lot of openness and exchanges of views. The result was that with everyone now using the same principles, the finance function moved itself from playing a minor role to performing on the center of the stage."[15]

Improve Communication and Teaching Skills

Communicating with analysts and investors is increasingly becoming a core competence for CFOs. According to Siegfried Luther, CFO of Bertelsmann AG, the German media company, "the CFO should be half accountant and half strategist and, to an increasing degree, an efficient communicator in both roles."[16] But it is easy to get it wrong. as Anne Mulcahy discovered just after she had taken over as CEO of Xerox. "It was October 2, 2000—my second conference call with investors and a deep, dark time for Xerox,"she notes. "It was clear to me that a company that was losing money had an unsustainable business model. My intent was to say just that, as a recognition that we 'get it.' That is, we understand this can't get better by itself. I made a mistake. No question. And I have to say I was even warned. Colleagues have said 'Ooh, do you really want to say that?' But I was naive enough to think that you got rewarded for being totally honest about the nature of your problems."[17]

Communicating complicated accounting changes is testing the skill levels of many CFOs. For example, the switch in 2005 to international accounting standards requires extensive consultation with the analyst community to explain the impact on company accounts. Analysts also want more dialogue around strategy. "All you can ask of a CFO is that they elucidate a clear strategy and execute it. You want them to show that they are in control of the risks and that they can control and explain what the other risks are. When a CFO does that, it gives an investor confidence and makes investing in that company easier," says Andrew Dickson, managing partner at a U.K. hedge fund.[18]

Boards are recruiting CFOs with exceptional communication skills. One CFO who clearly landed his job through his ability to communicate with investors was Philippe Crouzet, now CFO of French glass and building materials company Cie. de Saint-Gobain. Crouzet believes that investors want more than just numbers. "They want to hear stories about what is going on," says Crouzet. He was also prepared to listen and learn from investors. Previously he thought that maintaining high inventory levels was a smart way to serve customers, but after listening to investors' concerns about reducing inventories he tightened up on inventory levels. The result has been that, although sales increased by €2.5 billion, the company's working capital increased by only €100 million.[19]

CFOs are also realizing that there is a real and growing need for their finance managers to be effective communicators. They need to spend more time teaching their business colleagues the rudiments of financial analysis. This was the approach taken by the accountants at Caterpillar, who took on the burden of educating various divisions about what the numbers meant and how these numbers could impact them. The accountants developed a program called "Understanding the Business 101" that they presented to all eleven hundred salaried and all two thousand hourly people in one particular business unit. The employees learned what financial results are, how the accountants compiled the information, and how it was used to measure performance. The accountants explained how a welder impacts the business and how a purchasing officer impacts the business. In effect, by communicating effectively, they helped to create thousands of businesspeople.[20]

Like CEOs before them, some CFOs are being turned into media figures as increasing numbers of financial news networks search for interviews and other content to fill their schedules. This also tests their communication skills, since few financial journalists seem to be able to understand complex financial issues. According to David Devonshire, CFO of Motorola, "I think their understanding has improved, but it's still not near where it should be . . . I hope they'll start to see that the one thing that keeps you honest is cash flow."[21]

Ensure That Finance Managers Understand the Business

Some CFOs are making sure that finance professionals gain the right experience by placing them within the business teams rather than in central finance or geographic locations. Others provide extensive training and development programs. Intel, for example, has a project under way to develop its finance employees' skills. This includes building leadership abilities and training people to think strategically. According to Leslie Culberston, VP of finance, "changing the way finance operates requires people at all levels of the function who can help drive change. Additionally, finance needs employees who can communicate with other parts of the business. A big piece of this is to have the ability to have a good network inside the company and working relationships with the rest of the senior managers within the corporation so that you're viewed as a supportive role, helping the business make the right call.[22]

Cathy Ross, CFO of FedEx Express, speaks for most enlightened CFOs when she says "I encourage people within finance to leave the division and work elsewhere in the company. It helps the company and it broadens the individual."[23]

Building a Top-Quality Team at GE Capital

GE Capital is renowned both within the General Electric group and across corporate North America for having a superb finance operation. When asked what was his greatest accomplishment after fifteen years as CFO at GE Capital, Jim Parke said that is was to move from a net income of around $950 million when he first became CFO in 1990 to over $9 billion in 2005. "It's all about how to grow the business over those fifteen years and do it in a way that involves acceptable risks over various economic cycles," he says. He has little doubt that this success has been based on the quality of his people. The company has developed a financial management program that is the envy of other large corporations. Parke tells us how they do it:

For me, the quality of the people is the name of the game. We've established several developmental programs that are, I think, quite unique. One is that we have a financial management program that hires talented undergraduates. It doesn't matter if they know anything about debits and credits (I didn't when I came on board). This is a two-year program in the basics of finance with rotational assignments and classroom studies. We also have an audit group that is really a leadership development program. When they graduate from the financial management program, we encourage the best to go on the audit staff. Audit also takes high-potential people from other functions as well. It is a two to five year program; every year you either go up or out.

The big cut is after two years (the maximum is five). I know this sounds inefficient and that they don't have enough experience, but I'll put that group of people over the years against any audit group in the world. They are the best. They have free rein to do what they want and go where they want. They set their own agenda, which they coordinate with our external auditors (KPMG). It's a 24/7 very intense work program. They are away from home 95 percent of the time, but the good news is that there's light at the end of the tunnel. When they finish the program after four or five years, they invariably go into senior finance positions. There is a culture that accepts that talent, knowing what they've gone through, and knowing what their predecessors have done. It also means that people have judged you to have the talent—whether you have the experience or not is less important—so they know that they're getting smart people who know the culture and the business. It is also rigorous, probably one of the most intense learning opportunities I've ever seen.

This program is counterintuitive to almost everyone until they've had the opportunity to experience it. We recruit from around the world (50 percent have non-U.S.

passports). At my insistence, after two years they have to decide whether to focus on financial services or the industrial/service part of the company. We require half of them to focus on financial services because auditing and understanding risk is different from the rest of the company. It has allowed us to produce a lot of people who have good understanding of various GE businesses, and the risks in each of them. After the audit assignment, these people find senior roles right across the GE group.[24]

Use Technology to Deliver High-quality Information

The finance team will lack credibility unless it can use technology to provide a fast, integrated information system that delivers relevant knowledge and timely reports to operating managers. The design and implementation of these information systems is critical. The reason most new tools and systems fail to live up to their hype is that they are implemented from the center and are therefore seen by frontline troops as just another control weapon in the battle between head office staffers and frontline teams. The result is lack of buy-in and enthusiasm. In one survey, 53 percent of companies said they had the right ERP systems but didn't use them well.[25] The level of wasted investment is huge.

The trick is to involve local teams at the thinking and planning stage. If they can be convinced of the needs and benefits of ERP systems, then there is a fighting chance that they will support them. But if all they see are training programs and many more reports to prepare, against which their performance will be assessed, then you can say goodbye to the prospect of any goodwill, especially because those reports are likely to add to their existing workload.

If finance fails to get involved in the design and procurement of new systems, then it will only have itself to blame if these systems fail to deliver what the organization needs. In other words, what will be delivered will be the "default" management information system offered by the IT vendor. whose vision for finance is too often rooted in Vision A—more detail, drill-downs, and micro-management. The CFO needs to take charge of systems design and demand that IT deliver what managers need; that is, fast, relevant information. Cisco CEO John Chambers notes the benefits of this approach when he says "I can now close my books in twenty-four hours. I've known for a month what my earnings are for this weekend. I know my expenses, my profitability, my gross margins, my components . . . Once I have my data in that format, every one of my employees can make decisions that might have had to come all the way to the president . . . Quicker decision making at lower levels will translate into higher profit margins. So instead of the CEO and CFO making fifty or a hundred different decisions a quarter, managers throughout the organization can make millions of decisions. Companies that don't do that will be noncompetitive.[26]

Develop Integrated Systems

The HealthSouth case provides a sharp reminder of what can happen without integrated systems. Incredible though it sounds, a stream of five CFOs shielded a systemic fraud from investors over a six-year period as around $2.7 billion of faked revenues were booked to protect earnings and share price. But key to making this fraud possible was the disconnection between business-unit accounting systems and the corporate accounting system (the WorldCom case was similar). The consolidation of group accounts was done by hand, just like a 1960s manual private ledger kept under lock and key (I remember many of these from my early auditing days). Thus the checks and balances that normally flow from the finance team observing the transaction traffic through the consolidation system were absent. Auditors Ernst & Young noted in the 2001 accounts that "management is dominated by one or two individuals without effective oversight by the board of directors or audit committee."[27]

While this might be an extreme case, many organizations suffer delays and high error rates because information systems are fragmented and disconnected. Most cannot talk to each other. This problem is often the result of a series of acquisitions over several years. But software vendors are now shrinking the problem by providing reporting and consolidation capabilities that can draw data from disparate systems and make it look more like an integrated system. The ultimate goal is to have one unified system for the whole organization. One immediate advantage is the time saved in rekeying data as well as reducing the need for huge numbers of month-end journals.

Another advantage is that finance can use integrated platforms to build business rules and structures, then modify systems as their business evolves, easily accommodating changes such as extra locations, new or discontinued product lines, or restructured cost centers. Many of these systems have powerful modeling capabilities that enable teams to flexibly devise, compare, and assess alternative business scenarios. Such systems allow teams to build models in days rather than months. Data definitions can be imported from other sources like ERP and general ledger systems. They also enable cross-functional models to be built.

Tomkins is one company that has used technology effectively to deliver tangible results. CFO Ken Lever explains how:

> We make extensive use of the Internet to improve the speed and processing of transactions. The groupwide transaction processing system has enabled us to improve efficiency enormously. All the operating businesses can download their own information into this system. This, together with our consolidation system, sits on top of the systems that the individual businesses run. We have many different operating businesses that use their own ERP system. So what we have done very effectively is to use technology to transfer data from those systems into our central reporting system as seamlessly as possible and we now do very little rekeying of data from one system to another. This has saved us an enormous amount of time and cost. I'm

not saying that we don't do any rekeying of data but it has reduced dramatically, and we are continually looking at ways of eradicating this type of work. We've also used technology in other areas. For example, our capital investment appraisal process is now fully automated. This has speeded up the investment process considerably. Whereas previously we had a lot of manual documents floating around the system, this is all now done electronically.[28]

Integrated systems also reduce the dependency on closing the books quickly at the end of the month or quarter. In fact, while some best-practice companies close the books at lightening speed (in some cases within one day), many others do not depend at all on a fast close. Jim Parke, CFO of GE Capital, doesn't think it's all that important because managers have most of the basic information that they need when they need it: "We just don't have the final net income figure. We know our operating costs; we know what people we have (that's our biggest cost); we know our interest expense and we know the value of our assets. We can get at these numbers at a moment's notice. So not closing the books quickly doesn't slow us down or in any way handicap our business decisions. Getting it all together quickly is only a problem for external reporting."[29]

Another benefit of integrated systems is the enhanced effectiveness of decentralized decision making. While those at the corporate center can see patterns, trends, and exceptions, they need to interfere only when they see movements that trigger a dialogue. This leaves local managers free to spend all their time developing the business rather than dancing to the tune of top-down control systems such as budgets and variances.

Reduce the Dependency on Spreadsheets

According to a 2003 IBM survey of 450 CFOs, spreadsheets continue to dominate planning processes in over 80 percent of organizations.[30] While this is fine for local requirements, spreadsheets can cause problems when they need to be aggregated across and up the organization. It is also apparent that in large organizations, different units use different assumptions, algorithms, and software. This makes it difficult to combine and consolidate forecasts. According to Gary Crittenden, CFO of American Express, "spreadsheets are great for individual productivity work but they cause problems when there is a lot of sharing and aggregation going on. Using driver-based forecasts together with dedicated systems and Web technology enables hundreds of managers to work on forecasts together and aggregate the outcomes to the highest level, thus providing more control than ever to the board. The new approach has enabled us to standardize on a single methodology and align key assumptions and algorithms across the organization."[31]

Sarbanes-Oxley is also driving another nail in the spreadsheet-as-integrated-planning-tool coffin. In theory at least, every change to a formula or even a number of rows needs to be documented. This will undoubtedly make it more difficult for organizations to rely on traditional spreadsheets. Even Microsoft recognizes the problem. "There's an inherent tension between the 'power-to-the-people' origins of Excel and the role it is increasingly called on to play," says Marc Chardon, CFO of Microsoft's Information Worker division (which is responsible for Excel).[33] Needless to say, Microsoft is working on a new version that is better suited to collaborative work.

Building a Fast, Integrated Information System at Cognos

Cognos is a world leader in business intelligence and performance planning software for the corporate performance management (CPM) market. Before joining the company as CFO in 2001, Tom Manley just didn't realize how technology could improve both the quality of information and how it could be delivered in a much more effective way to key people around the organization. "Over the past two to three years we have become a test-bed for all our own products," notes Manley. "In the early phase we had disconnected business intelligence and were not really working toward a single view of the business. We had too much data and too little knowledge."[33]

So he and CEO Rob Ashe kicked off a program called "CPM at Cognos." But it was not only about optimizing the use of their own products; they also wanted to learn how they could move toward a better CPM environment and take their customers with them on the journey. After designing their corporate strategy map and scorecard they communicated it to the entire company. Employees were told that they all had access to the corporate scorecard, including descriptions of the detailed metrics, so everyone knew how they fitted into the strategic picture. Then each of the functions built its own strategic road map to fit in with the corporate one, and then enriched the entire environment with thoughtful reports. At the same time, they provided lots of information so that people could do their own analyses and make sure that they were making the right decisions relative to the overall strategy.

But the real key to getting full acceptance was the reform of the planning system. Up to this point many people felt that they spent half their lives feeding a planning system that provided precious few benefits. Manley and Ashe wanted to turn this around by providing a system that would minimize people's input time and leverage their knowledge to influence their future direction. Manley explains:

> I envisioned an environment where the information network was so efficient that our people could just absorb key information every day. New information would be a simple act of updating the plan, which was designed for handling constant, dynamic input. The planning environment would become a value-added support system for decision making. Instead of drowning in numbers, I wanted managers to focus on how they were going to allocate resources and what they were doing strategically to improve their performance. I wanted people to be focused on what they could influence as opposed to doing a lot of analysis that they put in a drawer and never looked at again.

Let me give you an example from my own perspective. I come in every morning, turn on my computer, and go straight to my BI [business intelligence] environment, where I see five different reports. The first report tells me every deal that we've closed in the last twenty-four hours. The second report tells me about any deals in the pipeline that have changed in the last twenty-four hours with some threshold. The third report tells me about any deals that have slipped from one quarter to the next. The fourth report tells me about all the big deals that we are tracking in a quarter so I know to whom we're selling on an ongoing basis. And the fifth report is a summary that basically tells me where we are from a revenue point of view. That takes me only ten to fifteen minutes because when you're used to the reporting framework you're just looking for the changes and the exceptions.

The real challenge was to hold people accountable for that information. But I have to say that with all the current attention on compliance, the integrity of the data is getting stronger every day. Yet I know that's not sufficient on its own. We also need to break the traditional mind-set that the planning and budgeting process is a game of negotiation instead of being the outcome of good planning. Best-in-class planning solutions support the activities of how management works—which in most cases means thinking about the next actions and the go-forward view of the business. Only a small portion of a manager's time is spent analyzing the historical results. I think that as more information becomes readily available and people are looking at information differently, the ability to negotiate starts to dissipate. And I think that's starting to happen.

Provide Effective Decision Support

The CFO and the finance team need to be independent and objective participants in the decision-making process. They should always ask the awkward questions and, where appropriate, be prepared to challenge conventional wisdom. They should also be prepared to go beyond the obvious numbers and look at the wider ramifications of particular decisions. They should look at hidden costs and best practices elsewhere.

Be a Skeptic, Not a Cynic

The CFO should maintain a staunchly independent view about management decisions. It is too easy to go with the flow, especially when the firm appears to be making profits and growing rapidly. Many companies have seen their good run come to a grinding halt through one poor decision, perhaps based on a misjudged acquisition. Every acquisition is based on long-term forecasts—usually showing synergy, cost savings, or other benefits of combining two organizations. But these long-term forecasts are often self-serving and difficult to challenge. One writer has this advice for CFOs looking at long-term forecasts: "Distrust computer-driven models that convey a spurious air of authenticity to the exercise but are based on no-less suspect assumptions that any more mundane approach. Distrust elegance and complexity. Prefer judgment to technique."[34]

The CFO is often placed in a difficult position with regard to the board and especially the CEO. Many CEOs are serial acquirers who see their role as creating shareholder value instead of managing the business. They are often egged on by investment bankers who keep telling the board that the company's share price will continue to underperform unless the organization can grow more rapidly. This is not easy without an acquisition or two.

But according to a report by KPMG, only 30 percent of acquisitions add value to the shareholders of the acquiring company.[35] The CFO should be particularly skeptical about synergy-type benefits, especially cost savings. While such benefits look seductive on spreadsheets, the reality is that the pain and costs of restructuring existing and new businesses, and the collapsing morale it brings in its wake, outweigh any cost savings. Campbell and Goold have conducted extensive research into the effects of "synergy." This comment encapsulates their views: "This thirst for synergy creates optical illusions. Parent managers, often supported by business managers, believe that synergy already exists and that further initiatives will reveal more synergy benefits that up till now have been hidden from view. If parent managers *want* to believe that synergy opportunities exist, it is comparatively easy to make a case in favor—especially given the problems of precise cost/benefit analysis."[36]

The very mention of the word *synergy*, according to strategy expert Gary Hamel, should send investors running for the door. "It's time to beware when the CEO loads up the balance sheet with billions of dollars worth of fixed assets on the basis of something as ethereal as synergy," notes Hamel.[37] The reality is that few grand strategies come to fruition, and very few longer-term forecasts are worth the paper they are written on. In an unpredictable world, the emphasis should be on flexibility and speed of response rather than strategic planning.

Investing in knowledge management systems is another example of how the skeptical CFO can save the company from going with the flow and increasing complexity and cost. Instead of debating the merits of investing in expensive knowledge management systems, the wise CFO would be better advised to address these questions: "What is stopping us sharing knowledge?" followed by "How do we remove these barriers?"

The reasons that managers fail to share knowledge are often concerned with how performance management systems work. Managers are placed in business unit silos, told to meet a range of financial targets, and then given incentives to meet them. This approach guarantees that little knowledge will be shared across the organization, since every manager has a vested interest in looking after his or her own part of the business. Some see other business units as the real enemy, rather than the external competition. Another barrier to knowledge sharing is that measures are separated from the work people do. If senior management forces workers to follow procedures (assuming that knowledge is accumulated in the hierarchy), then it is hardly surprising that workers will unplug their brains when they enter the workplace and follow the rules.

John Browne, CEO of BP-Amoco believes that knowledge sharing must start by creating the right climate. The top management team must stimulate the organization, not control it. Its role is to provide strategic directives, to encourage learning, and to make sure there are mechanisms for transferring the lessons. "The role of leaders at all levels is to demonstrate to people that they are capable of achieving more than they think they can achieve and that they should never be satisfied with where they are now. To change behavior and unleash new ways of thinking, a leader sometimes has to say, 'Stop, you're not allowed to do it the old way,' and issue a challenge," notes Browne.[38] The CFO needs to follow Browne's advice and remove the barriers to knowledge sharing. He must recognize that investing in expensive systems may not be the right approach.

Challenge Conventional Wisdom

Is increased market share always good? Is every customer a good customer? Do sales incentives drive performance improvement? Is maximizing volume production the best way to reduce unit costs? On the face of it, most finance managers would answer "yes" to these questions, though many would also be alerted to hidden problems. Pursuing market share can drive up costs and bring in the wrong (unprofitable) customers. In a large population of customers, 20 percent are likely to account for 225 percent of profits, while 80 percent "lose" 125 percent of profits.[39] The problem is that managers have no idea which customers make up the 20 percent and which make up the rest. Sales incentives can be highly dysfunctional and attract mercenary salespeople who stick around only as long as they are making maximum bonuses. When these tail off, they move on to the next gullible employer and try their best to take their customers with them.

Putting quality before volume is a smarter way to improve long-term profitability as Toyota and others have discovered.

Let's just zoom in on one of these issues—"good" customers. To most marketing managers and salespeople, every customer is a good customer and every sale is a good sale if it covers its direct costs (thus making a contribution to overheads). The result is that the accounts receivable ledger grows like gangbusters and salespeople pursue every sales opportunity. What's missing is *a method of evaluating whether customers (or customer segments)—both existing and targeted—are worthwhile.* In other words, there is little concern with which customers to keep, which have untapped potential, which are strategic, which are unprofitable, and which should be abandoned. Most marketing programs are simply aimed at replacing the 20 percent of customers the firm expects to lose each year, without any consideration of whether resources would be better spent on keeping them than attracting the replacements. Fred Reichheld and Earl Sasser have noted that a 50 percent cut in defections will more than double the average company's growth rate.[40]

What advice should the CFO give? He should encourage marketing, sales, and finance to sit down together to review the customer portfolio (perhaps with representatives from service, support, and credit control). Among them they should look at whether customers are either strategic, profitable, neither, or both. Customers can be strategic for many reasons. It helps if they buy for reasons of "value" rather than "cost." Dell exited the first-time user segment of the PC market in the early 1990s for exactly these reasons. Its value proposition was geared to more sophisticated users who knew what they wanted and required relatively little support. There are other reasons why a particular customer may be strategic. For example, one customer may well influence others. Dealing with one customer in a particular area or technology platform can be the gateway to many others—whether a community, a territory, a group of companies, or perhaps an economic web. Many other strategic relationship questions spring to mind. Is the customer likely to grow? Can we learn from the customer? Can we follow a particular customer into a new market opportunity? Does the customer have special technology or excellent systems from which we can benefit? Unless the CFO and business-unit leaders ask these types of questions, the underlying importance of customers will remain unrecognized and their full potential unexplored.

Customers must also be profitable. Though most finance departments provide customer profitability analysis at the *gross* profit level (i.e., revenue less direct costs), few provide it at the *net* profit level (i.e., after charging all the "below-the-line" costs of serving and supporting customers). But to sales and marketing teams, this information can be priceless. They might realize, for example, that some of their largest customers are also their biggest loss makers. These are the ones that take all the special offers at the end of the quarter, soak up all the promotional budgets, take all the discounts and other benefits going, return goods at the slightest suspicion of a fault, demand special deals and inventory call-offs, pay late, and more generally take weeks of valuable management time.

What should be done with an unprofitable customer? Unless the case is hopeless, the first action is to try to make that customer profitable. There are usually reasons underpinning the profit problems. For example, transaction costs may be too high or delivery and support costs may be excessive. Every case needs looking at on its merits. Once armed with this knowledge, sales and support people can at least meet with the customer and work out ways of making the relationship more valuable for both parties. The ideal customer is both strategic and profitable. The team should build a profile of what such a customer looks like and then try to gradually switch the balance of the customer portfolio. After the review the team will be in a better position to pass all its nonstrategic, unprofitable customers onto its competitors.

Becoming a Valued Business Partner at American Express

Under the leadership of CFO Gary Crittenden, American Express has transformed its finance operation. Most importantly, Crittenden has raised finance's game to a level where the team is now an indispensable business partner:

> I think that finance is such an integral part of how the "business does business" that no one would think of doing anything without a clear understanding of what their options were, and it just happens to be finance's job to do that. So if you're on the outside trying to shoehorn your way in, that's a tough job. But if you're actually part of the business team constantly thinking ahead, operating managers will seek you out. They want to know what your input is before they have to make difficult choices. We provide the information and structure the options in a way that they need to make effective decisions. It's the same as having relationships with customers so that they *want to deal with you* instead of constantly trying to persuade them to buy your products and services.
>
> We have some really talented people, but the trick is to find the time for them to use their knowledge to support the business. We've done this by reorganizing the way we do things, especially in the back-office part of the finance process. One of the things I always say about our business unit CFOs is that presidents fool me into thinking that they work for me when in reality they work for their business-unit CEOs. I think these business-line CFOs recognize the accountability they have to the group finance function by ensuring that they have the right controls in place and are following consistently good practice. But their real focus is on supporting their business managers. And that's how it should be.[41]

Operating managers must value finance for its knowledge and contribution to strategic planning and execution before it can earn its place in the business development team. Upgrading the competences of the finance team and the relevance of the technology it uses are both key elements in this process. But how the team provides and communicates decision support knowledge is really what makes it an indispensable player. However, even greater opportunities lie ahead for the ambitious CFO who really wants to make an impact on the whole performance of the organization. Changing management behavior from managing numbers to improving the business is the big opportunity. The next four chapters will show what an ambitious CFO, backed by a competent and committed team, can really do if they try.

A CHECKLIST FOR THE CFO

- ☐ Aim to be a trusted and indispensable member of the business development team. But also recognize that this cannot be achieved unless effective accounting systems and controls are in place.

- ☐ Reduce the central finance function. Place more finance managers in operating teams. Make the core finance group a center of excellence, setting and maintaining the highest standards.

- ☐ Be careful when outsourcing. Don't go for the "my mess for less" value proposition. Agree with the service provider to work together to improve the process over time so that the mess (and the cost) is reduced.

- ☐ Build a high-performance team with good analysts and communicators who are also capable accountants.

- ☐ Start by recruiting the right people. Look for the right attitudes (team players) and communication skills first and technical skills second. Skills can be improved; attitudes are hard to change.

- ☐ Work to improve communications skills at every level. Turn finance managers into teachers and mentors who help business managers improve their financial knowledge.

- ☐ Ensure that finance managers understand the business. If the business structure allows it, give all key finance people experience in business teams.

☐ Develop integrated information systems that fit with your performance management vision. Focus these systems on the needs of
frontline teams.

☐ Use dedicated planning tools and reduce your dependency on
spreadsheets for planning, forecasting, and consolidations.

☐ Provide effective decision support by maintaining an objective,
independent view (be a skeptic, not a cynic).

☐ Challenge conventional wisdom where appropriate.

☐ Look beyond the numbers. Seek out hidden costs and look at the
strategic impact of key decisions.

CHAPTER THREE

THE CFO AS ARCHITECT OF ADAPTIVE MANAGEMENT

If you cannot *know what your customers will want or your competitors will offer next year—or even who your customers or competitors will be—you cannot develop an effective plan for achieving targeted levels of sales and profits.*

—Stephan Haeckel, *Adaptive Enterprise*

THE TYPICAL CFO presides over a performance management system that involves plans, targets, and resources that are *negotiated, annual,* and *fixed.* These systems were designed for stable trading environments in which suppliers could dictate to the market. But as most of us now know, markets are unstable and customers rule the roost. Just think of the airline industry in recent years. In the first quarter of 2001 the industry was flying high after several years of record profits; traffic was soaring; fares were high; most experts predicted nothing but blue skies ahead. But how wrong the experts were. Few predicted the depth of the economic downturn that began in the second quarter of 2001; fewer still the dramatic drop in business travel; and of course, no one predicted 9/11, the SARS epidemic, or the wars in Afghanistan and Iraq. The economic impact has been devastating—accumulated losses over the past four years amounting to over $20 billion, a number of airlines in Chapter 11, and over a hundred thousand job losses.

Despite a number of compelling reasons to move away from annual plans and budgets, many CFOs are reluctant to make the change. One of the reasons is that they cannot see beyond financial targets and budgets as a means of driving performance improvement and making managers accountable for results. Indeed the evidence suggests that these links are becoming even more pervasive.[1] But other CFOs recognize that there are alternative (and less dysfunctional) ways of driving performance improvement and making managers accountable for performance (we'll examine these toward the end of this chapter). Their focus is less on holding managers accountable for meeting a predetermined plan and more on giving them the freedom and capability to "manage reality." The new performance contract is one based on continuous improvement compared with internal and external peers and benchmarks.

To cope with these changes CFOs need to implement systems that provide managers at every level with the capability to make fast, well-informed decisions. They need to replace annual planning cycles with more regular business reviews that enable managers to see trends, patterns, and "breaks in the curve" long before their competitors and thus improve the quality of decision making. In particular, the CFO needs to:

- Design adaptive systems from the customer's perspective

- Manage through continuous planning cycles

- Make rolling forecasts the primary management tool

- Report key metrics daily and weekly

- Enable fast access to resources

- Focus accountability on the relative improvement of teams

Design Adaptive Systems from the Customer's Perspective

One of the reasons that many CFOs believe in setting financial targets and attaching management accountability to them is that they are trained to see the organization as a huge machine containing a set of interacting parts that create a result. If the machine malfunctions its faulty parts can be fixed (or "reengineered") thus improving the performance of the whole machine. This mental model has its origins in Newton's idea of a world ruled by a centralized notion of cause and effect (one gear turns, which makes another gear turn, and so on). Its logic enables systems to be run forward in time and to provide predictions.

But according to the late London Business School professor Sumantra Ghoshal, the extension of this worldview to human organizations is an egregious error.[2] He believed that business schools themselves must shoulder much of the blame, that this pseudo-scientific approach to management is a result of their attempts to make business studies "respectable." Academics do this by removing the subjective difficulties of analyzing company behavior in terms of human choices, instead looking for explanations in impersonal patterns and laws—a kind of business physics (Ghoshal was originally a physicist). Ghoshal believed that because human behavior and relationships can't be modeled, they are conveniently ignored. So you simply end up with equations based on financial numbers (often with simple cause-and-effect relationships). According to this mechanistic view of organizational behavior, a change in one part of the organization causes a corresponding and equal change in another part. For example, if profit equals revenue minus cost, then reducing cost by one dollar increases profit by the same amount. This explains why so many finance managers practice "management by numbers" or "remote-controlled management." But these assumptions and practices are seriously flawed.

MIT professor Mitchel Resnick is another academic who believes that the Newtonian model does not explain reality. In his view, a new set of decentralized models and metaphors is spreading through the scientific community and gradually into culture at large. Researchers now view a wide range of systems—everything from bird flocks to immune responses—less like clockwork mechanisms and more like complex ecosystems controlled by decentralized interactions and feedback loops.[3] In other words, we are beginning to realize that a system can restructure and transform itself either in response to its changing environment or as a challenge to it. This means that instead of basing our strategies and actions on *prediction and control,* with the development and implementation of a plan designed to take us from "here and now" to "there and then," we have to adopt a more *adaptive and devolved* approach to management, constantly reinventing ourselves to meet new realities.

While many leaders talk about adapting to change, few know how to change their systems so that they respond naturally to the external environment. Instead the ingrained belief in rationality and prediction and control causes them to expend huge amounts of time and energy aligning and realigning their strategies, structures, and systems as one reorganization follows another. This is a slow, difficult, and expensive process and a nightmare for many employees whose jobs are at risk.

This inability to cope with discontinuous change is, more often than not, caused by hardwired "plan-make-and-sell" business models. In other words, managers first decide which products to make and then spend huge sums on marketing and sales persuading customers to buy their output. In his brilliant article "Marketing Myopia," written in 1960, Theodore Levitt wrote that an organization must learn to think of itself not as producing goods and services but as *buying customers,* as doing the things that will make people *want* to do business with it.[4] Most organizations today fail to understand this point. Until a few years ago, U.K. retailer Marks & Spencer was a classic example. This is how one disgruntled shareholder reflected on the attitude of senior executives as they failed to listen to customers.

> The word is arrogance. Arrogance that for four decades, M&S refused to include the use of credit cards in its merchandising strategy. Arrogance that it refused to focus on the customer, but relied primarily on the judgment of senior corporate management for its merchandising decisions. Arrogance that it allowed the quality of its product mix to deteriorate despite customer complaints. Arrogance that it still has not moved to zero in on the real M&S customer. Arrogance that it ignored the growing competitive forces surrounding it. Arrogance that it dismissed a retail axiom: that a store's primary function is not profit but to satisfy the customer—and from that will evolve profit. Arrogance that it thought the name of Marks & Spencer was invincible. And the final arrogance is the report that, in spite of all of the failings, in spite of the inability to jump-start the company, the board is considering a bonus for . . . its chairman.[5]

One reorganization has followed another in recent years but the company has struggled to retain its former position as market leader.

This approach (sometimes known as a "push" system) is in stark contrast to the approach taken by "sense-and-respond" organizations. These organizations operate with a "pull" system, in which everything is pulled by the customer order, rather than being pushed by the plan determined by a production management system based on forecasts agreed much earlier. It's not that the pull system does not use forecasts. The important difference is that a forecast is used only to plan the likely capacity required in a period, but the entire demand chain reacts only to customer orders, not to the plan.

Toyota is a well-known example of a sense-and-respond organization. Instead of pushing products through rigid processes to meet sales targets, its operating systems start from the customer—

it is the customer order that drives operating processes and the work that people do. The point is that in sense-and-respond companies, predetermined plans and fixed-performance contracts are anathema and represent insurmountable barriers. That's why adaptive organizations like Toyota don't have them.

Perhaps the real lesson for the CFO is that if an organization really wants to sense and respond to individual customer requests then it must not only redesign its operating processes to enable this but it must also redesign its performance management model (e.g., how it sets targets and manages resources). Otherwise a fatal collision will be inevitable as managers respond to (vertical) functional targets that cut across (horizontal) customer-oriented business processes. If both systems are in harmony, the benefits can be huge. U.K. occupational psychologist John Seddon spells them out: "The systems approach creates an adaptive organization, as demand changes, people change what they do—something that is impossible to accomplish in a command and control design. It puts people back where they belong: managing relationships with customers."[6]

Manage Through Continuous Planning Cycles

Adaptive organizations believe that discontinuous change is now the norm. They see planning as a continuous, inclusive process, driven by events (such as the launch of a new product or a competitive threat) and emerging knowledge, and not constrained by the current financial year. Nor does planning require sophisticated tools. It relies on fast, relevant (actionable) information and responsible people who know what is expected of them and what to do in any given situation.

Herb Kelleher, chairman of Southwest Airlines, describes how this process works in practice:

> Reality is chaotic, planning is ordered and logical. The two don't square with one another. When USAir pulls out of six cities in California, they don't call and tell me

they're going to do that. Now, if we have established a big strategic plan that is approved by our officers and the board of directors, I would have to go to the officers and the board and tell them we want to deviate from the plan. They would want to know why I want to buy six more airplanes. The problem is that we'd analyze it and debate its merits for three months, instead of getting the airplanes, taking over the gates, and dominating California. The meticulous nit-picking that goes on in most strategic planning processes creates a mental straitjacket that becomes disabling in an industry where things change radically from one day to the next.[7]

While the strategic direction at the group level and market positioning at the business unit level need to be as stable as possible, frontline teams need to continuously plan how to improve their performance and respond quickly to changing events (where an organization draws the front line will depend on a host of factors, including competencies and information availability). Thus continuity of strategy and rapid change are not inconsistent. In fact, "the two go right together," notes strategy expert, Michael Porter, "if we make the very important distinction between strategic positioning and operational effectiveness in executing that position."[8]

What Porter means is that in order to create the conditions to make trade-offs between strategy positions, managers need continuity in the basic positioning—the types of products an organization offers, the essential core of the value it is delivering. But within that continuity, Porter notes, "should be a feverish and ongoing process of change. If one examines high-performance companies, and by that I mean those that regularly outperform their industries, one finds that they don't change their strategies. Instead of change, we see stability. We see continuity. But we also see a lot of change in the details—the product details, the service details."[9]

In today's fast-paced information economy, the people best placed to see the changes taking place within markets, competitors, and customers are frontline teams. They are the ones that have to respond quickly to emerging events and this means devolving to them the power and responsibility to take the necessary action. The degree of freedom depends on the maturity of the model. At Handelsbanken, branch managers have significant freedom but this has gradually been extended over many years. Although the bank has five product-based subsidiaries and a central product development group, there are no product-based targets in the regions and branches. Though they have flexibility over prices, discounts, and which products they sell, branch teams work within well-understood cost and profit ratios.

Jim Parke, CFO of GE Capital, explains why planning needs to be flexible and owned by the local team: "Once the year is under way we review performance twice a quarter. We ask questions about how we are doing, what's changing in the marketplace, what are the new opportunities that have arisen, and so forth. We might then produce a new estimate based on the latest knowledge. Plans never work out the way you expect so you have to adjust as you go. There are new risks and opportunities arising all the time especially in financial services. The key performance measure we look at each quarter is improvement over prior year."[10]

The key change in this more devolved management model is the move toward a more continuous, or event-driven, planning cycle. In organizations subject to continuous change it might be appropriate to set regular (monthly or quarterly) strategic reviews, or to make a review dependent on some significant event. Such events can be positive (e.g., introducing new products or a new business model) or negative (e.g., reacting to supply chain disruptions or environmental disasters). The whole point is that these reviews are not time-dependent and thus can occur as and when needed. The typical planning cycle within a business unit has four steps: check, aim, plan, and act (see figure 3-1).[11]

1. *Check.* The cycle start with the questions, Where are we right now? What does the short-term future look like? What is the competition doing?

2. *Aim.* In the next step, we ask, What is our purpose? What does success look like? Are we on a trajectory to meet our medium-term goals? Does our strategy need to change?

FIGURE 3-1

Planning as a continuous process

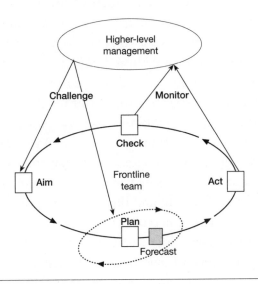

3. *Plan.* The third step focuses on the questions, What actions (if any) do we need to take to improve our performance? What resources do we need? What impact will these actions have on our performance?

4. *Act.* In the fourth step, the issue becomes, How should we execute the plans and manage the existing business?

You will note that nowhere in this check-aim-plan-act cycle has the team made a commitment to a higher authority to reach a specific target. In other words, there is no fixed-performance contract. All the commitment to improve is within the local team. This taps the power of intrinsic motivation. It is the team that sets the goals and plans, and it is the team that has the drive to make them succeed. The role of the corporate center is to set strategic direction together with clear operating guidelines and performance standards. It also has a clear monitoring role, using trends and rolling forecasts to check that the units are within bounds in terms of agreed indicators, and interfering only if they are not. This local check-aim-plan-act cycle is typical of many adaptive organizations. But the key to its success is that it is *driven locally* by people who want to improve their relative performance.

How does this cycle work in practice? Imagine you have just been appointed as a branch manager at a retail bank. You have inherited a poor situation. First you *check* where you are; you are at the bottom of the league table and your cost-to-income ratio is lagging behind your peers. Second, you *aim* for an improvement goal; you consult with your team and your regional managers and you decide to set a goal to improve your cost-to-income ratio by 30 percent over two years (this has to be a real stretch goal if you are to overtake your peers, who are also striving to improve). Third, you *plan* what to do, discussing with your team the options available for achieving this goal, and then test the options by examining their likely forecast outcomes. You also have a dialogue with your regional manager about the range of options available and ask his advice. He may ask questions about assumptions, risk, and time-scales and may even provide some input about best practices elsewhere. You then acquire (or reduce) the resources you need to put the plans into action. Finally, you *act,* choosing those initiatives that offer the best chance of success. This cycle repeats itself endlessly as the branch continuously tries to improve its performance.

Leading organizations share some common attributes that enable the devolution of strategy.

- They make accountability for strategy clear down the line. Teams know their scope of authority and the results they are accountable for.

- Teams share a common language for discussing strategies and a common process for developing them.

- They have skilled strategic thinkers who engage in a continuous dialogue about strategy.

- They actively encourage and support free, rigorous, and fact-based debate. There is a "no-blame" culture that enables ideas to circulate freely.

- They provide a climate where people can pursue long-term performance goals. Thinking strategically requires a more extended perspective than managing for quarterly results. Though the policies, style, and incentives of an organization should reward this kind of outlook, they most often do not.

Managing Through Quarterly Business Review Cycles at Telecom New Zealand

Telecom New Zealand is an innovative telecommunications company that provides a full range of Internet, data, voice, mobile, and fixed-line calling services to its customers. In the two years to January 2005 its share price increased by 66 percent. Through 2003–2005, led by CFO Marko Bogoievski, it implemented a major overhaul of its financial planning and reporting systems. This involved abandoning the bottom-up annual planning and budgeting cycle and moving to a new planning process based around quarterly rolling forecasts. Bogoievski explains how the new process works:

> Each quarter we complete a forward eighteen-month forecast for the business that focuses on a few key relative performance measures (financial and nonfinancial measures are used), and there is no difference in the way we approach each quarter. We do perform an abbreviated annual strategy review. This process involves a brief top-down review of the longer term (three-to-five year horizon) and that is more about which markets and adjacent industries we want to be in and how much capital we want to allocate to these new opportunities. The two processes combined look and feel very different from what used to be the annual planning process. So we still find that one of the issues with these rolling eighteen-month forecasts is that business units don't take the time to lift their heads up, so we do like the balance of business units looking ahead eighteen months and having a top-down strategic review every year, including which markets they should enter or withdraw from and overall how we are going to reallocate our capital within our group portfolio. Inside each business

unit we have more fluid mechanisms for reallocating capital and operating capacity as a result of these forecasts. Some business units are doing a better job of reallocating capital dynamically than others but that probably reflects their market position more than anything else.

The forecasts are consolidated, and that's what we present to the board. We also compare these forecasts to other relative benchmarks in the financial markets and against other telcos. We report actual performance against the latest forecast and against last year as opposed to any budget as we did previously. And in some areas we also compare our growth rates against market growth rates. That's the emphasis of monthly reporting. The actual reporting also looks quite different. So when a quarter rolls around, all we're really looking at is the performance trajectory. If we're aiming to grow at twice the rate of the industry for a certain service line we really only need to present a one pager and look at whether we're making progress against that target or not.[12]

Make Rolling Forecasts the Primary Management Tool

Most CFOs want to spend more time managing the future rather than dwelling on the past. So the ability to help managers to prepare quality forecasts is fast becoming a core competence. But most finance teams have much to learn. The mistake that most of them make is assuming that forecasts are about predicting and controlling future outcomes. The purpose of forecasting is to inform decision making (to help shape future outcomes), not to predict the future. In reality, forecasting is necessary only because organizations cannot react instantly to changing events. That's why fast reaction is more important than (even accurate) prediction—because accuracy is rarely achieved. Indeed, the only certainty about a forecast is that it will be wrong. The question is by how much. Narrowing that variation comes from learning, experience, decent information systems, and ultimately, judgment.

The more practice managers have at preparing short-term forecasts, the better they will become. That's why adaptive organizations focus less on annual budgets or long-term views and more on *rolling* views—usually rolling forecasts that always look twelve to eighteen months ahead. Rolling forecasts, if well prepared, form the backbone of a new and much more useful information system that connects all the pieces of the organization and gives senior management a continuous picture both of the current position and the short-term outlook. In effect they are the aggregate of business-as-usual forecasts (extrapolations of existing trends), all the action plans in progress, and all plans in the pipeline. In other words, forecasts should be "baseline plus anticipated events," with the effort being focused on "events." An honest view has no bias, so managers should expect to see half of their forecasts to be on the high side of actual outcomes and half on the low side. The ideal forecast has clean data that enables managers to improve decision making. Forecasts must not be seen as commitments, otherwise bias and distortion will be inevitable—that's why implementing rolling forecasts under the umbrella of fixed targets (usually focused on "closing the gap") rarely works. If managers at any level interfere with the forecasting process on the basis of giving it "more stretch" or "bridging the gap," the outcome is almost guaranteed to be a dangerous distortion of reality.

Figure 3-2 shows a typical 5-quarterly rolling forecast. Let's assume we are just approaching the end of quarter 1. The management team gets the rough figures for that quarter and starts to review the next four quarters. Three of those quarters are already in the previous forecast, so they just need updating. A further quarter, however, needs to be added (Q1 for the next year). More time will be spent on the earlier quarters than the later ones, using as much relevant knowledge and business intelligence as can be gathered.

Leading organizations are placing forecasting at the center of the management process. It becomes an essential tool for business

FIGURE 3-2

A 5-quarterly rolling forecast

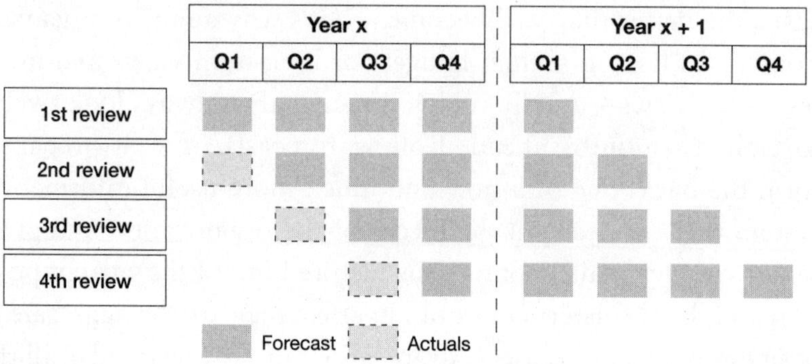

	Year x				Year x + 1			
	Q1	Q2	Q3	Q4	Q1	Q2	Q3	Q4
1st review	■	■	■	■	■			
2nd review	▢	■	■	■	■	■		
3rd review		▢	■	■	■	■	■	
4th review			▢	■	■	■	■	■

■ Forecast   ▢ Actuals

managers to support their decision making, not just another management chore that needs to be done to feed the corporate beast. Focusing on only a few key drivers, the process should take no longer than a day or two and it should be done not by specialist finance people but by the business team itself.

Make Forecasting a Management, Not a Measurement, Process

Forecasts must not be seen by senior managers as a tool for questioning or reassessing performance targets. Nor must they be used to demand changes or improvements. What happened at Procter & Gamble in 1999 was a classic example of mixing forecasts with targets. After abandoning the budgeting process for 1998–1999, the company introduced "stretch" forecasts and asked their managers to set their goals at more ambitious levels than they would have done under the old budgeting system. So managers did just that. They estimated revenues and resource requirements at a higher level; this obviously pleased their bosses, but in the event caused great damage to the company's reputation with suppliers, customers, and shareholders. The forecasts were far too optimistic, causing costs and inventories to inflate and ending in huge write-offs.[13] The problem was that their forecasts were just that—forecast numbers unrelated to the reality of the business. Managers gave supervisors what they wanted to hear rather than what customers were telling them. And despite suspending the budgeting system, the ingrained culture of negotiation and gaming was still intact—it simply moved into the stretch-forecasting process. In best-practice organizations, leaders neither demand certainty from managers, nor do they expect them to use single-point forecasts.

If forecasts are used by senior managers to demand immediate action from frontline teams, then trust and confidence will rapidly evaporate. A senior manager at a large French company made this point: "Forecasts and targets must be independent if we want to obtain both relevant action plans and reliable forecasts allowing risks and opportunities to be identified and relevant corrective actions to be taken. They must not be produced for control purposes. There should be no wishful thinking. It is also important to be realistic. Forecasts should reflect the fact that some businesses are cyclical and thus cannot always grow, even if this is politically incorrect."

How long should forecasts take to compile? In a financial services business, for example, with no physical supply chain and inventories to manage, there is no reason why forecasts should take longer than a day. However, in a fast-changing, capital-intensive business, where forecasts are used to make key decisions about capacity requirements often involving significant capital sums, forecasts can take several days.

Just as there is no precise amount of time it takes to create a forecast, there is no precise answer to the issue of the forecasting horizon or revision intervals. These depend on how long it takes to make and execute key decisions about operations, capacity, and capital spending. In other words, if it takes two years to bring new facilities onstream or deliver new products, then this might be a reasonable guide. At an airline where changes are happening at lightning speed, it would be advisable to revise forecasts each week or month. In a public-sector organization, quarterly forecasts would normally be sufficient. Most adaptive organizations spend more time and effort on near-term periods and less on the longer-term ones.

To be useful, forecasts should tell managers something about the trajectory they are on compared with their medium-term goals and thus whether further action is necessary. That means they are concerned with constantly "managing gaps" rather than closing them to reach a fixed target (as noted earlier, this invariably leads to tampering). Medium-term goals are best viewed in terms of ranges of desired outcomes rather than specific targets.

Managers should also learn from their forecast record. Borealis always carries out post-mortems on its forecasts. The purpose is not to attribute blame but to learn if forecast accuracy is improving and how it can be further improved. Forecasting inaccuracy can be seen in the same light as process variability; teams therefore need to better understand the causes of that variability and work to reduce them.

Using Rolling Forecasts to Manage the Business at Tomkins

At Tomkins, managers used to produce what was called a financial digest. It was due on the eighth working day following the month-end and was geared to explaining variances from budget and whether any further action was needed to meet agreed year-end targets. While six-quarterly rolling forecasts were part of this process, not much attention was paid to quarters beyond the fiscal year-end. They were also the last thing to be done during the monthly closing process and usually by the finance people. In other words, they were neither taken seriously, nor were they treated as a key part of the management process.

In recent years, however, this has changed radically. The forecasting process is now the *key management tool* for managing the business at every level. As CFO of global operations Dan Disser notes, "there is now as much energy put into preparing the forecasts as closing the books." That's why Tomkins has decoupled the monthly forecast process from the month-end close.

While there is still an annual strategy-formulation process, during which the big issues are discussed (e.g., Have we got the right products? Are we focused on the right markets? Have we got the right value proposition?), action planning is now a quarterly event. These quarterly business reviews, together with supporting six-quarter rolling forecasts, are completed around three weeks after the quarter end. Forecasts have been separated from performance measurement (and targets—there are no targets), thus taking much of the gaming out of the forecasting process. Although an annual financial plan remains, it is simply the four quarterly forecasts that fall within the fiscal year. This is what is communicated to analysts.

Another important element of the forecasting process is the monthly "flash" forecasts, which are prepared in the middle of each month (when there is more time available) and look to the end of the current month and a further two months ahead. So senior managers now receive monthly results and short-term forecasts for the following two months, the current quarter, and the full year four working days *prior* to the month-end. Given that average organizations take six days to close the books, a further eleven days to finalize reports, and fifteen days (concurrently) to prepare forecasts, this is a real breakthrough in information management.

According to Group CFO Ken Lever, the impact on managerial behavior has been dramatic: "Managers now have no option but to strive for maximum performance," he said. "Whereas before they would spend weeks negotiating targets, they now spend their time improving the business. All the gaming that we had to accept as part of the old process has also gone. There is no number to game. Better still, there are no excuses and no time wasted explaining variances against a useless budget. They are all now focused on what action to take to improve customer and shareholder value."[14]

Implementing Driver-Based Rolling Forecasts at American Express

American Express has learned a great deal about forecasting techniques and has now developed a "driver-based" rolling forecast model. Changing direction from its old forecasting system was not easy. Each of its three operating segments—Travel Related Services, American Express Financial Advisors, and American Express Bank—had its own approach to forecasting using simple spreadsheets based on their different markets (75 percent of forecast data had to be manually keyed in). The company then had to consolidate the data from these individually prepared forecasts. It took weeks to prepare the forecasts, making the end result redundant rather than relevant. CFO Gary Crittenden relates how the company went about implementing a new forecasting system:

> In my opinion, the key lesson is to cut out the detail and focus on key drivers. Under the old system, it took one business unit alone eight weeks and hundreds of person-days to assemble the bottom-up forecast. This made doing meaningful business reviews and timely investment analysis almost impossible. To create the framework for a new system, business units had to identify key performance drivers based on company-specific algorithms. The key question was: How would $1 in billings or one additional card member impact the bottom line? Previously, the staff had focused much of their attention on the impact of salaries and benefits on net profits. Managers had believed that all they needed to know was the cost of adding or eliminating an employee. However, they found that these numbers only had a 5 percent effect on the net figures. What they needed to identify were the volume drivers, those that influenced 80 percent of the numbers. This turned out to be only fifteen lines on the profit and loss statement. We found that billings were what really drove American Express's businesses: how much card members spent at restaurants, on airline tickets, and for major purchases. Two specific drivers behind this volume were the number of American Express cards and the average spending per card. Knowing those two items allowed business teams to calculate the billings numbers. These numbers, in turn,

affected quite a few other items on the profit and loss statement. From billings numbers, they could project the rewards usage, level of delayed billings, amount of interest income, measure of risk for bad debt, and so forth. The trick was to create the algorithms that accurately forecast the billings.

Using driver-based forecasts together with dedicated systems and Web technology enables hundreds of managers to work on forecasts together and aggregate the outcomes to the highest level, thus providing more control than ever. The new approach has enabled us to standardize with a single methodology and align key assumptions and algorithms across the organization. [15]

Report Key Metrics Daily and Weekly

To become truly adaptive, an organization requires fast, relevant information based on a few key performance indicators (KPIs) at every level. Handelsbanken uses a *daily* leading indicator based on the pattern of customer transactions. It doesn't conduct extensive customer surveys. Its knowledge comes from one hundred thousand customer transactions per day. Employees are used as its eyes and ears; they act as scouts, constantly feeding back information about customer problems and competitive actions. Information systems act like radar scanners showing patterns of change. Acquisitions, defections, discounts, profitability—these are the signs that tell managers' what's happening in the marketplace. KPIs represent the critical indicators for the adaptive organization, providing managers with advanced warning signals that there are problems looming ahead and that action needs to be taken.

A good KPI has a knock-on effect on, for example, improving quality, lowering defect rates, speeding up inventory turns, and ultimately increasing profitability. Take the story about Lord King, ex-chairman of British Airways. King set about turning BA around in the 1980s, reportedly by concentrating on one KPI—if a BA plane was delayed he was notified, wherever he was. The senior BA official at the relevant airport knew that if a plane was delayed beyond a certain threshold, they would receive a personal call from the chairman. It was not long before BA planes had a reputation for leaving on time. This had a significant knock-on effect on the bottom line. Late planes increased costs in many ways, including additional airport surcharges and the cost of accommodating passengers overnight as a result of planes being "curfewed" due to noise restrictions late at night. They were also a primary cause of dissatisfied customers and alienated the people meeting passengers at their destination (possible future customers). They used more fuel because planes had to circle the airport when they missed their landing slots. And they would disrupt servicing schedules, resulting in poor service quality and increased dissatisfaction of the employees who had to deal with customer complaints. The British Airways "late-plane" KPI immediately illustrated the need to focus on recovering lost time. As a result, cleaners, caterers, ground crew, flight attendants, liaison officers, and traffic controllers would all work together to save precious minutes.

While KPIs are usually nonfinancial indicators, leaders can also gain tangible benefits from producing fast financial information that, in turn, enables fast response. Take Slim·Fast, a slimming products company based in Florida with sales of around $700 million in 2004. Between 1996 and 2003, the company's sales grew at a compound rate of approximately 20 percent p.a. The driving factor behind its stellar growth rate was what owner Danny Abrahams called the 20:20 approach. The goal was to always achieve 20 percent top-line growth and return a 20 percent operating margin. The biggest issue for the finance team led by CFO Carl Tsang was producing information in real time so that the board could react quickly. So they decided to produce a *daily* profit and loss statement, which allowed them to compare the same day or week this year with last year and constantly monitor their performance progress.

What they did was work on the daily order intake. Orders were cut off at 5 p.m. so the team was able to print a daily profit statement by 7 p.m. The key metric was order intake that day compared with the same day last year. Tsang's team knew the company's gross profit on every order, so they could compute the actual gross profit based on the total order intake. Then they estimated the general and administration costs from the most recently closed monthly financials to arrive at the net profit. It wasn't perfect, but it was pretty close. And there was no fudging the numbers—for example, no one would put orders in just to please the boss.

The daily profit and loss account enabled Abrahams and Tsang to monitor sales trends and regulate spending. For instance, if the first ten days of a month this year compared with last year showed that business was flat or even declining, they would put a hold on spending in order to achieve their 20 percent margin. If they could trim general and administrative costs by 1 percent, that saving didn't go to operating profit, it went toward more advertising to fuel more growth.

Enable Fast Access to Resources

If business-unit teams are expected to use their intuition and judgment to adapt to emerging threats and opportunities, they must have fast access to resources—especially to new operating capacity, including people and technology. Handelsbanken branch managers can hire staff according to prevailing demand. When branches were given this discretion, skeptics thought that staff levels would rise, but the opposite happened. Managers, conscious of their need to raise profits, were no longer inclined to hold onto staff when demand began to fall (on the assumption that it would be hard to regain approval to rehire people). Thus staff levels and costs fell significantly. The lesson is that when resources belong to the corporate center and are negotiated through budgets, people feel little responsibility for them. But if they are accessed by the local team as part of their action plan, ownership and responsibility become much more personal. At Swedish distributor Ahlsell, local managers are accountable for beating the competition, with league tables driving competitive results. The degree of autonomy is considerable. Local managers can decide about recruiting or terminating staff, the level of salaries for their staff, and the prices at which to sell materials to customers.

At Telecom New Zealand, CFO Marko Bogoievski realized that despite moving away from annual budgeting the company still wasn't reallocating resources dynamically. As he explains:

> Though we were updating our forecasts on a quarterly basis, our performance incentives and resource decisions were still geared to the annual cycle. You might say that that's pretty obvious but it really wasn't at the time. People still liked to think that they were making more dynamic decisions on a daily basis. But when we looked at our operating and capital expenditure processes we realized that once they were locked into the annual plan they were really difficult to change or move between business units. Now we've done away with the old delegated authorities and given business units decision-making authority within reasonably tight operating bands based on return-on-invested-capital criteria. They are free to make choices provided they stay within those bands. These choices also apply to the reallocation of operating and capital expenditure again provided that their forecasts show that they are within those agreed operating parameters. There's quite an element of trust in all this. It's probably harder for the board to move to this new way of managing than for business unit leaders.[16]

Focus Accountability on the Relative Performance of Teams

Implementing adaptive management systems will be ineffective unless the CFO takes action to deal with target setting and performance evaluation. Ken Lever, CFO at Tomkins, is adamant that abandoning negotiated targets was the key to achieving a high-quality forecasting process: "It meant that people would spend more time looking at the quality of their forecasts and what they meant for action planning. Previously, managers would be thinking more about what their forecasts meant for their targets and performance evaluation than for their actions and this would distort the numbers. We wanted forecasting to become part of management rather than measurement. That was the key mind-set change."[17]

By setting annual group targets and then sharing them around each division and business unit, fixed-performance contracts give leaders the illusion of control. In other words, they believe that it is *their leadership* that drives and controls performance, and that without this process managers would fail to raise their game. But this goes against the grain of everything we've learned about motivation and performance. People will set higher goals and be more committed to achieving them if they set them themselves without the specter of a performance contract hanging over their heads. The point is that targets and incentives can be used to get people to do something they might not otherwise do, but this is a far cry from making people want to do something because it is the *right* thing to do. It is the difference between what social scientists call extrinsic motivation (where the task is seen as a means to an end, a prerequisite for receiving a reward or avoiding a punishment) and intrinsic motivation (where the task itself is appealing). In other words, it is not the *amount* of motivation that matters, but its *type*.

Extrinsic motivators come with the baggage of gaming and low commitment. The way to win the target-setting game from the operations perspective is to negotiate a lowball target, with plenty of slack in case things don't work out as planned. The way to win from the senior management perspective is to set a highball target that stretches performance. The result is a compromise. But the real loser in this game is the shareholder, because the compromise invariably undershoots performance potential by a wide margin.

Many finance people say that if managers don't have a number to aim for, how do they know what to achieve? This sort of question gives the game away. The answer is surely that all managers should maximize their performance every month, quarter, and year. They shouldn't *need* a number to aim for. In fact, providing a number immediately diminishes performance potential, since there is no effective way to set a financial target when the future is unknowable. It can only be a guess that will either be approximately right (same weather tomorrow as today), in which case, why bother? or disastrously wrong (we didn't predict the hurricane) in which case it's a liability. In both cases, it is not worth the candle.

There are a variety of ways of managing without targets. At the World Bank, for example, managers are now given spending directions based on staying within agreed trend lines (e.g., plus or minus 2 percent). These guidelines only change if a strategy review resets the spending levels. This goes a long way to overcome the "spend it or lose it" mentality that is so pervasive throughout the public sector. Managers at Tomkins work within three parameters that define what success looks like: return-on-invested capital, net-profit on sales, and sales growth. Others such as Handelsbanken compare performance with *hindsight*. They define success not by meeting agreed targets but by beating the competition and consistently being at the top of their peer group league table.

The performance contract changes from one based on *fixed performance* to one based on *relative improvement* (see figure 3-3). In the fixed contract, all the pieces of the performance management system (e.g., targets, budgets, and measures) are locked together and therefore make it difficult for managers to respond to change. In the relative-improvement contract, the pieces— goals, measures, rewards, and forecasts—are all disconnected from one another. This means that managers have less fear of failure and are thus more likely to set aspirational goals and be more committed to achieving them. And forecasts are more honest because managers are not worrying whether their superiors will use this information to change their targets or metaphorically give them a beating.

FIGURE 3-3

Contrasting the fixed-performance and relative-improvement contracts

Fixed-performance contract	Relative-improvement contract
Fixed targets lead to incremental goals	*Relative measures* lead to stretch goals
Fixed (individual) incentives lead to fear of failure	*Relative (team) rewards* lead to confidence to take risks
Fixed planning leads to a focus on meeting the numbers	*Continuous planning* leads to a focus on creating value
Annual resource allocations lead to cost protection	*Resources on demand* lead to cost minimization
Coordination based on central plans leads to slow response	*Coordination based on local plans* leads to fast response
Variance controls lead to excuse culture	*KPI controls* lead to improvement culture

Despite the demands of analysts and investors for earnings forecasts, increasing numbers of CFOs are getting the message and have stopped giving guidance (a 2004 U.S. survey concluded that 55 percent of 385 respondents said they had given some guidance against 72 percent in 2002).[18] Organizations such as Handelsbanken, GE Capital, Ahlsell, and Tomkins have moved from fixed-performance to relative-improvement contracts. Short- and medium-term goals are self-imposed by local units (with some challenge from the top), but they are not fixed commitments. I have given many reasons why fixed targets don't work. However, as confirmed by goal-setting theory, there is nothing wrong with a goal if it's *self-imposed*.[19] When you set a personal (or team-based) target, what's the point of setting it too high or too low? And what's the point of cheating? In leading organizations, teams are given the responsibility of setting their own targets without the contract and constraint of having to report against those targets to a higher level. And under these circumstances teams tend to shoot for high goals instead of focusing their efforts on negotiating a safe, low goal. At the end of the period, even if they fail to make the aspirational goal, the likelihood is that they will still have outperformed the lowball target they would otherwise have negotiated. This enables them to constantly manage reality rather than stick to an agreed plan. It is a world of continuous improvement, adaptation, and self-regulation. There is no need for protracted periods of negotiation. The system runs itself.

It also makes sense at the group level. If you were to ask investors what sort of performance qualities they were looking for, the likely answer would be (a) reliability (steady improvements over time) and (b) relativity (to be consistently near the top of the peer group). What merit is there in striving to meet a number promised a year earlier when the market has improved and competitors are showing much better results? The share price will only be marked down; an MIT study showed that earnings estimates twelve months in advance tend to be optimistic, noting "as the calendar ticks forward, the numbers are gradually revised downwards."[20] Over time, it is relative performance that matters. Such a measurement system should be familiar to fund managers who find their own performance reflected in performance league tables over different periods of time. It seems rational that fund managers want to back long-term winners—those companies that are at or near the top of their peer groups year after year.

Base Accountability on Fair Criteria with Hindsight

"If we don't set targets how will we hold managers accountable for their performance?" is a question that most CFOs struggle with. The answer is to design a report card (rather like an end-of-term school report) based on fair evaluation criteria and then use evidence from a range of sources to make an informed assessment. In other words, performance should be judged after the event rather than based on a predetermined target. Unilever's finance change leader, Steve Morlidge, believes this is a critical change: "It is only after the event that you can judge whether performance is good in the context of actual market conditions, for example, how stretching the target *actually* was. What was the inflation rate? What impact did the floods have? What was the impact of our biggest customer going bankrupt? It is only after the event that you can determine whether in achieving your goals you have beaten the competition or lost ground against them."[21]

Some organizations are building performance evaluation report cards for a range of teams including, for example, senior executives and business units. Jean-Marie Descarpentries had great success with this approach turning around the fortunes of two French companies: Carnaud Metal Box in the late 1980s and Groupe Bull in the mid-1990s. His success was based on separating target setting from performance evaluation and rewards, and measuring business-unit performance based on an evaluation formula (see table 3-1). This focused attention on a range of success indicators including growth, profitability, debt, and quality.

Each evaluation criterion in the formula was given a weighting according to its importance. The weighted score for each metric was then produced and the aggregate of the weighted scores was the final result. Both the corporate president and his executive committee independently reviewed performance. This assessment was used to set the bonus levels of all managers and employees within a particular business unit.

The amount of subjectivity and judgment involved in this type of assessment process is not to everyone's taste. But as Steve Morlidge

TABLE 3-1

Performance evaluation formula for a business unit at Groupe Bull

Key metric	Weighting	Score	Weighted score
Growth versus previous year	20	50	10
Growth versus competition	20	40	8
Profit versus previous year	20	60	12
Profit versus competition	20	50	10
Debt versus previous year	10	80	8
Quality factors versus previous year	10	60	6
Executive committee evaluation			**54%**

says, "while the process of calculating rewards is based on judgment, it is done using a rigorous process, one which is transparent and one which is immune to the exercise of prejudice or favoritism. It is, in effect, like the exercise of the law, using laws of evidence."[22] Some of this evidence is provided by a range of performance metrics, but these are subject to analysis, interpretation, and judgment. The metrics themselves, however, should not be presented with any judgmental comments; just presenting the raw numbers is sufficient to drive self-questioning and action for improvement.

While this approach can be universally applied, it needs to be tailored to fit the company and the team. Take an executive team that is primarily responsible for delivering group financial results and providing value to all their business units as well as to investors. The evaluation criteria might reflect some measure of financial performance (e.g., return-on-equity or net profitability) compared with prior years and with peers, and some measure of leadership competence (perhaps based on a rating by business-unit managers). A business-unit team is primarily responsible for executing its strategy successfully. One large organization uses three principal criteria for evaluating performance: (1) *current year in context*, taking into account economic factors, market factors (e.g., market share), other external factors, and structural factors; (2) *sustainability*, taking into account growth, price, investment, and margins; and (3) *strategy execution*, taking into account portfolio management, operational excellence, "getting more from the core," and brand focus.

If the performance evaluation framework is well designed and implemented, the organization will have also created a way to compare the performance of teams across the organization. This is where the weighting of evaluation criteria is crucial (some factors might be very important in one team but not in another). If this can be done successfully, then the power of peer pressure can be harnessed. In some cases, this means that producing performance league tables may be sufficient to drive continuous performance improvement. In other words, teams may not need a reward for achieving a high or improving performance. This is how the system works at Handelsbanken.

This approach relies more on peer pressure than on direct incentives. No self-respecting managers would want to go to a meeting of their peers knowing that they have underperformed, let down the whole team, and possibly drained the bonus pool. Internal and external league tables enable a framework for performance evaluation that provides a powerful force for continuous improvement as one business unit strives to improve its position against its rivals.

Peer pressure can be either positive or negative. Negative peer pressure leads to a fortress mentality. Local vested interests are paramount as managers seek to gain the maximum advantage (e.g., the most resources) from the corporate center. Other similar business units are seen as the enemy. Positive peer pressure is about improving faster than rivals but within a climate of cooperation and sharing. Achieving a balance between competition and cooperation needs to be carefully managed. The defining difference is the rewards system. If rewards are at the whole business level, then individual units have little need to act with a fortress mentality.

It is important to note that most social scientists criticize incentives as applied to individuals. They are less concerned about teams. In this context, rewards are seen as a share of success (like a dividend on human capital) rather than a "do this, get that" type of incentive linked to a target. A team in this context is any group that represents an *interdependent value delivery network*. For example, at Handelsbanken and Southwest Airlines the team is the whole company; at Tomkins and Ahlsell it's a business unit. Anything less than this, to some degree or other, is likely to be divisive. Rewarding the success of the business unit or firm as a whole is not intended to manipulate behavior, but to demonstrate that all are in the same boat, all pulling in the same direction, all dependent on each other.

Some people will say that moving incentives to the level of the work unit is a charter for "free riders"—those managers that keep out of the limelight yet produce little by way of results. The experience at Toyota, Handelsbanken, and Southwest Airlines, however, suggests that this is not as big a problem as most people fear. In a team-based system driven by continuous improvement, free riders are exposed very quickly and replaced by people more willing to commit themselves to real performance challenges. As one comprehensive review reported, "Under conditions described by the theory as leading to free riding, people often cooperated instead."[23]

When I talk about devolving planning and abandoning fixed targets in seminars I often see people smile and say, "That sounds great in theory, but it would never happen in our organization. Our executives have typically spent years climbing the corporate ladder and wouldn't react kindly to someone suggesting that they give their new control toys away." But I get a different reaction from operations people. They say, "Most of our people unplug their brains immediately when they enter the workplace. They do exactly what they're told to do and no more. They save all their creativity for social activities and voluntary work, and of course their expense accounts!"

What most business leaders struggle with is that organizations don't need central coordination and control. If the causes of dysfunctional behavior are removed, then managers across the organization will work more collaboratively to maximize results. However, persuading leaders that they don't need to coordinate and control actions from the center is not an easy task. Indeed, in command and control organizations it is their *main* task. But in more organic, flexible organizations, their main task is to get the most out of their people and this means devolving decision making to them. Adaptive organizations understand the power and benefits of the performance accountability approach. Relative-improvement contracts and adaptive processes are the primary mechanisms that enable these changes. They provide the framework for a new vision of the performance management model.

A CHECKLIST FOR THE CFO

☐ See performance accountability not in terms of meeting agreed targets but in terms of relative improvement compared with prior years, peers, and benchmarks with hindsight.

☐ If you cannot see the problems with targets, look at the evidence from such firms as Enron and Tyco and from within your own organization. Gaming is rife at every level (the aim is to agree the lowest targets, etc.). Targets stifle ambition and innovation; they don't stretch or motivate.

☐ Design processes from the outside-in to enable managers to sense-and-respond to customer needs. Abandoning top-down targets will at least enable managers to focus on meeting customers' needs profitably. Redesigning processes is a bigger job, but this is a good first step.

☐ Make planning an inclusive and continuous process not an annual event (use the check-aim-plan-act cycle).

☐ Make rolling forecasts the primary management tool. Consider two cycles: the first looking only a few months ahead and the second twelve to eighteen months ahead. Do forecasts mid-month rather than at the month-end. They should be done for local managers, not for corporate.

☐ Make these forecasts light-touch (a few days' work). Focus on a few key drivers rather than lots of detail.

☐ Avoid turning forecasts into commitments. Ensure that forecasts are separated from target setting and performance measurement.

☐ Make resources available on demand, not through annual budget allocations. This can be done through an "internal market" for central services. Another approach is to release project funding monthly according to current priorities rather than apportion it annually in advance.

☐ Coordinate cross-company interactions dynamically according to prevailing demand, not annual plans. All units need to coordinate plans with other units that they depend upon to execute those plans.

☐ Base controls on daily/weekly leading indicators (KPIs), rolling forecasts, trends, and relative performance indicators, not variances against plan. Report key metrics daily or weekly.

☐ Set aspirational goals based on continuous relative improvement, not on fixed targets. Devolve goal setting to local teams. This harnesses the power of intrinsic motivation and builds ownership and commitment to succeed. But avoid turning those goals into contracts.

☐ Recognize and reward shared success based on relative performance with hindsight, not on meeting fixed targets. Define success as being the best organization, division, business unit, department, sales team, and so forth.

☐ Focus performance evaluation on teams rather than individuals. Harness the power of the team esprit de corps. Share team recognition and rewards with all its members.

CHAPTER FOUR

THE CFO
AS WARRIOR
AGAINST WASTE

*True efficiency improvement comes when we produce zero
waste and bring the percentage of work to 100 percent.*

—Taiichi Ohno

S OME CFOS GIVE the impression that the war on
waste has been won (surveys show that cost reduction has fallen down the CFO wish list). Nothing could be further
from the truth. There is strong evidence to suggest that huge
amounts of work in every type of organization add no value for
the customer. Nor is this non-value-adding work particular to the
production process. It occurs in research departments, in sales
divisions, and in administrative departments. One leading U.S. IT
vendor, for example, found that only 10 percent of a salesperson's
time was spent in front of the customer. The balance was spent
progress chasing, traveling, and undertaking clerical duties. A
major U.K. aerospace contractor identified only 20 percent of

R&D costs as related to product development; almost 80 percent related to meetings, documentation, and supporting manufacturing operations.

While the restructuring and reengineering of the past ten to fifteen years has certainly had an impact, too many organizations have failed to deal with bloated bureaucracies and badly designed processes that hide swathes of non-value-adding costs. Compared with truly lean enterprises such as Toyota, Handelsbanken, Dell, and Southwest Airlines, the cost-reduction efforts of most organizations have barely scratched the surface. Too many programs have focused on restructuring (closing offices, plants, and divisions), and not enough attention has been paid to whether or not processes (and their supporting costs) add sufficient value.

Most managers understand intuitively that a very small number (say, 20 percent) of events in a business account for most of the results (perhaps 80 or 90 percent). Indeed the Italian economist Vilfredo Pareto taught us this in the nineteenth century, and Peter Drucker reminded us what the real implications of this meant in 1963 when he said that, "while 90 percent of the results are being produced by the first 10 percent of events, 90 percent of the costs are being increased by the remaining and result-less 90 percent of events."[1] In other words, *economic results are directly proportionate to revenue, while costs are directly proportionate to transactions and activities*. The trouble is that by looking at the conventional profit and loss account and related subanalyses, it would be almost impossible to know which costs are in the 10 percent (good costs) and which are in the 90 percent (bad costs) category.

This is Drucker at his brilliant best. He knew that many costs incurred by organizations didn't add value and should be eliminated but that accounting systems couldn't identify them. In the typical large organization, between 30 and 40 percent of costs disappear into management black holes, causing untold damage to profitability. Some of these costs are generated by the poor connections between functions and departments across the organization. Others are caused by the obsession with planning and control; firms spend fortunes on budgets, supervision, inspection, and control systems in their efforts to connect high-level decisions with frontline actions. And still others arise from the inappropriate use of tools and information systems, adding cost and complexity to already overloaded systems, driving up stress levels, and reducing quality of work.

Most CFOs have failed to understand Drucker's insight. While revenues relate to individual customer orders, costs are related to a host of activities, many of which have nothing to do with customer orders. The more activities that people do (and the wider the variety of those activities), the greater will be the costs incurred. Consider the implications of this view of costs and resources for a typical company. It means that a handful of customers produce all the profits; a few salespeople produce the bulk of "good" orders; a small number of products, services, and distribution channels produce all the profits; and a small proportion of the work done in the research labs, the factory, and the office actually adds value to customers. Because few accounting systems make any attempt to connect indirect costs with revenue streams (other than by largely arbitrary methods of allocation), managers have little hope of discovering which costs and value streams are worthwhile and which are not.

Leading-edge organizations incur only costs that relate directly to customer orders. That's why companies such as Toyota, Southwest Airlines, Dell, and Handelsbanken are the most cost efficient operators in their peer groups. In this chapter we will look at a number of ways that the CFO can learn from these organizations and identify and eliminate unnecessary costs. Using their examples, the CFO should aim to:

- Dismantle head office bureaucracy

- Manage processes and flow rather than functions and activities

- Manage fixed costs through directional goals and ratios rather than cost budgets

- Make central services responsive to internal customers

- Match capacity to current demand

- Ensure that all projects are necessary and add value

Dismantle Head Office Bureaucracy

Most organizations are wired for control rather than speed. Their structures remain stuck in a time warp of command and control. Though many have restructured and reengineered, the benefits have been neutralized by performance management systems (e.g., how they set targets, budgets, and measures) that remain attached to boxes on the organization chart (e.g., functions and departments). These systems have continued to deflect managers from focusing on how work is organized and performed, and how the resources of the workforce can best be used. In short, managers have failed to understand the nature of costs, how they arise, and how they can be reduced without demoralizing the workforce and upsetting customers.

Organizations like GE Capital, Handelsbanken, and Southwest Airlines have all gone to great lengths to clear out their stifling bureaucracies—dismantling the strategic planning apparatus, corporate staff empires, head office directives, and all the machinery that makes big-company operations predictable but complex, costly, and slow. Before 1970 the planning process at Handelsbanken took three months of full-time work, and over fifteen hundred people were employed at head office (excluding IT). Now the organization has around three hundred people at head office. This amounts to about half a head office person per branch—against around five per branch for its competitors. Another early change was to flatten the management structure and shorten the lines of communication. There are now only four layers—from branch office worker to branch manager to regional manager to chief executive. And the only organization chart at the bank is the internal telephone book.

These organizations have all developed process-based structures built around teams. In the lean organization, teams are the principal creators and deliverers of value to the customer. Though many organizations support the team-based approach, most fail to appreciate its nuances. Many managers assume that structural changes by themselves will naturally lead to common understanding of, and a collective sense of responsibility for, customers' needs. Managers typically underestimate the power of the functional mind-set and how, unless it is tackled head-on (and quickly), team members will continue to carry out their old jobs, albeit within a team-based system. Special attention must be paid to restructuring incentive systems, reconfiguring the work space, or redesigning jobs and procedures within the process-based units to encourage collaboration and collective responsibility.

Effective teams have a number of essential characteristics including a set of common values and objectives, a measurement system set by and *owned* by them, and the tools (e.g., information technology) and resources necessary to fulfill their task. Their members must be dependent on one another, and they must rise and fall on their collective performance. Teams have leaders who take charge of and are accountable for performance.

Toyota provides a classic example. The Toyota Production System is built around teams of between 20 and 30 people. A team comprises 5 to 8 group leaders, 3 to 5 team leaders, and 12 to 18 team members. Team members perform manual jobs to standard and are responsible for solving problems and improving their work. Team leaders take on a number of jobs traditionally done by white-collar managers such as keeping the line running, producing quality parts, covering absenteeism, training, and meeting production goals. Group leaders perform many functions usually done by support functions in human resources, engineering, and quality, including manpower and vacation scheduling, production planning, shift coordination, and process trials. There is no such thing as a "hands-off" leader at Toyota.[2]

Under the system in most firms, problems are identified through the information system and high-level people are responsible for solving them. This is a slow and expensive way of dealing with problems, many of which have serious knock-on effects down the line. At Toyota, problems are solved when and where they occur, at the level of the frontline team. Teruyuki Minoura, former president of Toyota North America, neatly summed up the paradoxical benefits of this process when he said "if some problem occurs in one-piece flow manufacturing then the whole production line stops. In this sense it is a very bad system of manufacturing. But when production stops, everyone is forced to solve the problem immediately. So team members have to think, and through thinking team members grow and become better team members and people."[3]

We need look no further than the Handelsbanken example for evidence of the major cost benefits that result from reducing management layers and managing through processes and teams. Frontline teams don't need a head office bureaucracy sending daily directives about what managers can and can't do. They don't need multiple management layers to meddle with decisions and manipulate information. They don't need detailed budgets to control their actions. And they don't need endless meetings that absorb their time and prevent them from serving customers. Handelsbanken has operated with the devolved management model for over thirty years, and it consistently has cost-to-income ratios some 15 to 20 percent lower than its rivals (its cost-to-income ratio was 45 percent in 2004!). Just think of what this lower cost level would mean in your organization. For $1 billion of revenues, costs would be $150 million to $200 million lower! Leaders, especially in finance, just need some faith in the capabilities of their own people.

Manage Processes and Flow Rather Than Functions and Activities

One of the principal reasons CFOs and their colleagues struggle to root out unnecessary costs is that the finance function sees costs through the lens of budgeting and general ledger reporting systems based on functions and departments. Few realize that most cost budgeting systems *protect costs* and *hide waste*. Line managers are well known for including contingencies in their budget estimates. The amounts will vary according to the level of uncertainty, ranging from 10 to 20 percent up to 50 to 70 percent or even more. The nature of a contingency means that it may or may not be needed depending on unpredictable outcomes. But it is not available for the rest of the organization to spend (by definition, it's hidden!). Suppose that the contingency amount is 50 percent and the probability of not being met is 40 percent. This means that 20 percent of the budgeted amount is excess and will probably be spent toward the end of the year to protect the budget for the following year. The typical game is that, because they know this goes on, accountants try to cut the budgets back. Managers preempt this tactic by increasing the contingency amount. Whatever the outcome, the result is wasted expenditure in one part of the business while other parts that desperately need funding go without. This is a classic problem of traditional budgeting and is particularly prevalent in the public sector.

Translating general ledger costs into process costs is likely to reveal many opportunities for cost reduction. Imagine you are the manager of an IT department and you are about to submit the departmental budget for the following year.[4] Cash is tight and you have been told to reduce the coming year's costs by 10 percent. Your accountant reckons that six jobs will have to go, but you fail to see how next year's targets can be reached without these people. Last year's expenditure and next year's budget are presented for your approval (see "General ledger view" (left-hand columns) in figure 4-1). Your inclination is to accept the inevitable and cut the six jobs. After all, the only alternatives are either to cut salaries rather than jobs but this would upset all the remaining staff, or to cut certain discretionary expenses that would have only a limited effect. But before making the final decision, you ask for a different presentation of the department's costs. This is shown in the "Process view" (right-hand columns) in figure 4-1.

The revised analysis shows that the costs that add value for the customer amount to only 60 percent of last year's total; 40 percent of the costs were attributable to work that should not have

FIGURE 4-1

A look at the process view of costs

General ledger view			Process view		
	$m this year actual	$m next year budget		$m this year actual	%
Salaries (60)	3.20	3.30	New systems	2.60	
Staff cuts (6)	0.35	—	Customer support	1.00	
Travel	0.90	0.80	Value-adding costs		60%
Expenses	1.05	0.90	Rework and corrections	2.00	
Telecoms	0.50	0.40	Non-contract user help	0.40	
			Non-value-adding costs		40%
Total	6.00	5.40	Total	6.00	

been necessary in the first place (e.g., poor design and analysis, sloppy maintenance, excessive downtime, and ineffective customer support). If only 25 percent of these non-value-adding costs were eliminated, the cost reductions demanded by head office would be achieved—and with no job losses. Looking further ahead you can also see how the productivity of the department could be improved if all this unnecessary work was eliminated.

Most budgets are invariably approved on the basis of percentage adjustments to the previous year's figures. But, given the alternative (process-based) analysis, what now happens? All the costs hidden within accounting descriptions (such as salaries and traveling), whether of value or not, are adjusted in the same way. Let's assume that a 10 percent increase is agreed in the budget with no acknowledgment of the alternative process view. What's the result? A 10 percent uplift in the budget for unnecessary and wasteful costs! For example, the budget for "reworking and corrections" increases by $200,000. This scenario demonstrates that budget holders who are rewarded on their ability to stay within the agreed levels have little incentive to ask searching questions concerning the strategic and work-based issues that should underpin the whole process. The net result is a huge wasted opportunity.

Seeing the organization through a horizontal process lens enables managers to identify and eliminate these wasteful costs. In *The Machine That Changed the World,* the landmark book that spawned the "lean manufacturing" movement, authors Womack, Jones, and Roos describe how the Toyota Production System uses less of everything compared with mass production—half the human effort in the factory, half the manufacturing space, half the investment in tools, half the engineering hours to develop a new product in half the time. It also requires half the inventory, results in many fewer defects, and produces a greater and ever growing variety of proucts.[5] That in a nutshell explains why Toyota is the fastest-growing and most profitable auto manufacturer in the world today.

While American and European firms were pursuing strategies based on economies of scale, Toyota was concentrating on "economies of flow." One of the stories told about Taiichi Ohno is that when he returned from America in the 1950s (having studied U.S. manufacturing methods) to set up a new plant in Japan, he didn't have much capital, so he had to manage with a few small machines. Thus his primary task was to reduce changeover times. Within a few months he had reduced the time it took the Americans from ten days to ten *minutes*. He then had a counterintuitive moment—*his costs went down.* He, like others, assumed that smaller batch sizes would lead to higher costs. But he soon realized that his costs had reduced because he had less inventory and fewer quality problems to correct.[6]

Ohno's ideas have been taken up by Dell in personal computers. Its direct sales model has enabled Dell to become the lowest-cost producer in a cutthroat industry and, in contrast to almost every other Western computer maker, has enabled the company to compete aggressively in every market in the world. Dell continuously finds ways to cut costs ($1.3 billion in 2002 and another $2 billion in 2003) as it continues to improve operating processes. The secret of Dell's success is improving its supply chain. According to Jeffrey Clarke, product group vice president, "We manage the supply chain end-to-end, from order to delivery. When you outsource part of it, you're averaging out, because the outsourcer will also be doing it for someone else. Our competitors do that to compete. But the supply chain is our competitive advantage—why should we outsource? Over the past five years Dell has reduced its supply chain costs by 60 percent."[7]

But the benefits of removing unnecessary work through lean thinking are not confined to the shop floor or the supply chain (as the IT example illustrated). The story that John Seddon tells about a U.K. bank is typical of the cost saving opportunities in service organizations. The bank closed hundreds of branches and recruited lower-cost people to fill three call centers (one thousand people each). The savings looked enormous. After six months the demand was so great, it opened a fourth. When the CEO asked why another was needed the reply was, "because customer demand has increased. Customers clearly like it because they keep calling." The CEO called in a consultant who analyzed the calls. There are basically two types of calls: those that relate to order taking or customer support (they add value); and those that drive customers crazy because they need to call several times to get through, get someone to call back, get an order agreed, get someone to turn up, or get something sent that's been ordered (they add no value). The consultant found that the "non-value calls" comprised roughly *half* of all the call center traffic. So that's how the bank got to five call centers.

This pattern is not unusual; it is common to most call centers. The same consultant found failure rates of between 20 and 45 percent in the police service and telecommunications companies. And in the public sector it ran as high as 50 to 80 percent. When those in charge of these systems were questioned about these extraordinary results, the common reply was, "well that's the industry standard, isn't it?"

Why does this happen? The primary reason is that most call center agents are driven by targets and measured on how well they perform individual activities (all metrics borrowed from the factory). These activity targets are based on the number of calls taken, the time to answer, the average time a call takes, abandon rates, and how much work each agent does in a day or week.

Now these types of information are useful when planning for the resources needed (number of people, etc.), but as measures of performance they are counterproductive. If agents can't meet their targets they start to cheat.

Consider what leaked confidential documents reveal about the effects of targets at a large U.K. energy company. Difficult customer inquiries, once dealt with by the sales staff, are now routed to a separate service department that is struggling to cope. Call length is a primary target. Over a five-week period, two call centers handled 750,000 calls at an average call length of 432 seconds and 450 seconds, respectively. Under new targets for the third quarter of 2005, the service center staff is expected to deal with calls 10 percent faster than before, with a target of 420 seconds. The "wrap" time—how long a staff member can deal with a customer's problem after the call has ended—is included in the 420-second target, and has been cut to a maximum of 230 seconds. To avoid missing these targets, the staff may not answer up to fifteen hundred customer calls on busy days. Instead, they send a letter saying they tried to call the customer back, and inviting the customer to return the call.

On the sales side, service staff members face disciplinary action if they regularly fail to make twenty product sales a month. Service assistants failing to sell less than this are sent for retraining. Those persistently failing to reach the new sales targets will, in the company's own words, be "exited out of the business." To earn their £1,500 ($2,700) annual bonus, service center staff must achieve at least thirty-five sales a month, as well as hit call time limits. Good customer service makes up less than half of the "scorecard" that results in a bonus.

The call center worker who leaked the documents alleges that the staff is increasingly working under a "climate of fear." He says: "As staff are becoming increasingly desperate not to lose their jobs, they are doing things they wouldn't have in the past. They typically earn £15,000 ($27,000) a year—so what have they got to lose by putting through a few false sales? If the targets rise again, then incidents of mis-selling will only increase."[8] At a time when the company, by its own admission, is hemorrhaging customers and battling to preserve profits, the use of targets is contributing to its woes.

Though many senior managers would deny it, I suspect that this story is typical of what happens in most call centers. However, the problem, lean thinkers claim, is not the people, it's the system. Deming calculated that 95 percent of the non-value-producing activities are caused by the system and only 5 percent are concerned with people.[9] Yet as we have just witnessed in the call center story, all the attention is on employee performance appraisals. Managers typically change targets and incentives, put people on training courses, and threaten them with their jobs, but in reality they are working on only a fraction of the problem.

To eradicate the non-value-adding calls, lean organizations examine the work flow from the customer's perspective. They find out why products are not being delivered on time and why customers are not being called back. They know that if they can get to the root cause of these problems (e.g., by eliminating targets and measuring the customer experience) they will begin to make real headway. By achieving these relatively simple changes, firms will either create huge amounts of extra capacity or avoid building that capacity in the first place.

These ideas were used by the Liverpool Council to transform itself from one of the worst performing local government councils in the United Kingdom to one of the best. Nine human resources systems and two hundred people have been streamlined into one system and seventy-eight people. Thirty ways of claiming car expenses have become one. The number of departments has been collapsed from eleven to five, and the council is continuing to collapse systems down. But this couldn't have been done without dealing with customer service. The myriad delivery departments of the past have gone. There are now just two channels: a call center that accounts for 70 percent of customer contact and a network of one-stop shops providing access to the council's 770 services. The surprise package is the call center. "Liverpool Direct" boasts of being the highest-paying call center in the United Kingdom. It also has the lowest staff turnover, at 2 percent. All staff are experienced council workers (hence the high costs) but the value they provide can be seen in the number of calls that are dealt with successfully at the first point of contact. They measure repeat, or "failure," calls, and these are a fraction of the industry average. The whole project is seen as a winner, saving £120 million p.a. for the council.[10]

The impact of lean thinking on most organizations is so compelling that we have to wonder why it has taken so long to take root. The likely answer lies in the deeply ingrained way our organizations are managed. One report identified that the key barriers are attitudes to change within a company, lack of understanding of lean, shortage of the right lean skills (at management/supervisor/workforce levels), and cultural issues.[11] Another problem is that as project leaders migrate lean thinking from operations up the organization, they come across the functional, hierarchical mind-set that runs counter to the environment required for lean thinking to flourish.

We need to remind ourselves that in most organizations, decision making is separated from the work. This creates a void that is filled with mixed messages and political behavior. To bridge this gap, firms spend huge sums on complex planning, budgeting, scheduling, and control systems that program every action and activity on a daily basis at the front line. Lean organizations don't operate this way (and thus don't incur the attendant costs). Everyone at Toyota is involved in business improvement planning. They have regular meetings to discuss their progress and consider new initiatives. Everyone is expected to contribute and everyone's ideas are listened to. There are no suggestion boxes anywhere because people are not afraid to talk about new ideas, no matter how radical they are. On one of author Jeffrey Liker's visits to Toyota's plant in Kentucky, he discovered that over a one-year period employees had made eighty thousand improvement suggestions—and the plant had implemented 99 percent of them![12]

Manage Fixed Costs Through Directional Goals and Ratios Rather Than Cost Budgets

Cost budgets should be renamed "cost protection budgets" because that's what they do. No self-respecting manager is going to allow his or her costs to be reduced from last year's numbers. You win the budget battle by getting more resources, not by accepting less. "How can you justify increasing training by 20 percent?" "Why has parking gone up by 10 percent?" "Why do you need another 15 percent for marketing?" are all typical budget negotiation points. The justifications are easy—you simply tell your supervisor that you can't run your business with your current resources. And you also spend your entire budget allocation every year to justify the need for next year's increase.

Many CFOs will question how they control fixed costs without budgets. World Bank CFO John Wilton describes how: "We can ensure that spend levels stay stable and affordable over the medium-term by setting spending parameters that define aggregate and unit-level costs over time. We will do this by holding management accountable for ensuring that costs do go in the intended direction and by taking corrective action quickly and decisively if and when necessary." He questions the efficacy of cost control by budget:

> Most people, including board members, have spent the majority of their careers using traditional budget tools, and think that control comes from providing funds in thousands of small buckets, then making sure that managers spend no more than these amounts . . . What they don't see of course is all the creative accounting that goes on around where expenses are allocated in the system. Once one bucket is full, most managers will simply define that bucket's expenses to another bucket with spending room still available. So control at this level of detail is an illusion, and it's expensive. We can of course control spending with much larger buckets, but more importantly, we need to educate everyone to see controls more in terms

of managing strategic risk. If we can make fewer mistakes and turn more of our resources into value-adding outcomes, then I'm sure we'll all be happier.[13]

Organizations such as the World Bank are moving to cost management systems within which no up-front allocations are made to cost centers. Instead, business units draw on central funds as they need them and are responsible for ensuring the level of spending follows an agreed path. Costs are charged to the unit as they use them.

The role of senior management is to give units clear indications of the resources that business-unit managers can anticipate over the medium-term given the strategic priorities agreed. These indications are typically in the form of three-year expenditure directions set in relation to the latest twelve months' actual expenditure. The message is this: "your current spending level is following this trend. Over the next three years you should manage your resources so that the level of spend moves in this direction."

The direction is usually expressed as a percentage change in the level of spending on a rolling twelve-month basis, measured over *any* twelve-month period. Thus the control lever is relevant over any set of twelve consecutive months. This sharply contrasts with using the absolute yearly (or more often depending on performance) dollar targets that encourage the gaming behaviors we noted earlier. The indicative spending trend line is a ballpark destination in terms of both size and timing (see figure 4-2). There is deliberate imprecision in the goal on both the time and spending level axes. This approach also negates the importance of the fiscal year-end and the "spend it or lose it" mentality. Rather, spending by the unit is to be at an approximate level at an approximate time. The degree of satisfaction at the actual level of spending and what has been achieved using those resources is assessed retrospectively, whenever appropriate, with the benefit of hindsight.

Business-unit leaders make their plans on the understanding that resources will be made available, to the level indicated, when they are needed to implement agreed strategies. This means there

FIGURE 4-2

Setting directional spending guidelines

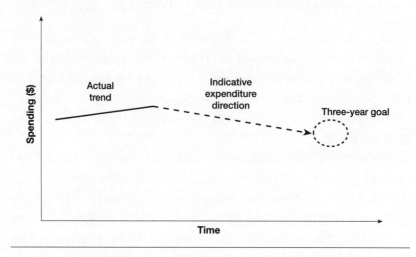

needs to be explicit agreement about how long the strategy will be supported (for example, three years). This approach transfers the responsibility for cost management from the corporate center to the frontline team. This transfer of ownership changes the spending mind-set. Instead of local units spending "corporate" funds to which they are entitled following the budget negotiation, they are spending *their own* money—with due care and attention. They also know that they can overspend and underspend as long as they keep within agreed parameters over time. At Handelsbanken, these parameters are defined by the cost-to-income ratio. At the World Bank they are defined by a percentage change in the trend line (for example, plus or minus two percent of the existing spending level).

Some organizations also support these directional spending controls with monthly prepared rolling forecasts that look two or three months ahead (see figure 4-3). When aggregated, these forecasts should be reasonably accurate, providing senior managers with another control lever—early warning of any spikes that are likely to occur. Borealis used this approach successfully to reduce its fixed costs by 30 percent over five years.

FIGURE 4-3

Controlling directional spending

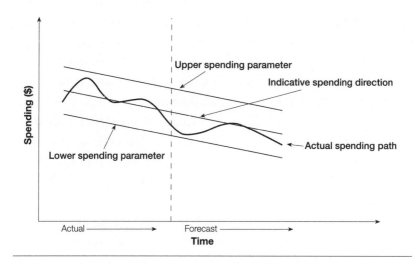

The real benefit of this approach to cost control is the disappearance of all the gaming of the management process, both at the front end (e.g., protecting costs through large contingencies) and back end (e.g., spending every penny of the budget to justify an increase for the following year). The potential savings are huge, and the control systems are arguably tighter and more relevant as both local and senior managers constantly monitor that spending is linked to value-adding work and strategic initiatives.

Make Central Services Responsive to Internal Customers

In the process organization, central services become centers of excellence that support operating teams. But the benefits of centralizing back-office functions will be limited if these services are simply allocated to operating units based on some arbitrary and often opaque formula. That's why some organizations are moving away from the annual allocation of central costs toward systems that enable business-unit teams to access operational resources closer to the point of need. This reduces much of the waste endemic in the traditional system.

One approach is to create an internal market whereby internal customers buy services from internal service providers. Some have used service level agreements to define this supplier-customer relationship, but this can suggest more of a legal obligation to support central services units than simulate a real market with choices and conditions of customer satisfaction. Another problem is how internal services are defined and invoiced. For operating managers, there is nothing worse than receiving unfathomable internal service invoices. The invoices just make these managers suspicious and resentful about the head office burden their business units have to carry.

The golden rule is to keep the basis of charging as simple as possible. For example, an IT department might provide the services shown in figure 4-4 together with a clear basis for charging out these services. Operating units can then clearly understand the basis of charging and, more importantly, how they can influence the costs that they incur. Thus if they are incurring high charges for a service they don't value they can use it less or complain and demand that it is improved. This transparency exerts far greater pressure on central costs and makes them feel much more like external suppliers with customers to satisfy.

It sounds obvious, but knowing who is the customer for central services—who is using the service and do they have a cost budget and the authority to pay for it—is important. Thousands of employees, for example, have PCs and laptops but only department heads have a budget to absorb the cost. Listening to the needs of customers is critical, but in large organizations there are often hundreds and thousands of them, so how can this be done? We will see in a moment from the Handelsbanken example that follows that hundreds of customers' views can be represented by just a few appointed people who have the scope and authority to agree services and prices.

There are some common services that can't readily be applied to one particular internal customer or another. Recruiting an

FIGURE 4-4

Menu of central services

Service description	Basis of charge
Application development service	Number of hours
Application maintenance service	Number of hours
Mainframe processing service	Number of CPU units
Distributed processing service	Number of servers
Network service	Number of network ports
Ad hoc data requests	Number of hours
Desktop equipment leasing	Number of desktops
Laptop equipment leasing	Number of laptops
Online report viewing	Number of online reporting log-ins
Remote access service	Number of subscriptions
Intranet support service	Number of hours support
E-mail service	Number of accounts
Imaging service	Number of seats
Basic telephone service	Number of extensions

employee or providing a training course can clearly be related to a particular unit. But senior executive costs, IT development costs, and some R&D costs cannot easily be identified with particular operating units. In these cases, a share of such costs would be shown as "unit-sustaining costs," a figure shown after all "controllable" costs.

Be Wary of Transfer Pricing

Many organizations use various forms of transfer pricing when they move products and services from one organizational unit to another. But it is easy to lose clarity and transparency in the performance measurement system through a poorly designed transfer pricing system. The problem is that accountants are desperately trying to make *financial* sense of business units (spread costs and profits and minimize tax) whereas it is *behavioral* sense that organizations now need. Each company must agree a set of rules governing the management of and accounting for business units.

Teams should know in detail how measures are constructed. Such measures should be clear and transparent so people have confidence in them. The CFO needs to be extremely careful with transfer pricing, especially if profit markups are involved. There are basically four pricing options: variable costs only; full cost (variable cost plus a proportion of overheads); full cost plus a profit markup; and full market pricing. Let's look at each option.

VARIABLE COSTS. This is the lowest level transfer price and represents only those costs that vary directly with the product or service (e.g., material, labor, and other direct costs of production). They do not include overheads. While it is simple to use, the variable cost method is unlikely to lead to a fair accounting result for the upstream or downstream unit. And the price is likely to be unstable, since variable costs can change significantly with volume output.

FULL COST (VARIABLE COST PLUS A PROPORTION OF OVERHEADS). This is the method preferred by most organizations. It means that each cost center (usually a unit with no external customers) clears its costs over a year and breaks even in accounting terms. It has the advantage of being relatively simple and avoids the adverse behavior often associated with the next option (i.e., where a profit figure is included).

FULL COST PLUS A PROFIT MARKUP. This option is used by some organizations to "motivate" managers in non-customer-facing units by giving them profit targets. The idea is to simulate market prices and give upstream unit managers incentives to maximize performance. But the opportunities for bad practice and gaming are wide open as managers cut corners or manipulate prices to achieve their numbers. I've heard it said that "every business unit made a profit, it was only the whole company that made a loss."

FULL MARKET PRICING. This option is used by organizations that have independent business units that also sell their products and services to external customers. They are likely to have price lists that can be used for transfer pricing purposes. Thus they charge the same price to other group businesses as they would to external customers (i.e., the market price model). Most oil companies operate this way.

Managing Central Services Costs Through an Internal Market at Handelsbanken

Handelsbanken uses the second transfer pricing option (full cost) using a kind of process standard cost to charge products and services from central units to regions and branches. All central services costs (only 2 percent of the whole cost base) are roughly "cleared out" each year (including some allocations such as IT costs). Within branches there are a number of processes such as opening new accounts and processing mortgages and loans. The time required to perform these has been measured using a system based on predetermined standard times for the individual elements of work involved in each process. These process costs then form part of the menu of transaction charges that are applied to branches each time they execute a standard process. Thus, for example, each Internet transaction has a standard cost. However, this is the one cost that changes regularly depending on the volume of transactions. So the higher the volume, the lower the cost to the branch.

It is because each transaction is also related to a customer (and each customer is fixed to a branch) that the system is able to compile and produce instant profitability statements for customers, branches, regions, and the whole bank. Thus there is a "notional" set of accounts based on these estimates that allows fast results (group and branch profit statements are available online). These accounts are reconciled annually. It is important to recognize, however, that there are no profit markups in the system. There is only one set of revenues and costs or "one truth."

Handelsbanken provides a good example of how the internal market can work. All central costs are absorbed by profit centers such as regions and branches, but they are not simply presented as a fait accompli. There is an annual round of negotiations whereby cost estimates and the services underpinning them are presented and discussed with representatives of all those involved. Regional and branch managers have every right to challenge these costs and even to reject them. It is an internal market where the central service "sellers" meet the business-unit "buyers." Buyers check the prices against similar services in the marketplace and ensure that they receive value for money. CFO Lennart Francke tells us how it works in practice:

> The internal market is a system designed to put central services under the same sort of market pressures that customer-facing teams operate under. Where possible, market rates (or lower) are determined using benchmarks for the prices of the outputs of the central service departments. Under my supervision as well as the group controller, four representatives of "sellers" (central service functions) and four representatives of "buyers" (profit centers such as regions and branches) meet to hammer out a price for each possible process or transaction (around five hundred prices in total).
>
> Each transaction within the internal market is charged to the branch immediately through a "shadow" accounting system. This means that branch and profit center managers have a fairly good view on a continuous basis of what is happening. This is one of the really great advantages from having a decentralized organization like ours. Managers can always act on their own numbers, they don't have to sit and wait for management to make any important strategic decisions before making decisions. Every transaction in a branch has either an income or a cost or both. All central and regional costs are roughly cleared to branches each month. So that if you add up all the branch income statements they will give you the total figures for the whole bank (although there are some head office costs like directors salaries that are not charged).

But we shouldn't confuse our approach with service-level agreements. I suspect that most service-level agreements are a sham in that they talk about service commitments but in reality they are just contracts driven by central services that have the power to inflict them upon business units. In that sense you probably couldn't apply our system to other centralized organizations because then you don't have the independent buyers that actually are empowered to negotiate transfer prices. The thing to remember is that we have buyers that actually have an income statement that they have to guard and they can act as almost independent buyers. So if a branch doesn't want to buy your product or service they can either buy somewhere else or just discontinue buying your services. It's up to them— they are responsible for their costs and profitability.[14]

Match Capacity to Current Demand

One of the greatest sources of waste in any organization is excess capacity (e.g., underutilized buildings, plant, people, and technology). In the traditional model, capacity is fixed well in advance, thus determining much of the product cost before the first item is made. Michael Dell put the traditional capacity problem well: "The typical case in our industry is the factory building ten thousand units a day, day in and day out. First the machines stack up in the warehouse, and then they stack up in the channel. And all of a sudden, the guy at the end of the chain hollers, 'Whoa, hey, we've got too many of these. Everybody stop!' And the order to stop flows back through the chain until it reaches every component supplier. It's literally stop and start, because if you have a ninety-day lag between the point of demand and the point of supply, you're going to have a lot of inefficiency in the process. And the more inventory and time you have, the more variability, and the more problems. In our industry, there's a lot of what I call bad hygiene. Companies stuff the channel to get rid of old inventory and to meet short-term financial objectives."[15]

The perverse effects of the standard costing system and the overhead recovery mentality can lead to management decisions that defy rational belief. Consider the following situation. A consumer goods company recently launches a fifth variant of a range of kitchen knives. Production capacity is set at ninety thousand units per month (the budget for the new product is five thousand units). But the new product doesn't sell and is quickly dropped from the range. What happens next? The automatic pilot of the cost allocation system moves into gear, and the capacity costs originally charged to the dropped product are reallocated to the four remaining products. The result is predictable (if difficult to believe)—the fourth product is now marginal. This downward, or "death," spiral can easily occur through a blind adherence to an overhead recovery mentality.

Lean manufacturers work hard to eliminate overheads and remove waste. Taiichi Ohno defined capacity as work plus waste. In other words, if we can identify and eliminate waste then "free" capacity is released into the system. This can either sit there until absorbed by additional work or be eliminated altogether. Some firms use spare capacity to take special orders for fast turnaround and thus gain a real competitive advantage. Lean manufacturers tend to use twelve-monthly rolling forecasts (updated every month) to review capacity requirements. There is one forecast for each product family. The operations capacity is then established for each month, taking into account the revised product mix forecasts and any bottlenecks within the value stream. The team makes today what customers require today. Materials and components are pulled into the system just-in-time, resulting in low inventories and perfect on-time delivery. To accomplish this there must be spare capacity. Once the forecasts have been prepared, the management team looks at forecasts versus capacity. If further capacity is required, it simply provides additional people. If there is not enough capacity, it needs to think imaginatively how this can be made available—through further lean improvements, changes in the production process, changes to the manning of production cells, acquisition of additional equipment, or the outsourcing of some products. If the capacity problem is immediate the team would work overtime or maybe get help from another value stream.[16]

At Toyota, planning is a continuous process. By the early 1990s, while each plant forecast what its likely output (and thus capacity) would be, detailed planning was only one month ahead with, for example, March's planned production being set in the second half of February. Because Toyota has now moved to a single common platform in nearly all its global plants (these can handle up to eight different models, never mind varieties of the same model!), it has even more planning flexibility and is able to reduce cycle times even further. The cycle time from order to finished product is moving toward a staggering five days.[17] This additional speed and flexibility reduces costs even further, making it even more difficult for competitors to catch-up.

Ensure That All Projects Are Necessary and Add Value

Another major cause of waste is the number of ineffective projects that are instigated without a rigorous process of establishing their worth. This error is compounded when little thought is given to exit strategies if the project doesn't meet its projected returns. In fact, decision making in large organizations is anything but rational. Gary Hamel once said that resource allocation was the last bastion of Soviet-style central planning and can be found in *Fortune* 500 companies. "Big companies are not markets, they're hierarchies," according to Hamel. "The guys at the top decide where the money goes. Unconventional ideas are forced to make a tortuous climb up the corporate pyramid. If an idea manages to survive the gauntlet of skeptical vice-presidents, some distant CEO or chairman finally decides whether or not to invest."[18] Hamel's scathing attack rings true. These decision-making processes are too often based on company politics rather than management common sense. Thus new ideas are stifled in favor of pouring good money after bad into loss-making projects.

Capital expenditure decisions are usually based on financial criteria—invariably involving some hurdle rate based on the cost of capital. Thus the system is biased against high-risk projects that cannot easily establish predictable and precisely calculated returns. Other problems are evident. Projects can become highly political as managers champion their own pet initiatives. It is likely that less than half of major projects support a company's strategy. That means that half the capital expenditure budget is adding little value. Leading-edge organizations derive initiatives from strategy reviews, then they prepare the investment case thoroughly and implement quickly.

Derive Improvement Initiatives from Regular Strategy Reviews

Many initiatives are driven by the vested interests of local teams whose primary aim is to maximize their own resources compared with their business-unit rivals. This leads to many investments that have little or nothing to do with the firm's strategy; at one large U.S. bank, Kaplan and Norton found that few initiatives passed the strategy test.[19] With often hundreds of initiatives in play at any one time within large organizations, this can be a huge problem and represents a significant waste of resources. Initiatives are, more often than not, easier to start than finish. Thus many projects often linger on well past their sell-by-date.

One software company actually took an inventory of how many strategic initiatives it had placed on the organization and found around 450! And a lot of them were overlapping—they were just expressed differently. Since it had only a few thousand employees, the company began to wonder how it could possibly move in its chosen direction with this level of complexity. So after preparing a strategic road map, it boiled those 450 strategic objectives down to just 13 high-priority objectives.

Improvement initiatives are often caught up in corporate politics as one business unit competes with another for resources from the corporate center. Jan Wallander of Handelsbanken notes that there has been quite a lot of research in the Scandinavian countries about how investment decisions are made. These studies show that in real life the documents on which decisions are based are colored by a lot of irrational and subjective considerations by those who have formulated the memos, assembled the facts, and made the analyses. What staff and technical experts will deliver is something that mirrors their need for prestige, and their envy and jealousy toward other people and other divisions in the company. However, Wallender is also aware how difficult it is to avoid this problem, given the tendency to gain outline approval for longer-term investments that then grind their way through the system until the cash is spent.[20]

The World Bank is starting to manage its business with strategy and performance contracts (SPCs). Under the contract, each business unit is responsible for defining its overall strategic objectives, the key business lines through which it intends to achieve them, and the trade-offs or choices it is making by focusing on these lines. The contract also defines the risks facing the unit as it implements its strategy and identifies the indicators that will be used to monitor performance as it moves forward. According to CFO John Wilton,

> We wanted to focus on a different agenda. If that's the strategy, what are the priorities and which business lines are we going to engage in? And how are we going to allocate resources to those business lines? These are very different questions from asking people to "give us your detailed budget for the next three years." So we moved to a multiyear system that enabled us to better align our resources with our strategy. We asked each VPU [vice presidential unit] to prepare a strategy and performance contract. We said to them that this would be "valid until no longer valid" and "updated when necessary." This allowed managers the flexibility to change direction when necessary instead of being driven by the planning and reporting cycles. The monitoring process would move to a higher level based on a longer time perspective with more

use of historic and indicative trends and more effort to understand the strategic story. Rolling twenty-four-month histories and medium term indicative targets for key indicators would provide the context for on-going discussions about unit and institutional performance. These were the major changes.[21]

The SPC is written with an explicit understanding of the indicative level of resources available. Once an SPC has been agreed with senior management, performance management becomes a continuous cycle (see figure 4-5). Actual performance is tracked regularly in relation to the indicators, and strategic objectives and choices are reviewed as necessary. In the case of some units that are operating in volatile circumstances this provides the flexibility to make frequent changes. But in most cases the strategic direction is unlikely to change from one year to the next. Senior managers believe that these contracts will provide the basis for a continuous discussion about strategy and decision making and will lead to fewer (costly) strategic mistakes.

FIGURE 4-5

The links in the strategy and performance contract

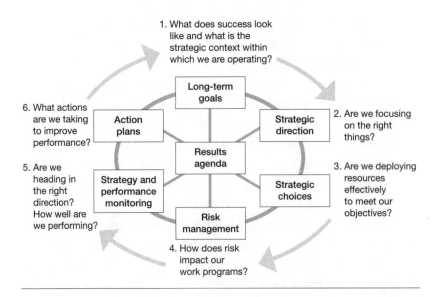

While this approach is similar to that of the balanced scorecard in that it focuses management attention on strategic goals and direction and action plans to support them, there are important differences. For a start, the SPC does not follow an annual cycle. It needs changing only when strategy changes ("valid until invalid"), and in many organizations this happens infrequently. Nor is it driven by detailed measures that tell managers whether they are on track or not to meet some short-term target. Performance evaluation is a mixture of both hard and soft measures that together with other feedback enable senior managers to form a judgment about overall performance. The SPC forces business leaders to think deeply about their strategies (even in back-office units such as finance and human resources) and provides them with a governance framework within which they can take decisions and prioritize resources.

Prioritize Projects According to Their Strategic Impact and Value Creation

Some organizations have taken the idea of strategic alignment of resources several steps further. One large financial services organization is moving to a system of *investment optimization* in which it takes all the dollars that it spends every year on operational improvement and instead of just giving them to businesses in the form of annual budgets, it regulates them in the form of thousands of small projects. Business leaders now know that they have to justify all their spending plans; they don't get them as a right. The trade-off is that they can put new projects in for approval at any time to support their latest initiatives. Instead of four quarterly reviews with only three opportunities during the year to release investments, there are now twelve. An Australian utility has taken discretionary spending (which used to be allocated through the budgeting process) away from business units and holds these funds at a higher level. This avoids placing spending on an automatic pilot whereby budgets for expenses such as "training" or "parking" are spent mindlessly just because they are there. In a large multidivisional business the savings can be huge—

this organization has saved around A$30 million per year. In essence, what it did was fund core expenses but make each unit bid for discretionary spending. And what was most interesting was that the units had to do this in front of their peers, so everyone could see fair play and only the high priority bids were approved.

CFOs are also realizing that a significant element of their capital expenditure is wasted. Just think how quickly, and with such scant knowledge, that some major investment decisions are made. This particularly applies to acquisitions, where enormous risks are taken based on fluffy estimates of cost savings and additional market penetration. Huge investment case packs are prepared full of numbers and charts that justify the bottom line estimates. But too often there is a political motive behind the proposal rather than a compelling (and rational) strategic case. It is no wonder that most acquisitions fail to create wealth for the acquiring company's shareholders.

Enlightened CFOs are aware of these problems. They focus on two criteria: *impact* (whether it is global, regional, or local) and *value* (whether it is strategic or nonstrategic).

1. *Global/strategic.* These projects are likely to benefit many business units and thus should be decided and funded by corporate. A new corporate branding exercise or the implementation of an enterprisewide computer system would be examples.

2. *Global/nonstrategic.* These projects also impact a number of business units, so again a corporate decision is appropriate. A new office building is an example.

3. *Local/strategic.* In this case the impact of the initiative lies within a particular business unit. Because it is strategic, corporate will want to know about the proposal and ensure that it complies with its definition of a worthwhile strategic investment. At Tomkins, for example, business units are provided with a "sustaining capital pool" each year. This is based on their four-quarter forecast for the

fiscal year usually available during the last week in October. They can use this pool for their spending plans without recourse to head office. Only new projects above $500,000 need express approval, and this can often be done with a conference call. So access to capital is swift and enables unit teams to respond rapidly to new opportunities. Each business is self-sufficient in terms of support services. There are no shared services in the group.

4. *Local/nonstrategic.* If decisions involve relatively small sums and need to be made quickly then that is exactly what should happen. Teams should look at the options and decide. This is the process at Tomkins. New initiatives can be agreed and started at any time, provided they meet a number of criteria (modified rate-of-return, cash payback, consistent with strategy, pass holistic criteria, and pass risk assessment tests). Investment proposals include capital requirements, start-up costs, and operating costs as well as income streams generated. Whereas in the previous regime, capital expenditure submissions were made *after* bid proposals were agreed (e.g., for a potential major order), now they must be agreed *in advance* of bids. To facilitate this accelerated timing, senior executives regularly make themselves available for video or teleconferenced oral presentations of the business case supporting the bid and give the nod right there if it passes muster (Tomkins's flat management hierarchy makes this possible).

When capital is rationed, many organizations use some sort of ranking criteria to choose investments. The U.S. bank Wells Fargo developed such a balanced ranking model for its Online Financial Services (OFS) business.[22] The executive team had identified three strategic platforms: (1) attract and retain high potential value customers; (2) increase revenue per customer; and (3) reduce cost per customer. The initiative identification process started by sorting initiatives into two categories: "strategic" and "business as usual." The team developed three criteria for approving a strategic initiative:

(1) it helps OFS achieve a strategic objective (as listed on the balanced scorecard); (2) it builds a competitive advantage; and (3) it builds a sustainable point of differentiation.

To qualify as strategic, an initiative had to score highly on each criterion (initiatives that were rated medium to high were considered to be "major" projects; initiatives that rated medium to low were considered to be "minor" projects, and initiatives that rated low were considered only as "activities"). Once the projects passed the initial screening process, the team segmented them into two groups: those that were function-specific and shorter term, and those that were cross-functional, relatively expensive, and longer term. The team used three questions in this segmentation process:

- Does the initiative reallocate resources within other functional units?

- Does the initiative cost more than $500,000?

- Does the initiative take more than three months to implement?

Only those initiatives that received a "yes" to *any one* of these questions would pass through this screen to the initiative ranking model. Of the complete list of over one hundred initiatives, only eleven survived the first two screens. At this stage the proponents of each project would be asked to prepare a more detailed business case proposal. As table 4-1 shows, six criteria were used to rank initiatives and these were weighted according to importance.

It is rather pointless going through an extended decision-making process only to find that essential resources are not available. Leading organizations calibrate initiatives with available resources. At a large French company, each business team had to produce around twenty to twenty-five strategic actions that would support their chosen key value drivers and be implemented over the next few years. The resource impact of each action plan had to be shown on an impact matrix, which would show how processes contributed to the achievement of each strategic action—high, medium, or low. When completed, this matrix gave a complete

TABLE 4-1

Investment approval criteria

Criteria	Definition	Weighting
Strategic importance	Fit with strategic platforms outlined in balanced scorecard	40%
Cost	Cost of implementing the initiative (from conception to deployment)	15%
NPV	Present value of net benefits (three-year time horizon)	15%
Elapsed time	Implementation time period (from conception to deployment)	10%
Interdependencies	Degree to which the initiative is dependent upon other initiatives or other parties	10%
Risk/complexity to implement	Operational risk Technology risk	10%

picture of the resources demanded and whether or not these demands were realistic. This led to the prioritization of actions and avoided potential bottlenecks such as overloading key people or IT resources.

Preparing Investments Thoroughly and Implementing Quickly at Toyota North America

Alex Warren of the Kentucky Toyota plant observed: "If you've got a project that is supposed to be fully implemented in a year, it seems to me that the typical American company will spend about three months on planning, then they'll begin to implement. But they'll encounter all sorts of problems after implementation, and they'll spend the rest of the year correcting them. However, given the same year-long project, Toyota will spend up to ten months planning, then implement in a small way—such as with pilot production—and be fully implemented at the end of the year, with virtually no remaining problems."[23] When Toyota purchased some land for a test track in Arizona, the U.S. lawyer acting for the company was amazed at how thorough its planning was, commenting after the deal: "Toyota stands out as the preeminent analyst of strategy and tactics. Nothing is assumed. Everything is verified. The goal is getting it right."[24]

At Toyota, the emphasis is on thorough preparation. If a decision fails to live up to expectations, then management will be tolerant, but if the preparation is sloppy, it will not—a reprimand will likely follow. There are five major elements in the Toyota decision-making process:

1. Find out what's really going on.

2. Understand the underlying causes that explain surface appearances—ask "Why?" five times.

3. Consider alternative solutions and develop a convincing rationale for the one preferred.

4. Build consensus within the team.

5. Use simple, efficient methods of communication.[25]

Taiichi Ohno developed the idea of asking "Why?" five times. He gives the example of a machine breakdown:

1. *Why did the machine stop?*
   There was an overload and the fuse blew.

2. *Why was there an overload?*
   The bearing was not sufficiently lubricated.

3. *Why was it not lubricated sufficiently?*
   The lubrication pump was not pumping sufficiently.

4. *Why was it not pumping sufficiently?*
   The shaft of the pump was worn and rattling.

5. *Why was the shaft worn out?*
   There was no strainer attached and metal scrap got in.[26]

Repeating *why* five times can help to uncover the root cause of a problem or reveal the core issues within an investment proposal. Ohno tells us why this is so important: "To tell the truth, the Toyota Production System has been built on the practice and evolution of this scientific approach. By asking *why* five times and answering it each time, we can get to the real cause of the problem, which is often hidden behind more obvious symptoms."[27]

Most companies write long proposals and memos to justify their case. This is not a learning process. It tells people why you have made a proposal that they should accept. Toyota has communication down to a fine art. All the information needed to make a complex decision is presented on one 11 × 17 inch piece of paper. It is called an A3 report, and typically has seven boxes: current situation, proposal, benefits, plan, implementation, controls, and time line.[28]

Toyota's approach to lean thinking and cost reduction has enabled it to become one of the best manufacturing companies in the world. It has been consistently profitable for over thirty years (the results of its rivals have gyrated between periods of profits and losses). Its cars are consistently at or near the top of the J.D. Power customer satisfaction ratings in most countries (according to a 2003 study in *Consumer Reports,* fifteen of the top thirty-eight most reliable models over the previous seven years were made by Toyota/Lexus).[29] It has risen to be the number-two carmaker in the world, and its net profits dwarf the combined profits of its big three rivals (General Motors, Ford, and Daimler-Chrysler).

One of the greatest services a CFO can perform for the organization is to wage a war on waste. But to do this effectively he or she needs to blow up the bureaucracy and challenge those resources often protected by some of the most influential people in the organization. Learning and applying the lessons of lean thinking will yield huge benefits, provided that managers have the scope and authority to make the necessary changes. They also need to see these changes as permanent rather than quick fixes, otherwise any benefits will be fleeting.

A CHECKLIST FOR THE CFO

☐ Think about Drucker's insight that business results are proportionate to revenues while costs are proportionate to transactions and activities. Don't be surprised to find that 20 to 40 percent of your costs relate to activities that add little or no value for customers. The challenge is to identify and eliminate them.

☐ Think about how budgets protect costs by focusing on general ledger cost categories such as salaries rather than the costs of delivering products and services to customers. Transfer accountability for resource usage to operating managers and either give them profit responsibility or provide directional spending guidelines (e.g., cost-to-income ratios). Don't give them detailed cost budgets that are just uplifts from the previous year.

☐ Dismantle the head office bureaucracy and see the organization as a system with core processes and subprocesses that create and deliver value to customers. Process teams should be joined together in supplier-customer relationships. This puts pressure on internal suppliers to reduce costs.

☐ Eliminate management layers and duplicate channels and shorten the time between planning and execution. But you will need the support of key influencers within the senior management group to make these changes.

☐ Embrace lean thinking. Do only work that adds value for customers (though some work needs to be done for other strategic and regulatory reasons). Recognize the distinction between value and non-value work (anything that's not done right the first time or that necessitates follow-up action—these costs can comprise over 50 percent of total cost).

☐ The improvement focus should be on the system rather than the people, since 95 percent of problems are concerned with the system. Eliminating common causes in a service center might involve understanding why products are not delivered on time and why customers' calls are not returned promptly.

☐ Move toward an internal market to put constant pressure on central services costs. Switch the power to business managers who demand low prices and high quality.

☐ Match capacity to prevailing demand. Use rolling forecasts to estimate future capacity and take early action to increase or reduce capacity costs.

☐ Derive projects from strategy reviews and align resources according to the highest priority initiatives. Eliminate those projects that have little or no strategic impact and create little value. Prioritize projects according to strategic impact and value creation.

☐ Prepare investment proposals thoroughly and implement them quickly.

CHAPTER FIVE

THE CFO AS MASTER OF MEASUREMENT

We would like to dethrone measurement from its godly position, to reveal the false god it has been. We want instead to offer measurement a new job—that of helpful servant. We want to use measurement to give us the kind and quality of feedback that supports and welcomes people to step forward with their desire to contribute, to learn, and to achieve.

—Margaret Wheatley and Myron Kellner-Rogers

WHAT IS IT that creates great performance in organizations? If you believe the answer is leadership, commitment, creativity, learning, teamwork, and quality (all behavioral factors), then it begs the next question. Which measures have you found that maximize these behavioral factors? None, is the likely answer. Wheatley and Kellner-Rogers believe that they are all performance factors that depend on the prevailing culture. They emerge as key capabilities when people feel connected to their work and to each other. Each of these factors is a choice that people make. Depending on how they feel about the organization and their own team, they will choose how much to give of themselves.[1]

W. Edwards Deming was also a skeptic about the value of measurement. He once observed that less than 3 percent of what influences final results can be measured. Nevertheless, American managers, according to Deming, tend to spend over 97 percent of their time analyzing measures and less than 3 percent on what really matters—the unmeasurable.[2] When managers talked to him about particular measures he would ask, "How do you know? How can you possibly assess things with the minuscule little elements you're looking at here? How do you know?"[3] This is a disturbing question for all those involved in performance measurement.

Despite Wheatley, Kellner-Rogers, and Deming's misgivings, we need effective measures so we can tell if we're improving or not, as well as evaluate management performance. *But we only need a few of them.* Most organizations have far too many measures; this invariably undermines the behavioral factors just mentioned. Measures should be used to stimulate inquiry and help teams to improve their performance rather than command and control their actions from some remote location. But targets and measures are becoming more pervasive. The rise of balanced scorecards and customer relationship management systems has released a surge of measurement energy as finance managers seize the opportunity to impose even more targets and measures and control performance against them. But, as noted in the previous chapter, managers are more likely to be focusing on only 5 percent of the improvement opportunity (people and activities) rather than the 95 percent (process flows). The root of the problem is that leaders believe that the "right" measures give them control. They focus on setting targets and agreeing performance contracts rather than giving managers the freedom and capability to satisfy customers' needs profitably.

Enlightened CFOs recognize that performance measurement is a minefield of misinformation and often a driver of the wrong actions and behavior. But liberated from the fear of failing to meet fixed targets, teams will see measures as a friend that guides them rather than a whip that controls them. They will use them to ask questions and drive dialogue about context, purpose, meaning, and action. Leaders will look at patterns and trends and open up information to everyone who is able to make sense of it and contribute ideas and suggestions.

The CFO has a key role to play in changing the measurement culture. In this chapter we will suggest that the CFO needs to:

- Measure to learn and improve

- Choose the right measures

- See measurement as patterns, trends, and abnormalities

- Provide external reality checks

- Use a range of measures to inform a dialogue about management performance

Measure to Learn and Improve

A water utility has a manual of standards that defines excellent performance. Service staff must respond to problems within two working days. There are targets for the time it takes to phone customers, send a surveyor if there's a structural problem, and send a plumber to fix the problem, as well as for performing each activity according to detailed specifications. But the customer's experience is not on the measurement radar screen. A customer with a leaking drain can suffer interminable delays waiting for this system to take its course while the water meter is ticking and the house is damaged. But measuring each activity allows the company to claim that its standards of service are excellent. The gulf between measurement rhetoric and reality can be huge.

If the saying "you can only manage what you measure" has any truth, then it is little wonder that our management systems are so ineffective. If we insist on measuring performance against a fixed target and budget, it should not surprise us when we fail to adapt to unforeseen events. If we insist on measuring activities such as how many sales calls we make or how many orders we process then it shouldn't surprise us if we fail to satisfy and retain key customers. Managers are rewarded for compliance rather than results. I have made this point time and again. If measures are aimed at evaluating performance against predetermined targets, people will focus on meeting those targets rather than meeting the needs of the customer. This is a perfect example of Goodhart's law (when a measure becomes a target, it ceases to be a good measure).[4] Goodhart's law is a sociological analogue of Heisenberg's uncertainty principle in quantum mechanics. Measuring a system usually disturbs it. The more precise the measurement, and the shorter its timescale, the greater the energy of the disturbance and the greater the unpredictability of the outcome.

Targets are the blunt instruments of command and control. Jan Wallander knew what he was doing when he allowed teams to set their own goals but measured their performance in a completely different way—that is, relative to peers. This idea has been at the core of the company's success for over thirty years. Why don't other leaders see the point? The likely answer is that setting annual targets and measuring performance against them is deeply ingrained in the management practices of the vast majority of organizations. But such a system is deeply flawed. It emphasizes measurement over management, ends over means, blame over risk, result over method.

What matters to managers is *soft and timely feedback* rather than so-called hard numbers. As we have seen in countless examples of measurement abuse (HealthSouth, WorldCom, etc.) and the elasticity of generally accepted accounting principles, accounting numbers really aren't that "hard" at all. As Wheatley and Kellner-Rogers point out, there are some important distinctions between hard numbers and soft feedback (see figure 5-1).[5] They follow the line of Vision A and B set out in the introduction to this book.

Vision A suggests that senior management "experts" are the ones with a monopoly of wisdom and should be in charge of the

FIGURE 5-1

Contrasting two visions of measurement

Vision A (Measurement as hard numbers)	Vision B (Measurement as soft feedback)
• One size fits all	• Context dependent
• Imposed; criteria are established externally	• Self-determined; the system chooses what to notice
• Information is in fixed categories only	• Information is accepted from anywhere
• Meaning is predetermined	• The system creates its own meaning
• Prediction and routine are valued	• Newness and surprise are essential
• The focus is on stability and control	• The focus is on adaptability and growth
• Meaning remains static	• Meaning evolves
• The system adapts to the measures	• The system co-adapts with its measures

information system, and that allowing information to flow around the organization in an uncontrolled way is potentially dangerous, since managers might fail to interpret it in the "right" way. Vision B assumes that most managers are mature enough to interpret and analyze information in a sensible way and use it to make effective decisions. Once again, we see the fault line between top-down control and frontline decision making.

The CFO's dilemma is that the tighter the target and measurement coils become, the greater is the distrust and dysfunctional behavior in the system. While the short-term results might show an improvement (depending on how poor the performance management system was before), the longer-term result is likely to be declining performance. The answer is to disconnect measurement from targets and rewards. Thus the focus of measurement should be on self-improvement rather than top-down control (effective control is maintained in terms of monitoring patterns, trends, and abnormalities—we will discuss this later in the chapter). The CFO should also open up the information system so that managers can extract what they believe is useful to them rather than have it prescribed by someone else. That's what brings newness and surprise, and enables adaptability and growth.

Open and high-trust organizations tend to be consistently strong performers. But to get there is, to some degree, an act of faith. For many CFOs, it is a real challenge to forgo their detailed control and monitoring systems. Their instinctive reaction is that it is these controls that enable them to drive improvement. What they fail to appreciate is that human organizations are full of interdependencies that cannot be easily unraveled to show cause-and-effect. The results can be seen in only the performance of the whole.

Take the example of Tomkins, which switched from annual targets to a broader framework of performance expectations (based on its "10:10:10" formula). Managers had to strive to maximize their improvement over the prior year. There was no number to meet. Bonuses were based on the increase over prior years with no upper limit. But Tomkins's performance didn't suffer at all. In fact, it improved significantly.

In this system, performance improvement is the responsibility of local teams. That's why they need only a few simple measures to provide constant feedback to continuously learn and improve their performance. This also leads to another important principle. Measurement should be integrated with the work. It must not be top-down or remote from the process. Staffers in white coats with clipboards checking activity time or quality is not the right approach. Contrast this with one Hewlett-Packard factory years ago, where four out of every thousand soldered connections were defective. Not bad for those days, but engineers were called in— and they cut the defect rate in half by modifying the process. Then HP turned to its workers. They practically rebuilt the operation— and slashed defects a thousandfold, to under two per million.[6]

Integrating measurement in the work means that many top-down controls are not required. Targets, budgets, standard costing systems, quality procedures, and other control systems that exist to link high-level decisions with frontline work are superfluous to requirements. Overheads shrink dramatically. Measurement becomes much more transparent. And without so many overheads to allocate, even activity-based costing becomes unnecessary as product and customer costs become easier to extract.

Measurement at Toyota is based on learning and improvement at the front line. That's why Toyota, despite having an excellent accounting system that allows it to comply with regulatory authorities, actually has no standard cost accounting system. The only measures inside the plant are visual ones. Toyota doesn't drive operations with the numbers. It doesn't measure to check where they are against some target. It follows a different, deeper logic. Measures are used only to enhance awareness of how the work is flowing.[7] Otherwise, visual controls, kept on daily graphs and charts, tell everyone at a glance if work is being performed to critical standards. Such controls might show where items belong, how many belong there, what the standard procedure is for doing something, the status of the work-in-process, and other information critical to the flow of work. These controls are not about meeting plans and targets. They are integrated into the work. The visual aspect means that anyone can see if work is deviating from an agreed standard and enable immediate corrections to take place. For example, by just observing minimum and maximum levels of inventory compared with the standard enables managers to be highly effective.

Finding the right number and balance of measures, however, is not easy. A single measure is invariably too simplistic, while a wide range of measures is likely to lead to contradiction and confusion and make it difficult to prioritize what's important. Managers at any level shouldn't need more than six or seven measures. Harvard professor Robert Simons's rule of thumb for accountability systems is that individuals should be accountable for no more measures than they can remember—usually about seven.[8]

While the CFO should not decide which measures local teams will use, he should provide some guidelines for the selection of measures. For example, an effective measure should pass the "SMART" test: it should be *s*imple (easy to understand); *m*easurable (the data can be readily collected); *a*ctionable (it leads to action/behavior change); *r*elevant (to level, purpose, and strategy); and *t*imely. A whole measurement system should be balanced between leading/lagging, financial/nonfinancial, and short-term/medium-term metrics;

show results relative to peers and prior years; and focus on trends and abnormalities.

Choose the Right Measures

Measures should be appropriate to the management level (see table 5-1). At the *process level* they should be derived from the purpose of the process and focus on process flows (i.e., the performance of the end-to-end process) rather than individual activities. These will invariably be KPIs that enable self-regulation and improvement within the process team. At the *business-unit level* they should be derived from strategy and focus on the customer value proposition. These will be a mix of leading and lagging indicators and focus on improving business-unit performance compared with peers and prior periods. At the *company or group level* they should be derived from the best way of communicating results to a range of stakeholders including the board and external investors. These will usually be a range of financial measures that tell a complete performance story.

TABLE 5-1

Choosing the right measures

Level	Business process	Business unit	Company (and group)
Derivation	Process purpose	BU strategy	Investor relevance
Focus	End-to-end process results (measures integrated in the work)	BU results	Group results
Mix	Operational KPIs (leading)	Operational/financial KRIs (lagging)	Financial KRIs (lagging)
Management appraisal focus	Process improvement	BU improvement relative to peers and prior periods	Group performance relative to peers and prior periods

Focus Improvement on Process Outcomes

Perhaps the most important principle of an effective measure is that it is derived from purpose or strategy (see figure 5-2). When activities become the primary focus of measurement, dysfunctional behavior will be the likely outcome (however, we need to estimate activities for planning and resource management purposes).

Consider measuring traffic wardens on the number of parking tickets they hand out. Now the purpose of having traffic wardens is presumably to keep the traffic flowing smoothly. But as soon as they are measured on the numbers of tickets they issue, they become more aggressive and are likely to hand out tickets to taxi drivers, delivery vehicles, undertakers, emergency plumbers, and even firemen. The same behavioral outcomes will result if police are measured on the number of arrests they make instead of crime prevention. Yet the government prosecution service is encouraged to take on only those cases it is sure to win (because it is measured on convictions).

When the purpose becomes "serve the customer" instead of "meet this activity target," measurement and management attention is completely transformed. Doctors and nurses can focus on treating patients and the police department can focus on preventing crime. Measures should focus on flow (the end-to-end customer delivery cycle) rather than how much of any activity has been completed. The result is that everyone focuses on improving the work by applying their own and other people's knowledge.

Most process teams have a reasonable idea of which measures are critical to their success. If they are given the scope and authority

FIGURE 5-2

Deriving measures from purpose and strategy

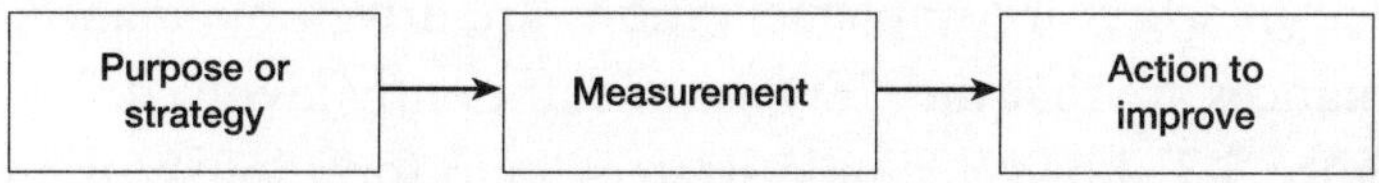

to find these measures they often approach the task with enthusiasm and imagination. Trial and error are part of the process. But the point is that these measures are owned *by the team*. They have not been imposed on them by a higher authority. Measures must not be turned into targets or commitments. Even if this is not the intention, some teams will interpret measures as targets against which their performance will be assessed. If this happens, the wrong behavior will result.

Focus on Business-Unit Results

So far we have talked about process (or operational) measures. Effective process measures, usually known as key performance indicators (KPIs), have some element of predictive capability. As we noted in chapter 3, KPIs are usually defined as measures that are taken daily or weekly. They represent a manager's dashboard or radar screen. But we also need other measures at higher (more aggregated) levels of the organization. These lagging measures are usually known as key result indicators (KRIs) or key business indicators (KBIs). They are invariably collected weekly and monthly and are used by managers to monitor progress toward medium-term goals.

At the business-unit level, metrics should also be derived from strategy. Some business-unit teams use the balanced scorecard for this purpose. They first set the strategy, derive key measures from the strategy, set goals to improve on those measures, and then decide how to achieve those goals through action plans. However, too many scorecards go off the rails on goal setting. In other words, the link between goals and measures becomes a contract that, in turn, undermines the continuous feedback loops that should be one of the key strengths of a vibrant scorecard process. The CFO needs to be involved in setting the guidelines for a successful implementation of the balanced scorecard—but only around 20 percent of scorecard implementations are driven by finance, thus the chances are that the CFO is not sufficiently involved.[9]

Figure 5-3 shows a simple strategy map for a low-cost airline. To increase profitability (the financial perspective) the airline

FIGURE 5-3

Deriving key measures for a low-cost airline

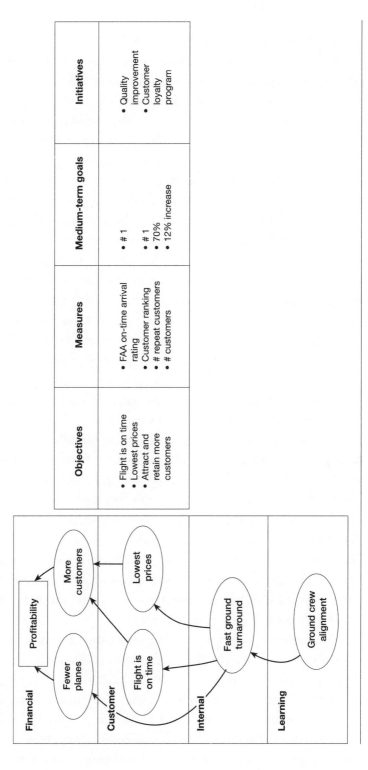

needs to both operate with the minimum number of planes and increase its volume of customers. To win more customers it must ensure that flights are on time and that it offers low prices (the customer perspective). To operate with low prices it must turn planes around quickly at the gates (the internal perspective). To turn planes around quickly it must train ground crews and align their performance evaluations with this objective (the learning perspective). Figure 5-3 zooms in on the customer perspective to show how objectives, measures, goals, and initiatives are derived and aligned. Notice that goals are derived from objectives and measures, and that actions follow goals.

If we focus on the customer perspective, then another way to think about key metrics is to look at the *customer value proposition,* or how the business distinguishes itself from its competitors in the eyes of the customer. The three classic value propositions are: *product leadership* (best product), *operational excellence* (lowest-cost product), and *customer intimacy* (best customer solution). However, determining a core value proposition is not always easy. Most senior managers like to think their company is good at every one of them. However, while this might be true, the theory goes that each business unit needs to be *exceptionally* good at one of them, and it is this one that distinguishes it from its competitors.

The primary objective of companies that compete on product leadership is to produce innovative products and services and bring them to market faster than the competition. Customers expect the latest, state-of-the-art products and services. Key metrics include time-to-market, rate of product introduction, percentage of sales from new products, cost of product development, number of patents filed, R&D as a percentage of sales, and the number of talented people who accept job offers.

The primary objective of companies that compete on operational excellence is to be the lowest-cost producer. Customers look to buy products and services on the basis of low price and convenience. They still demand high quality but they are not prepared to pay premium prices or go out of their way to make a purchase. Key metrics include process measures (quality, cycle times, efficiency), productivity measures, and working capital turnover.

The primary objective of companies that compete on customer intimacy is to acquire the right customers, keep them forever, and provide as many related products and services to them as possible. Customers are interested in getting exactly what they want, even if they have to pay a higher price or wait a bit longer to get it. These customers buy from suppliers that they can identify with their own special needs. Customers see these companies as being responsive to their needs, and they repay this responsiveness with loyalty. Key metrics include customer satisfaction, customer retention, new customer acquisition, customer profitability, market share by segment and by customer, and employee satisfaction.

Many organizations have learned important lessons about scorecard measures. First, they can become overcomplicated, especially when strategy maps are too detailed. Managers need only a few key measures to understand what is happening within the business. Second, finding these measures is not easy and is often a process of trial and error. And third, desirable but unnecessary measures are often difficult (and sometimes expensive) to track with any degree of reliability (this is especially dangerous if incentives are attached to them); if this is the case, they are better left out. Many scorecards end up being too heavily weighted toward financial numbers—sometimes because the data for nonfinancial measures are too difficult to collect or line managers don't trust them. One survey suggested that many companies see the scorecard as just another "fad that companies feel compelled to adopt in order to stay current."[10] However, it turns out that the companies making these comments were still using predominantly (75 percent) financial measures, against only 20 to 25 percent as recommended by Kaplan and Norton.[11]

Look for Hidden Meaning in Financial Results

All organizations use financial (lagging) indicators to report their performance over a period of time (usually a month, quarter, or year). They often have a language of their own littered with acronyms: EBIT, ROCE, ROE, ROI, CFROI, NOPAT, ROS, EPS, TSR, MVA, and EVA. Many of these are useful measures that tell senior managers how well the organization has performed over a recent period and if their organization is heading in the right direction. They do not, however, tell them what they need to do to improve these results. Nor do they inform users of accounts about many intangible assets (such as the value of R&D, brands, supply chains, etc.) or contingent liabilities (such as financial risks inherent in the use of derivatives and hedge funds) that, for many organizations, have a huge impact on their market value.

Another problem is that, as we noted earlier in this chapter, accounting numbers can be easily manipulated. "Window dressing" and "creative accounting" are two expressions that spring to mind to describe this problem. So how is the CFO to get value from accounting statements? One way is to compare results with peers both inside and outside the organization. Another is to look at trends over time. I will examine both these issues a little later in this chapter. I want to focus here on a number of red flags, both strategic and financial, that will enable the CFO to glean some insights into the underlying performance of a company or its subunits.

STRATEGIC RED FLAGS. Gary Hamel has some fascinating insights into how financial indicators can be used to gain some understanding of the effectiveness of strategy execution. Hamel believes that managers often become obsessed with a single performance measure—share price, revenue growth, return-on-investment (ROI), operating margin, or some other measure—and notes how dangerous this can be: "A deteriorating strategy can be masked by vigorous revenue growth, steadily increasing earnings, dramatic improvements in ROI, or even a rising share price. In fact, a single-minded focus on any one financial measure blinds one to more subtle signs of strategy decay."[12] So where do you look for signs of creeping strategy decay? According to Hamel there are four red flags that indicate a seriously moribund strategy:

- *Earnings growing far faster than revenues.* Over the past few decades many firms have produced acceptable levels of growth based on improving efficiency and as a result have been paying little attention to the top line with the result that the growth in earnings has far exceeded the growth in revenues. But profit growth-through-efficiency gains have now run their course. The trouble is that many executive teams have forgotten how to grow profitably.

- *Revenues growing far faster than earnings.* Though many companies have forgotten how to generate profitable growth, it doesn't stop them pursuing growth strategies *unprofitably.* There are many ways to achieve this including engaging in price-wars, overpaying for acquisitions, and "buying" customers. As Hamel notes, "This reminds us of that old saw, 'We lose money on every sale but we make it up on volume.'"

- *ROI going up, price-to-earnings ratio (P/E) going down.* Contrary to current conventional wisdom, Hamel believes that the price-to-earnings ratio is the single best barometer of investor confidence in a company's ability to continue growing earnings into the future. He notes:

  [A] P/E that is rising, or that is significantly above the market average indicates a substantial degree of confidence—the market believes your strategy has its best days ahead of it. But the opposite is just as true. There are only two reasons a P/E falls, or grows more slowly than the overall market P/E: either investors think the risk associated with those future earnings has increased; or they expect your future earnings growth to taper off. In either case, their assessment is that your strategy has decayed. Other things being equal, a rising ROI coupled with a falling P/E suggests that a company is mortgaging the future to pay for the present.

- *Shareholder returns growing faster than market capitalization.* Again Hamel's views are controversial: "It is fashionable today to talk of 'unlocking' shareholder wealth." He notes:

  The metaphor is telling. The assumption is that the wealth is already there. It doesn't need to be created—it just needs to be set free. To unlock shareholder wealth you get out of bad businesses, spin off companies that

> *may command a significantly higher P/E than the parent*
> *company, and shed unproductive assets through out-*
> *sourcing. You acquire your rivals and whack out the*
> *shared overhead costs. You ruthlessly slash away at oper-*
> *ating inefficiencies. In short, you excise those things that*
> *destroy wealth. It's quite possible to "unlock" share-*
> *holder wealth without actually creating new wealth.*
> *There are dozens and dozens of companies that have,*
> *over the past few years, delivered healthy shareholder*
> *returns, but have at the same time experienced little or*
> *no growth in their overall market value. Shareholders do*
> *well, but growth in market cap is desultory—no new*
> *wealth is being created. In this case think of the firm's*
> *strategy as a capital asset that throws off interest, but*
> *never appreciates.*[13]

What makes Hamel's views so interesting is the amount of
accounting debate devoted to linking strategic and financial indicators—usually without any convincing result. Hamel's ideas
point us clearly in the direction of multivariant measures that
should indicate the strength of current strategies. Increasing sales
and profits faster than the competition is perhaps the key combination, with the P/E ratio remaining a key indicator of future performance. This conclusion has real implications for performance
measurement and management rewards.

FINANCIAL RED FLAGS. There are a number of signs in financial reports that indicate whether a company's reported numbers
paint too rosy a picture and should cause the CFO to demand further explanation. Some point to unethical management practices;
others to declining financial performance. While by no means an
exhaustive list, here are some common red flags that should merit
the CFO's attention.

- *Declining operating margins.* If operating margins (operating income divided by sales) are falling then this is a sign
  of deteriorating performance. A rule-of-thumb is that if
  margins decline by 10 percent or more over a year (say from

35.0 to 31.5 percent) then something is seriously wrong with the company's value proposition to the customer, production costs are rising, or the company's competitive position is being eroded.

- *Falling free cash flows.* Some financial analysts prefer to monitor free cash flow (operating cash flow minus capital expenditure) rather than earnings per share (they believe it provides a more reliable performance indicator because it is harder to manipulate). Growing free cash flows indicate a healthy business that can pay its debts on time, reinvest in the business and pay dividends. Conversely, declining free cash flows suggest that the business is under increasing pressure and heading for tough times. There are exceptions to this rule if, for example, a major investment has just been made in growth capacity. But, more often than not, a trend line of falling free cash flows represents a major red flag.

- *Rising net income but falling operating cash flow.* Operating cash flow (roughly translated as net income plus non-cash expenses such as depreciation) is another key figure to monitor. If it is falling but net income is rising, this might indicate that inventory or accounts receivable levels have risen. Either of these two reasons points to other problems (see next point).

- *Accounts receivables rising faster than sales.* Receivables usually mirror sales (i.e., if sales increase by 30 percent you would expect receivables to also increase by 30 percent). If sales grow faster than receivables then it suggests that managers are performing well. But if the opposite happens the CFO should be alerted to potential problems including inefficient invoicing and collection processes, dissatisfied customers who are withholding payment, potential bad debts, and a business buying its customers by offering over generous terms or providing products on sale-or-return terms.

- *Rising levels of debt.* While there is nothing wrong with taking on more debt if cash flow is strong and improving, excessive levels of debt can turn a performance blip into a full-blown crisis. What is acceptable varies from industry to industry, but a rule of thumb is to keep the debt-to-equity ratio well below 1:1. When debt is rising at the same time as free cash flow is falling, the CFO should be on red alert.

- *Rising fixed costs-to-sales ratio.* Every organization should be working relentlessly to reduce its fixed costs-to-sales ratio. If this is rising, it can suggest declining levels of operational efficiency, too many management layers, poor quality, dissatisfied employees (e.g., high levels of employee absenteeism and staff turnover), and too much under-utilized capacity.

See Measurement as Patterns, Trends, and Abnormalities

According to Deming, the central problem in management and leadership (including finance) is the failure to understand the information in variation.[14] The theory of variation has been at the heart of world class manufacturing since the 1950s and it has had an astonishing effect. Toyota, for example, gave up making things "within tolerances" decades ago, instead making things "more and more alike," reducing variation and thus reducing the chances of failure.[15] There are two types of variation in any system or process. The first springs from common causes—faults in the system such as poor design, poor working conditions, poor supervision, and lack of information that can be identified and eliminated. The second is triggered by special causes—one-off or fleeting events.

Think about how long it takes you to get to work each morning. Maybe it takes you forty-five minutes on average but this can vary ten minutes either way. That's a common cause variation and it is predictable. Now suppose on one day you suffered a flat tire, causing an extra forty-five-minute delay. That's a special cause. The distinction between common and special causes tells you something about what to do differently. To eliminate special causes you need to examine why the flat tire happened and ensure that it doesn't happen again. Eliminating common causes means a thorough reexamination of the process of getting to work. Using a car, bus, or train, or a combination of them are all possibilities. Starting earlier or later is another option.

Use Trend Reports

These principles can also be applied to higher-level reports. Measures should not just tell a story about what has happened over a single period of a week, month, or year. They should also paint a picture of performance over an extended period of time (e.g., a rolling three-year period). Often single period and multi-period results are shown as trends and moving averages. Trends show performance directions and tell managers something about likely outcomes and whether further action is necessary for improvement. Trends also show a more complete picture of performance evaluation. Many strategic decisions take a year or more to have any impact. So judging a team on one year alone cannot take into account the full impact of their strategies. Also if the management has changed, the new team's first-year performance may well be based on the decisions of the previous team.

Table 5-2 shows how actual and forecast outcomes can be used to present a moving picture of performance (of course they can also be shown as graphs). Managers can immediately see what progress they are making toward their medium-term goals. They can see trends and whether forecasts are consistent and robust. As a result, they can direct their attention to the effectiveness of improvement initiatives and are in a better position to influence future outcomes. This gives leaders more control than they ever had before, a point reinforced by Gary Crittenden, CFO of American Express, when he said that, "paradoxically, you have more control in a rolling process than in a static process. In a static process you use the plan as the reference point for control, whereas a rolling process is constantly informing and regulating itself about what's happening."[16]

TABLE 5-2

Measures as trends

	Q0	Q1	Q2	Q3	Q4	Q5	Q6	Q7	Q8	Q9	Q10	Q11	Q12	Goal
					HISTORY						FORECAST			
Key financials														
Orders	290	300	312	324	290	302	314	326	339	353	367	382	397	500
Sales	280	290	300	312	324	290	302	314	326	339	353	367	382	500
Gross profits	84	81	90	87	97	84	90	91	98	102	106	110	114	167
Gross margin	0.30	0.28	0.30	0.38	0.28	0.29	0.30	0.29	0.30	0.30	0.30	0.30	0.30	0.33
SG&A costs	50	55	57	56	58	52	51	56	59	58	60	59	61	67
Net profit	34	26	33	31	39	32	39	35	39	44	46	51	53	100
Cash flow	44	37	44	42	51	42	49	46	51	56	58	63	66	115
Key cost goals														
SG&A costs (% sales)	0.18	0.19	0.19	0.18	0.18	0.18	0.17	0.18	0.18	0.17	0.17	0.16	0.16	0.15
Packaging costs (% sales)	0.06	0.06	0.05	0.05	0.05	0.05	0.05	0.05	0.05	0.05	0.04	0.04	0.04	0.03
Transportation costs (% sales)	0.04	0.04	0.04	0.04	0.04	0.04	0.04	0.04	0.04	0.04	0.04	0.04	0.03	0.03
IT costs (K per employee)	3.6	3.6	3.6	3.3	3.3	3.3	3.3	3.3	3.0	3.0	3.0	3.0	3.6	2.4
Key operational goals														
First-time through rate	86%	86%	84%	85%	84%	85%	87%	87%	88%	88%	90%	90%	92%	96%
On-time delivery	87%	87%	88%	85%	88%	89%	90%	88%	89%	90%	91%	92%	94%	98%
Customer retention	66%	67%	70%	68%	72%	74%	75%	75%	77%	80%	82%	84%	84%	90%
Inventory (number of days)	65.0	66.0	66.0	64.0	62.0	62.0	60.0	60.0	55.0	50.0	45.0	40.0	35.0	30.0
Accounts receivable (days)	92.0	90.0	90.0	88.0	82.0	82.0	84.0	84.0	82.0	80.0	78.0	76.0	75.0	60.0

The result of these measurement practices is more insight (and foresight) at every level. Instead of focusing on results against a plan, managers (or the board) are now focusing on such questions as "Where have we come from?" "Where are we now?" "Where are we going?" and "How are we progressing toward our medium-term goal?" When information is presented in this way, it is more difficult for managers to get away with bland promises and overoptimistic forecasts. In other words, the focus of the discussion turns to continuous improvement and action planning. Operating managers are more in the spotlight because there are no excuses about why they failed to make the numbers (especially if the reporting package also includes peer group comparisons).

When asked about the benefits of using trends and forecasts instead of standard budget-based reports, Ken Lever, CFO at Tomkins, said: "Instead of just looking at static information at one point in time, we are now looking at trends. We can see patterns and pictures of how things are changing, and this enables us to ask a lot more relevant questions about performance. One of the things I track is moving annual totals on operating profit and cash flow for each of the businesses. If I see the two moving out of line I then ask what's happening. And that triggers a constructive dialogue with the business-unit team. It might, for example, mean that a business is overinvesting, in which case we need to pull back. We also do some scenario-planning exercises and we use the forecast information to support them."[17]

Provide External Reality Checks

Most measures are aimed at checking progress against an internally agreed target and plan. But this tells managers only about internal improvement. It does not tell them whether such improvement is good, bad, or indifferent. In other words, it fails to provide a *context for success* in a world of customer choice and investor impatience. The way to get this is by continuously comparing performance against peers.

Most leading organizations use some form of external benchmarking, whether it be high-level metrics based on best-in-class industry standards or more specific KPIs based on operational measures. Benchmarking at the operational level entails analyzing in detail the performance of companies deemed to be best-in-class in performing certain processes and activities. These companies need not necessarily be in the same industry as the analyzing company. The focus is on the ability to perform selected activities well; for example, billing, distribution, providing customer service, and using suppliers as partners. Performance league tables are the result, and it is these that drive the continuous improvement process. Finding that your business unit is lying in a lowly position in one or another performance league table should tell you where to look in terms of improvement. Jack Welch promoted benchmarking at GE for many years. He attributes much of the company's sustained success to breaking the barriers of internal thinking and benchmarking with other leading-edge companies. The result of this process is to prove to frontline managers that big performance leaps are possible and thus to build the confidence essential to their achievement.

At higher levels of aggregation benchmarking can provide an important context for success. Table 5-3 presents a typical performance league table at Handelsbanken. It shows how the bank is performing against its five nearest rivals on two key performance indicators: cost-to-income ratio and expenses expressed as a percentage of total assets.

How high-level peer groups are compiled usually means preparing a list of competitors; this should not be too difficult for any distinct business unit with external customers. The primary task is to draw up a list (or a league table) of six to ten key competitors. But when thinking about key competitors, it is advisable to think not just about common customers, but also about alternative companies in your business sector with whom shareholders might place their funds. In the case of multiple business units (e.g., multiple regions, divisions, branches), the competitive domain can include

TABLE 5-3

Relative measures at Handelsbanken

	Cost/income ratio	Expenses expressed as a percentage of total assets
Handelsbanken	43%	0.7%
Danske Bank	51%	0.7%
FöreningsSparbenken	56%	1.4%
DnB Nor	61%	1.9%
Nordea	61%	1.4%
SEB	66%	1.2%
Average (excl. Handelsbanken)	59%	1.2%

Source: Handelsbanken, *Annual report,* December 31, 2004.

other internal units (e.g., other branches) as well as similar external businesses. The objective is to create a performance league table at every level. It is the pressure that arises from a unit's position in the league table that drives performance improvement.

Handelsbanken operates with multilayered league tables of like branches and regions that appear every month, maintaining a strong focus on performance and harnessing the power of peer pressure. While at first this might appear to be divisive, this competitive network also operates within a broadly based rewards system, thus giving strong branches ample incentive to support those that are not performing so well. Thus knowledge and best practices are quickly shared. Handelsbanken measures its progress on three simple measures, which are used to create internal competition between branches and a sense of common purpose across the bank: return on capital employed, cost-to-income ratio, and profit per employee. Every employee understands these measures. And employees know that these measures will inform them about the bank's overall performance and roughly how it will impact their profit share.

Use a Range of Measures to Inform a Dialogue About Management Performance

While a measurement focus on business improvement is a relatively recent idea, the measurement of management performance is centuries old (though the focus on the income statement as opposed to the balance sheet is a twentieth-century phenomenon initially driven more by tax collectors than investors). Within most performance evaluation systems, accountability is focused on the individual, culminating in the completion of annual performance appraisals, usually in the final quarter of the year. But the history of business-unit performance measurement has been littered with unfair central management charges, transfer pricing (leading to false profits and losses), and gaming as local managers manipulate the numbers to reach targets and bonuses. Henry Mintzberg, for one, believes that the way organizations apply these measures can destroy businesses—and in education and healthcare, the effects can be devastating. He poses this question: "What would happen if we started from the premise that we can't measure what matters and go from there? Then instead of measurement we'd have to use something very scary: it's called judgment. A society without judgment is a society that's lost. And that's what bureaucracy does: it drives out judgment."[18]

Leading organizations are listening to Mintzberg and moving away from the traditional evaluation framework to one that focuses on whether managers have improved performance over time based on agreed assessment criteria that relate to some definition of success (we discussed this at the end of chapter 3). Performance is assessed retrospectively, not in relation to a predetermined target or budget, but in relation to a number of criteria over which management has a high degree of influence such as operational effectiveness and resource management. Though the assessment is underpinned by measurement, the final evaluation is based on judgment and takes account of many factors that paint a picture of management performance looking back over the period.

The business-unit focus is on profit centers in most commercial organizations, so derivatives of profit such as return-on-capital, cost-to-income ratio, and profit-per-employee are appropriate measures. In the not-for-profit world, these measures are not available. Some look at five areas of required excellence: strategy execution, resource management, operational effectiveness, people management, and risk management. These criteria should focus on critical success factors that, when combined, tell a story of what success looks like in the unit. The role of measurement is to inform this assessment. The context for measurement is to compare performance outcomes with peers, prior years, and benchmarks.

When designing these evaluation systems for business units it is important that accountability measures be aligned with the span of control that managers have over revenues and resources. This is sometimes known as the *span of accountability*. It refers to the extent to which a manager is expected to make trade-offs to achieve the desired level of performance.[19] Thus a branch manager in a retail bank who is responsible only for revenues and has no control over staffing, building, or IT costs should not be measured on costs and profitability. However, if we look at Handelsbanken branch managers, who are accountable for full profitability, they need the freedom and capability to make decisions about most of their costs (some central IT is allocated to the branch but they have some influence over them). There is a range of opinion about which central costs should be charged to a profit center. Most textbooks suggest that it should only be those costs that local managers *control*. However, I support the Handelsbanken approach and prefer the word *influence*. The higher the percentage of central costs that are charged to frontline units, the more these units will feel the burden of those costs and the more pressure they will exert to reduce them.

In many cases, measurement and spans of accountability are inevitably out of line. For example, if salespeople are measured on customer loyalty it is likely that many factors beyond the control of the salesperson will affect that measure. For example, if the quality of the product or service is poor, a customer is unlikely to repurchase. Likewise, a marketing manager might be held accountable for brand values. Again, this measure is affected by many factors (such as competitor's actions and product quality) that are outside the marketing manager's control. In fact, few measures fit precisely with any one person's span of accountability. That's why a more judgmental evaluation process using wider evidence-based criteria is preferable than the use of simplistic measures.

Performance comparisons (external or internal) provide a useful perspective for assessing business-unit performance. Once chosen, relative measures can remain in place for years as one unit strives to beat its peers. Remember of course that the benchmark figure itself is not static. It is, in effect, a moving target. The power of ranking one business unit against another (provided you are comparing apples with apples) should not be underestimated. Done well, it is a recipe for continuous improvement.

Using Relative Measures to Drive Improvement at Ahlsell

Swedish wholesaler Ahlsell provides a broad range of products for installation contractors, the building industry, public works, and retailers in the Nordic region of Europe. CFO Gunnar Haglund is the architect of the new management model. He led its implementation in 1995, and has subsequently developed it further. Since 1996 Ahlsell has acquired twenty-three companies that account in a static market for 90 percent of its revenue growth over the past nine years. Since decentralizing profit responsibility and moving to relative measures, Ahlsell has been steadily extracting advantages. These are now reflected in more satisfied and highly skilled employees, improved customer satisfaction, and superior financial performance relative to its competitors.

The key measures chosen for the frontline sales units were (a) growth in value created, (b) return on sales (RoS), (c) efficiency (measured as gross profit divided by salary cost), and (d) strategic performance (measured as market share). The performance of all units is ranked in league tables that are made visible to everyone at the same time. There are three leagues: the "Premier League," where units with a RoS in excess of a defined benchmark are measured on both growth in value and RoS; the "Qualifiers League," in which units that fall short of the benchmark are measured just on RoS; and the "Elite League," which measures success in the adoption of e-commerce. Trend information is also made available. Further, for internal control purposes, senior managers can compare the performance of different categories of unit (e.g., by size or location).

In determining the return on sales of the two hundred frontline units, the costs that are charged against sales include direct material costs and haulage charges, as well as all the local unit costs (such as staff, obsolete/redundant stock, stock losses, bad debts, rent, and depreciation). Units aim to reach the benchmark standard RoS figure. Performance of each unit is compared with all the other units. There are no fixed targets. There is, however, an incentive scheme with potentially quite large payments to good performers, but it is based on performance *relative to the previous year*. At company level, performance is measured relative to competitors.

Each month the performance of every unit is measured and league tables produced to identify the best and worst performers. The reporting system is fast and open. Everyone at every level in the company sees the results at the same time. Units are expected to use the information to govern themselves and control their own performance. There are no remote business controllers in Ahlsell who will do the job for the units. There is no place to hide—the exceptions where performance is not up to standard stand out clearly. At Ahlsell the culture is one of rewarding success (and learning from mistakes). Every month a bouquet of red roses is delivered to the home of every member of the best-performing unit. In addition, the unit may be featured in the in-house journal that is published six times a year. "Why roses?" you may ask. Well, the Swedish word for rose is "ros," which is also the acronym for return on sales (RoS)!

Ahlsell has an information system based on the highest ethical values. As Gunnar Haglund explains, "we established at the outset that one of our key principles was self-management and internal competition based on free access to information. We reduce all management reports to the simplest and most relevant content and format. Our reporting system has no middlemen "treating" the information or giving it some particular spin. Performance is transparent. We only use real numbers. Everyone can see relative success or failure. It drives knowledge sharing and the transfer of best practices."[20]

Most managers have already developed deeply ingrained mental models of measurement by the time they have completed their business school courses or their first few years of practical experience. However, the likelihood is that these models will be based on the command and control mind-set. In this model, measures are turned into targets and contracts that lead to performance evaluations, bonuses, and personal appraisals. Accounting numbers are treated as the gospel truth. But the reality is different. Measures only provide rough and ready performance guidelines. The skill is in the analysis and interpretation of what they mean and what action should be taken based on them.

The CFO has a major responsibility to explain the meaning of measures at every level of the organization. This is a key educational role and one that must not be shirked. But it requires communication skills of the highest order. The key message is that measures paint a picture of a performance trajectory that leads in a particular direction. And it is the role of the CFO to show the way.

A CHECKLIST FOR THE CFO

☐ Stop the spread of measurement mania.

☐ Use only a few key measures at every level (about six or seven).

☐ Focus on soft feedback rather than hard numbers. Hard numbers only tell part of the performance story and if wrongly interpreted (as is easy to do), they can lead to the wrong actions and fail to capture the true worth of management performance.

☐ Avoid turning measures into targets and performance contracts; otherwise they will lead to the wrong behavior.

☐ Focus measurement on self-improvement at the operating-team level.

☐ Open up the information system so that managers can extract the information they think is relevant and useful.

☐ Derive measures from purpose and strategy. Purpose informs measurement and measurement informs improvement.

☐ Measure the end-to-end process value rather than individual activities.

☐ Select operating measures on the basis of whether they help managers to improve the system. Any measure that doesn't pass this test should be questioned and probably abandoned.

☐ Devolve the selection of operating measures to local teams.

☐ Distinguish between key performance indicators (leading and predictive measures) and key result indicators (lagging and after-the-event measures).

☐ When using the balanced scorecard, be careful that measures do not become annual contracts.

☐ At the process level, use measures to reduce variation.

☐ Use benchmarking to provide a performance reality check.

☐ In a decentralized structure, ensure that local managers have the information they need to regulate their performance.

☐ See measurement in terms of patterns, trend, and abnormalities. Use reports to change the dialogue at business review meetings (to focus on continuous improvement rather than variances from plan).

☐ Use a range of measures to inform a discussion about management performance. Measures are like good pieces of evidence in an investigative case, but they are not the whole story.

CHAPTER SIX

THE CFO AS REGULATOR OF RISK

When we work together in organizations the tendency towards a blinkered view of the future is usually increased by various social pressures and management systems.

—Matthew Leitch

MOST CFOS HAVE BEEN trained in the disciplines of "internal control." These were usually concerned with setting clear authority levels, ensuring that financial processes were correctly managed, and meeting audit requirements. But this whole subject has exploded onto the corporate agenda in the wake of a number of high-profile governance scandals and the ensuing Sarbanes-Oxley (SOX) legislation. The new regulatory regime has forced CFOs to review their control systems, and many have been found wanting. Only 40 percent of CFOs believe that they have good visibility of accounting processes, systems, and controls in place throughout the company.[1]

And few finance executives have much confidence in the numbers that most public companies produce. According to a 2004 survey, only 27 percent said that if they were investing their own money they would feel "very confident" about the quality and completeness of information about public companies.[2]

New descriptive terms have come to the fore, including "corporate governance," "risk management," "uncertainty management," and more recently "enterprise risk management." The knowledge and expertise required of the CFO has expanded dramatically. He or she is now expected to be the chief compliance and chief risk officer rolled into one. To some CFOs, SOX has provided the excuse to revert back to command and control. They have interpreted the legislation as a license to impose more targets and detailed controls on the organization. Typical comments are: "If we agree detailed plans and budgets and comply with them, we will be squeaky-clean," and "If we set out all the risks we can think of and ensure that we have taken some action to deal with them, we will pass the SOX requirements." But this type of thinking does nothing to improve performance.

Too many CFOs have followed the letter rather than the spirit of the law. In other words, they have approached the problems from a procedural (or "check-box") perspective rather than a management (or cultural) perspective. But the primary problems are not with documentation and audit trails. They have to do with the causes of excessive risk taking, malpractice, and greed. The root causes are invariably the setting of aggressive targets supported by financial incentives and share options throughout the organization. They breed a culture of macho management and self-interest and a focus on short-term results. Another problem is that senior managers often demand certainty when discussing investment options; they do not want to hear the many caveats that most ethical managers would provide if they were encouraged to recognize the inherent uncertainties in their proposals. Most managers are too optimistic and then get drawn into a process of justifying their proposals rather than discussing upside and downside risks.

More enlightened CFOs have removed fixed contracts and created a culture of honesty and openness reinforced by strong ethical leadership. Teams at the front line are free to make decisions but are accountable for results within a fully transparent system. CFOs need to encourage managers to keep their minds open about the wide range of possible outcomes that could arise from their decision options.

This chapter looks initially at corporate governance, focusing on management behavior and reporting. It then looks at risk management and focuses on internal controls and uncertainty management. It will suggest that the CFO should:

- Set the highest standards of ethical reporting and behavior

- Regularly review the key pressure points for excessive risk taking

- Manage risk across the whole organization

- Approach uncertainty with an open mind

- Provide effective feedback controls

Set the Highest Standards of Ethical Reporting and Behavior

In 2003, a research team from the International Federation of Accountants (IFAC) looked at twenty-seven companies across the world from a corporate governance perspective. The companies represented a wide range of industries including telecoms, retailing, financial services, energy, and manufacturing. Of these, eleven were deemed to be successes. The sixteen failures included Ahold (Holland), Cable & Wireless (United Kingdom), Enron (United States), France Telecom (France), HIH (Australia), Livent Inc. (Canada), Marconi (United Kingdom), Marks & Spencer (United Kingdom), Nortel Networks (Canada), Peregrine Investments (Hong Kong), Saskatchewan Wheat Pool (Canada), D. Tripcovich

(Italy), Vivendi (France), WorldCom (United States), Xerox (United States), and YBM Magnex (Canada). The IFAC report concluded that these were the most common problems:

- Poor ethical standards at the top

- Aggressive targets and earnings management

- Misaligned incentives

- A CEO who was too dominant and charismatic

- A weak board of directors (too cozy with the CEO)

- Weak internal controls (e.g., poor resource management)

- A CFO who was too involved in aggressive M&A strategies

- A poor choice of strategy and lack of clarity

- Poor execution (especially unsuccessful mergers and acquisitions)

- Failure to respond to change quickly enough.[3]

The level of fraud and misrepresentation, triggered in large part by these problems, has been quite staggering. Enron, WorldCom, and Tyco have been only the highest-profile examples in a list of many others. The fall of U.S. communications company Lucent Technologies (its shareholder value fell by $200 billion in one year) was blamed by one former executive on "unreachable goals [that] induced the company to mislead the public."[4] During the 1990s Gillette engaged in "trade loading," or stuffing its distribution channels with goods at the end of quarters to push up sales figures.[5] Coca-Cola used capital gains from selling bottlers to smooth its reported earnings.[6] In 2004 Citigroup was hit by a series of scandals that resulted in an $8 billion special write-off.[7] In that same year a report on U.S. mortgage company Fannie Mae showed that between 2000 and 2004, executives had failed to account correctly for derivatives, resulting in $9 billion of profit restatements, and in one year had failed to disclose $200 million of expenses so that they could achieve full bonuses.[8] Both CEO and CFO were subsequently dismissed, and the auditors are facing a severe investigation.

A 2004 analysis of the financial filings of more than 120 companies representing close to 40 percent of the S&P 500 market capitalization revealed that misleading financial reporting remains a pervasive practice in corporate America (around one-third of filing statements do not represent the true financial position). Among the alarming trends are off-balance-sheet financing (used by 75 percent of companies), unrealistic pension assumptions (64 percent), and aggressive revenue recognition (28 percent).[9] Recent earnings restatements by firms such as Krispy Kreme, Nortel, and Fannie Mae, combined with an increasing number of enforcement actions, suggest that accounting irregularities remain commonplace.

Many accountants see the "sexing up" of accounts as a perfectly legitimate practice (provided they stay within some defensible interpretation of generally accepted accounting principles). Indeed, it is one of their most prized skills. As most experienced accountants are aware, profit statements and balance sheets can be made to sing and dance to different tunes at different times, depending on what is needed. The effects of fudging, manipulating, and spinning the numbers, like an addictive drug, can give managers a temporary fix (they can even be convinced that they change reality), but the problems quickly return as the next reporting period comes around.

The real worry is that these "flexible" standards are more prevalent than many of us realize. The pressure to meet the numbers at every level of the organization is causing people to prostitute their professional ethics in order, in some cases, to keep their jobs. Despite a forest of value statements and policy manuals, it is what leaders *do*, not what they say, that sets the moral and ethical standards throughout the organization.

Be Wary About Dominant CEOs Chasing "Shareholder Value"

One of the common characteristics of failed companies highlighted in the IFAC report was a dominant and charismatic leader.

CEOs come in all shapes and sizes. While most are talented individuals with a range of qualities, do they really make as much difference as they are given credit for? And should they accept the lion's share of the blame if things go wrong? Not according to the research done by Jim Collins. Indeed, few leaders are able to transform large organizations. Of the 1,435 companies that have appeared in the *Fortune* 500 from 1965 to 1995, he found that only eleven executives had transformed their companies from "good" to "great."[10] Perhaps investors should heed the advice of the "Sage of Omaha," Warren Buffet, who once said that, "You should invest in a company that even a fool can run, because some day a fool will."[11]

What most large organizations require today are leaders who can inspire people to raise their game and reach their potential, harness their emotional commitment, and set the highest moral standards of personal and business behavior. The belief that leaders have "visibility," can implement killer strategies, and are able to restructure their way to higher levels of shareholder value is hard to change. To many leaders (and investors), steady improvement sounds too dull; they require spectacular change. This often involves major acquisitions or reorganizations, leading to further disillusionment at the front line. Meeting short-term stretch targets at almost any cost can easily become the prevailing culture. It is often a white-knuckle roller-coaster ride of boom and bust, and should be avoided. The reality is, as Collins makes clear, that the image of the leader as hero is a myth (with rare exceptions). Professor Henry Mintzberg believes that while organizations may need visionaries to create them, they don't need heroes to run them. What's required are competent, devoted, and generous leaders who know what's going on and exude the spirit of the hive.[12]

What influence does the CFO have over a dominant CEO? Of course it varies. At HealthSouth the answer was "very little," as five consecutive CFOs failed to stop unethical reporting. But the CFO can at least point out the fallacies of chasing shareholder value rather than profitability. Whether the board is pursuing shareholder value or profitability can make a huge difference to a company's decision-making and risk profile (in the long run there should be no incompatibility, but in the short run there can be a significant divergence). For example, the share price can be impacted by announcements of such events as profit forecasts, acquisitions, new product releases, and even job cuts. An aggressive board with large share options can be tempted to over-egg these announcements, sending buy signals to investors. But none of these announcements has a quantifiable impact on profitability. Leaders in less aggressive organizations prefer to let their results do the talking. They do not get themselves into a position of taking actions to protect the commitments they've made to investors.

The CFO would do well to reflect on Deming's view of "constancy of purpose." He was referring to the unwavering pursuit of steady growth year after year with few shocks—such as boardroom coups or CEO defections—to worry investors or employees.[13] This seems to encapsulate the beliefs of successive leaders at such organizations as General Electric, Toyota, Handelsbanken, and Southwest Airlines. Perhaps leaders should act more like grandparents. Instead of looking for short-term gains to feed their ego and satisfy analysts' short-term cravings for good news, they should use their knowledge and experience to guide and support their younger managers and help them to grow and mature. That's what great leaders do. Like a relay baton in a marathon lasting many years, they hand on a stronger and fitter company than the one they inherited. That is the true legacy of leaders. While this will reflect in the financial strength of the business, this is not the sole measure. Building capable people and a culture of common-sense decision making at all levels of the organization is an even better measure of the inheritance handed on to the next generation.

The effects of the "marathon rather than a sprint" view of corporate governance must not be underestimated. If senior executives really see their role in terms of steady long-term growth rather than a quick dash for shareholder value, then they are more likely to take measured risks and provide the sort of governance framework and moral leadership that encourages people to be honest and open with each other.

Provide an Independent Internal Audit
Function Reporting to the Board

Sarbanes-Oxley has given the audit committee more teeth. As Professor Charles Elson has noted: "Whereas the CFO and the audit committee of the board once worked together collegially, it has now become an oversight relationship, with power moving to the audit committee."[14] The board is also responsible not only for setting up systems of internal control that adequately address the risks facing the organization but also for establishing a professional, well-resourced internal audit function. The problem is that as finance and internal control departments have been subjected to relentless benchmarking, they have cut costs and valuable resources. The accounting profession has indeed observed a substantial increase in control failures in recent years as firms downsize and cut out many previous checks and balances.[15]

Sarbanes-Oxley has also raised the profile of the internal audit profession. According to Bruce Nolop, CFO of Pitney Bowes, "internal auditors are like rock stars now. This is their day in the sun."[16] SOX now enables internal audit teams to look beyond making a subjective judgment about internal control systems. Instead, they can now compare them with a high-level model. (The most popular model is "COSO," which stands for the "Committee of Sponsoring Organization(s)" of the Treadway Commission.) This is a generic model that needs tailoring to each organization. And because the internal control framework focuses primarily on bookkeeping rather than risk management in its wider context, it is not about managing uncertainty; rather it is about evaluating after the event rather than integrating risk management with the work. Nevertheless, it is a positive step for the internal audit team. Instead of asking "Do these controls work?" teams can now ask "Do these controls align with the model chosen?"

However, in leading-edge organizations, the internal audit function doesn't drive the risk-management agenda. Risk management is a core part of the general management process. In other words, managers focus on *managing uncertainty* first and complying with rules second. Internal audit supports this role, but also audits what managers do. It is both proactive and reactive. In its proactive role, it will examine important forecasts, material risk exposure, and insurance cover. It will comment on plans and decisions. It is part of the management team rather than a detached inspectorate. That is not to say its views are compromised. It remains an independent force inside the organization, reporting directly to the board.

Regularly Review the Key Pressure Points for Excessive Risk Taking

Many CFOs are now rethinking their control systems and risk-management policies and practices. But just making a list of risks and noting how well or badly the organization copes with them is not the right way forward. The risk profile of any business is constantly changing, and managers must use all their knowledge and skill to keep on top of it. There are a number of pressure points in most organizations that provide fertile ground for risk assessment. These include looking at how targets and incentives are set, whether the gap between senior management and average employee pay is too wide, and whether information is open or kept within management silos.

Be Wary of Aggressive Targets and Incentives

Harvard professor Robert Simons notes that, "in good times, it's easy to forget about risk."[17] But that's the most likely time for poor decisions to be made and excessive risks to be accepted. These are also the times when messengers with bad news are most easily silenced. And these behaviors can lead to a multitude of growth initiatives that can overwhelm the management capabilities of the firm.

But it is the issue of executive pay for performance that has the potential to send the risk-monitoring system off the Richter scale.

Many boards tie executive pay to performance. This usually takes the form of financial bonuses and share options. How aggressive these contracts are is often a strong signal that excessive risk taking is being encouraged. It can also seduce the board into believing that high growth is possible every year. But this notion defies reality. In an article entitled "The 15% Delusion," Carol Loomis notes that leaders, "again and again . . . loudly tell the world about revenue and earnings goals they've set up—practically always the kind that consultants call 'big, hairy, audacious goals.' What follows, so much of the time, are big, hairy, ignominious failures."[18] The article was referring to the standard promise of 15 percent growth in earnings per share (EPS) over the next year. But few companies are able to deliver double-digit growth on a consistent basis. In fact, only three out of the top fifty U.S. companies in 1972 achieved over 15 percent compound growth in EPS over the subsequent twenty-five years.[19]

As the rewards for entrepreneurial behavior rise, so do the risks. Derivatives traders on huge bonuses, for example, are more likely to take excessive risks. Bernie Ebbers, ex-CEO of World-Com, borrowed hundreds of millions of dollars to support his personal share purchases in the company's stock. But when the company's performance went into rapid decline Ebbers went into denial; he and his CFO lieutenant put pressure on the finance team to cook the books so that the company could show that it was meeting its targets, thus (temporarily) protecting the share price. But eventually, time ran out.

The CFO should be aware that the link between incentives and performance is tenuous at best and misleading at worst. In 2002, CEO total annual compensation (salary plus bonus) rose by 10 percent, while total return as measured by the S&P 500 fell by 24 percent.[20] Over the past decade, according to Charles Handy, "incentives ended up consuming all the extra wealth they were supposed to generate."[21] One study undertaken by McKinsey & Company suggests that there is an *inverse correlation* between top executives' pay and innovation. They suggest that the secret of persuading people to focus simultaneously on developing new businesses and managing current operations may be to rely less on pay for performance.[22]

A number of influential investment advisers have started advising clients to vote against members of compensation committees or against compensation plans that exceed certain competitive benchmarks or are not tied closely enough to performance. Prior to a shareholders meeting of U.K. supermarket group J. Sainsbury, the National Association of Pension Funds was urging shareholders to vote against the bonus payments awarded to ousted chairman Peter Davis. It transpires that Davis was to be awarded 86 percent of a performance-related bonus in a year in which the group's profits and shareholder returns had actually fallen. The association said that "the company, and specifically the remuneration committee, has been remiss in approving [this award] . . . The board stated that it retained the right to upgrade or downgrade the award in the light of Sainsbury's performance against its peers. They have categorically failed to do this."[23]

Compensation committees have also come under the spotlight. But who sits on this committee is a key issue. Barbara Franklin chaired the Blue Ribbon Commission that looked into these issues. She says, "you can't expect compensation-plan experts to sit on the committee but you *can* expect people who are truly independent, psychologically independent—and who have a little bit of courage to stand up to the CEO when necessary."[24]

Some well-governed organizations have gone even further and either neutralized or abandoned the fixed performance contract with its emphasis on meeting numbers. As we discussed in chapter 3, some have moved to a performance measurement system based on fair and consistent criteria featuring relative measures, so there are no numbers to meet. Managers don't know how well they've done until they see the results of their peers. They have no option but to do their best right up to the end of the period.

In sum, aggressive performance contracts reinforced by financial incentives are probably the number one cause of over zealous risk taking and unethical financial reporting in organizations today. One accounting professor described the Fannie Mae debacle as "the kind of thing that shakes your confidence in financial statements."[25] The lesson is that setting unrealistic earnings targets and then resorting to every conceivable means (whether fair or foul) to meet them is likely to end in tears, as it has done for thousands of shareholders and employees in companies that have been destroyed by these actions.

Be Wary of Alienating Employees

The risk of employees making poor decisions or not informing senior managers about potentially serious problems is exacerbated by their increasing alienation from their leaders. Consider this staggering statistic. The ratio of average CEO compensation to the pay of the average worker in the United States went from 41:1 to 411:1 between 1980 and 2001.[26] What sort of attitude does this engender in employees throughout the organization? I would bet it is something like: "Why should we bother? If they can look after themselves first then why shouldn't we?" There is little doubt that fraud or corruption is much more likely to occur in organizations where people are disconnected from their leaders, who feel no responsibility for their actions, and who see greed and manipulation at the top as a license to act with the utmost self-interest. Nor does a wide gap in compensation necessarily lead to better results. A study in the American baseball leagues suggests that the greater the difference between the pay of the stars and that of the rest of the team, the less impressive the performance of the stars and the team as a whole.[27]

This type of alienation provides fertile ground for what Simons calls *rationalization*. He suggests that this is an essential ingredient for turning the pressure of alienation into the opportunity for unethical behavior. In other words, if individuals can convince themselves that their contemplated behavior is not wrong—using excuses such as "Everybody does it," "The effect is immaterial," "No one is hurt," or "I'm doing it for the good of the company"—then there is little to prevent the type of behavior that puts both the individual and the organization at risk.[28]

Organizations such as Handelsbanken and Southwest Airlines defuse these potential pressures by eschewing individual incentives based on hitting targets in favor of groupwide profit sharing schemes. This approach encourages cooperation and sharing and is seen to be fair and equitable. Both companies have the lowest staff turnover ratios in their peer groups.

Be Wary of a Silo Mentality Toward Information Management

Most firms don't know where they are today, never mind being able to anticipate what lies around the corner. It takes around six days to close the books and another five days to produce management reports. Another problem concerns the transparency of information. If information only goes to those people who "need to know" as dictated by senior executives, then the checks and balances that come from full transparency will be compromised. Author Meg Wheatley, for one, warns against this approach: "Think of organizational data for a metaphoric moment as a quantum wave function, rich in potential interpretations. If this wave of potentials meets up with only one observer, it collapses into only one interpretation, responding to the expectations of that particular person. All other potentials disappear from view and are lost by that solo act of observation. This one interpretation is then passed down to others in the organization. Most often the interpretation is presented as objective, which it is not, and definitive, which is impossible."[29] It is doubtful that the Enron debacle could have happened with truly transparent information systems.

Well-governed organizations know that a small percentage of people in every organization will abuse the freedom of information—they will abuse any system. But these organizations judge that the risk is worth taking. They realize that the benefits of providing the nourishment that everyone gets from being able to access any information when needed far outweigh the downside risks. Trust is the key issue—demanding strict conformance with the plan assumes an absence of trust. Their leaders take an optimistic view of human nature; they set rules for trust and are absolutely ruthless if they are violated.

Leading organizations have promoted information flows to new levels of openness and transparency. They have given their people access to the sort of strategic, competitive, and market-based information that was once the preserve of senior executives. And they have understood that all the numbers within the organization should stick to "one truth."

Using Devolved Decision Making to Provide Effective Management Controls at Handelsbanken

Finding the right balance between compliance and risk taking is difficult at the best of times but in the light of SOX it has become even more unbalanced. These problems are exacerbated in a bank. CFO Lennart Francke thinks this is one of the most important issues that he has to deal with right now. He tells us why and how the bank has approached the problem.

> Perhaps it's because we are a bank that compliance is generally thought to be a more complicated issue than in most other companies. The equivalent to Sarbanes-Oxley in Sweden does not provide us with any big problems. We have a corporate governing body to deal with that. We had to make very marginal changes, the most important of which was to establish a Central Board's Auditing Committee that we didn't have before . . .
>
> The problem is that the financial regulator—the FSA of Sweden—has a whole bunch of rules that it wants to apply. It's very much based on a centralized framework, which means that every regulator expects a bank to have highly centralized credit performance management systems (which we have never had). Incidentally, we considered our decentralized structure to be one of the main reasons why we have had such low credit losses. We expect all branch managers to follow our low-risk credit policy and to be conservative. That means that we get very few proposals

up to top management that are high risk. They are filtered
out before they get to group credit department, a department that consists of only nine people who are running
through all the big proposals—and that's just about
enough. But that's a problem because regulators believe
that you have to have hundreds of people to keep track of
all the credit rates that your business organization wants
to market. So we do have a compliance problem in the
sense that to be able to meet with the requirements of the
FSA we have to change instructions and take on new people to deal with all these regulations rather than a compliance problem itself.

We think one of the most important issues is transparency,
and this comes through having a flat, lean organization. We
only have three management layers. Some banks have
seven or eight! With only three layers it makes it so much
easier to maintain transparency. This makes control very
simple. For example, it's quite possible for me to really
understand what is happening in the branch office. I can
look at trends and see why this specific category of branch
offices is performing better this year than last year and I
can understand fairly well what's happening on both the
cost and the revenue side of different types of branches.
This knowledge reinforces the transparency I talked about
earlier. It means that the CEO, CFO, and other senior
managers are actually able to keep track of what is happening at the front line. And I think from the management
control point of view that is probably the big difference
between us and most other companies.[30]

The risk policy to which Francke refers is spelled out in the
Bank's annual report: "The Bank aims to delegate to the individual
employee the responsibility for transactions and the risks which
those transactions give rise to. The person who best knows the customer and the market conditions is also in the best position to evaluate the risk. In this way, full responsibility is taken for the business
operations and it is done as close to the customer as possible."[31]

This approach has been remarkably successful. The report notes that, "for a long time—and particularly in the early 1990s—the Bank's method of analyzing and managing credit risk and bad debts has led to significantly lower loan losses than for competitors in relation to outstanding loan volumes."[32]

Manage Risk Across the Whole Organization

As CFOs grapple with one unpredictable event after another, they are reminded that business threats can come from anywhere at any time. These include not only terrorist acts or financial disasters, but also strategic risks such as the emergence of a new competitor, a new technology, or a failure to predict marketplace shifts. But few of these major threats are measured or monitored.

Most CFOs realize that they need a more comprehensive system to manage such risks. Unlike traditional risk management, which tends to focus on financial and hazard risks, this more comprehensive approach covers operational and strategic risks and has recently become known as enterprise risk management (ERM). ERM involves mapping all of a company's risks in a uniform way and applying a cross-functional approach to managing them.

Some organizations have used ERM to prepare a risk-management matrix that grades all their operational risks according to severity and frequency on a chart. Risks are also analyzed into those that are wholly transferred (insured), those that are partially transferred, and those that have not been transferred (the company carries the risk). This was the approach taken by Peabody Energy, a $2.8 billion producer and distributor of coal. It was pioneered by CFO Rick Navarre to educate the audit committee. By showing the whole portfolio of risks the company was exposed to, he could explain how the company had dealt with them. "I wanted them to be comfortable that we had identified each and every risk we face and prescribed specific risk-transfer and -mitigation strategies for those risks we did not want to retain," says Navarre.[33]

Navarre polled more than a dozen executives at various levels to extract what each believed were the risks challenging their respective areas of oversight. Risks fell into four categories: operational, financial, strategic, and IT. Navarre and his team from treasury, operations, and the various other departments then calculated the expected probability of each risk in terms of frequency and severity, arriving at this assessment through a mixture of experience, intuition, and research. Using risk-mapping software developed internally, the team then plotted the risks on a matrix and color-coded them to indicate how each was addressed; red indicates that a risk has had little or no transfer; blue, that a risk has been transferred; and green, that a risk has been partially transferred. The software enables the team to drill down on a particular risk and show a detailed analysis of that risk from its relative importance in the risk hierarchy or, if it is transferred or mitigated, whose responsibility it is to manage the risk.

The entire process is dynamic: Peabody formed a cross-functional risk-management committee, with Navarre as chairman, that meets monthly to continually assess the company's risks. "If a new risk emerges—say we enter into a joint venture or acquisition—we meet to assess the inherent risks and feed them into the ERM process," explains Navarre. He is also clear on the benefits. "This is a broadly focused process that involves the entire senior-management teams across all functions to evaluate risk. Instead of looking at individual risks, ERM gives us the ability to assess all the risks of the company and understand them, separately and in relation to each other, potentially identifying risks we may not otherwise have identified, and then making a determination to either mitigate a risk or choose to accept it."[34]

ERM represents a shift from managing risks in functional silos to managing them across the whole organization. This gives senior management a better view of risks and enables a portfolio approach. The more unified a risk-management process is across the company, the more satisfied CFOs are with it. Likewise, the more closely risk management is tied to the strategic planning process, the more effective CFOs believe it is.[35] James Lam, the founder of eRisk and formerly the chief risk officer of Fidelity Investments, argues that one of the key ingredients of successful risk management is having the right reporting system. In his view, the ideal monthly risk report to senior management has only two pages and describes three issues:

- *Gross losses.* This helps management understand the operational, credit, and market losses the company has suffered, and shows the trends relative to revenues.

- *Risk incidents.* This identifies recent risk incidents that may or may not have resulted in loss, but are worth knowing about.

- *Management assessment.* This is a self-assessment on the part of management: What keeps me awake at night? What should I be concerned about?[36]

According to Matt McKenna, SVP Finance, PepsiCo, the drive for ERM has come mainly from the board's audit committee after the company saw a major write-off on its investments. "One goal of the new risk program is to ensure that finance works closely with the business units to manage the risks of their investments once the checks have been signed," notes McKenna. Peter Thompson, PepsiCo's vice president of finance, explains how the company's new program has focused on four issues:

- *Define/prioritize risks.* To help prioritize the company's many risks, PepsiCo has created three categories: (1) risks that could break the company, (2) risks that could damage the company, and (3) "noise"—relatively minor risks that don't warrant senior management time. Thompson emphasizes the need to ensure that short-term pressures don't cause the neglect of major long-term risks: "Perception shapes your risk focus, but that perception can be distorted, especially by quarterly earnings pressure."

- *Establish risk tolerance.* This involves determining what level of risk senior management is willing to tolerate for the corporation as a whole, and within business units individually.

- *Risk identification.* The main change in this area has been to alter the focus of internal audit to include more operational audits.

- *Risk management/mitigation.* PepsiCo's efforts in this area have focused on three activities. First, improvement in crisis management, which involves an improved understanding of all the company's business processes. Second, the finance function has worked to make its own processes more risk-focused. This includes increasing the number and frequency of informal risk reviews. Finally, McKenna is leading an effort to update financial policies, which concentrates on developing a new approach to managing investments.[37]

Some finance executives believe risk management can create competitive advantage in several ways. First, a company that can manage its industry's key risks better than its peers is in a stronger position to make or sustain a superior profit over time. Merck's mastery of product development risk is one example. Through a careful modeling of the risks in its product development pipeline, Merck has more insight into its central source of revenue. "This is a risk that we would never try to shift to financial products, because this is the risk that creates shareholder value," says Caroline Dorsa, VP and treasurer at Merck. "Anything you can do to provide management with additional insight into the management of the pipeline process should be—and I think in our case is—a contributor to our competitive position."[38]

Second, an ERM system helps CEOs and CFOs to evaluate project risks more thoroughly. Understanding the company's overall risk level and knowing how much aggregate risk it can bear makes it easier to recognize investments that fit the corporate risk profile. Without this knowledge, executives may not take a chance on innovation. "A lack of good risk management could result in your being overly conservative and not effectively deploying your capital into certain businesses," says Richard Osborne, chief risk officer (and former CFO) of Duke Energy, a North Carolina–based firm with operations in power generation and natural gas and electricity trading.[39]

Thirdly, integrating risk management and planning can help to identify projects that reduce the company's overall risk and thereby improve its performance. For example, Akzo Nobel, a Dutch chemicals and pharmaceuticals manufacturer, has identified risk-reducing opportunities in its chemicals and coatings businesses. One such project is the development of a line of water-based coatings—these products reduce the company's liability and employee safety risk, and also produce higher profits. According to Anders Bjarnehall, the company's head of risk and insurance, "If we can recognize certain environmental risks or risks to humans and be on the front lines in our product development, then we will certainly have an advantage in this market, where there is a demand for environmentally friendly chemicals."[40]

Integrate Risk Management into the Strategic Planning Process

Tomkins's Ken Lever speaks for many CFOs when he says he is frustrated by the switch in emphasis from strategic control to internal audit driven by the SOX legislation. As he explains:

> All that SOX does is to force us to have lots of detailed documentation to support our control systems. And then it forces management to keep testing them. This has added a lot of work for marginal benefit. To be fair, there are areas where it has identified a few control weaknesses that should have been addressed. But I do think that SOX is not addressing the real problem. I think that 90 percent of value destruction in businesses comes from strategic error, not from problems in control systems. I'd be very surprised if a weakness in any of our control systems gave rise to a material financial error, whereas making a big strategic mistake could cost a company and its shareholders tens of million of dollars. I think the problem with SOX is that it doesn't focus on the real issues. These are about risk. So we'll end up with lots of documentation and a testing regime so that the auditors and the SEC can

come along and make sure that we're doing it properly. Now, if that adds value to corporate America I'd be very surprised. It just seems to me that it's a big value-shifting exercise from shareholders to accountants and lawyers.[41]

Preventing big strategic errors is a real problem. Psychologists have shown that most managers tend to be overconfident in their predictions about future outcomes and that they think they have more control than they really have. This realization has led some companies to seek a closer integration between risk management and strategic planning. It's a shift that some have made explicitly. For example, Duke Energy has put strategic planning under its enterprise risk-management operation. "It's our responsibility to determine where the capabilities we have at Duke Energy can achieve the best risk-adjusted returns for our investors," says Richard Osborne. Other companies, including Akzo Nobel and Aventis, are linking planning and risk management in less formal ways, but with the same goal: using risk management to drive value creation.[42]

Some CFOs and risk managers spend time creating lists of risks that need to be dealt with. But risk doesn't lend itself to neat divisions and lists. Another problem is that risk analysis typically registers thresholds for action. But managers can't categorize risk so readily; for example, "risk of losing market share" could involve a wide range of events. Breaking risks down into divisions also encourages managers to avoid taking action by recategorizing a major risk into smaller subsets that fall below the threshold.

It is an increasing realization that by far the most effective control systems are those that prevent poor decision making. That's why many organizations are increasingly using strategic controls to hold managers accountable for their performance. This means agreeing with managers what their strategic goals are and then engaging in a continuous process of challenging plans and actions geared to achieving them.

Group executives have an important role to play in the development of strategy and the control systems that are needed to support it. For example, they set direction and guidelines for strategy development and decision making, and then challenge business-unit managers to justify key assumptions and risks. The process starts with business units being given clear guidelines and expectations (but not specific targets) that enable them to set their own goals and plans and align them with the group's aims; the role of the corporate center is to challenge and support, not to command and control. It then enables business-unit teams to deal with unpredictable events like a flood or customer problem and adjust plans and forecasts in real time. This is very powerful because it lets the organization respond effectively and quickly. It also improves speedy disclosure—a key SOX requirement.

Some organizations have used scenario planning not to predict the future but to be able to react quickly should a particular future scenario happen. Royal Dutch/Shell is said to have had a plan for the 1973 oil price hike and for the end of the Soviet empire in 1989. Author (and ex-Shell executive) Arie de Geus has said that, "scenarios act as a signal-to-noise filter" sensitizing managers to significant environmental signals.[43] This approach helps to open minds to possible future outcomes that would otherwise be overlooked. But there is a danger that it can exaggerate the remotest risks and distort spending toward expensive contingency programs.

Approach Uncertainty with an Open Mind

Professor Daniel Kahneman, winner of the 2002 Nobel Memorial Prize in Economics, has pioneered research into how decisions are made.[44] His conclusion is that individuals consistently behave in ways that traditional economic theory, predicated on the optimization of self-interest, would not predict. In fact, individual decision makers make irrational choices even when they have pretty good information. "Many of us who study the subject think that there are two very different systems, which actually have two very different characteristics," explains Kahneman. "You can call them intuition and reasoning, although some of us label them System 1 and System 2."

You would think that high-level decision makers, particularly those schooled in decision theory (usually involving decision trees with associated probability assumptions), would always use System 2 but, according to Kahneman, that's not the case. He believes that decision makers don't like decision analysis because it is based on the idea that decision making is a choice between gambles. Notes Kahneman: "Managers think of themselves as captains of a ship on a stormy sea. Risk for them is danger, but they are fighting it, very controlled. The idea that you are gambling is an admission that at a certain point you have lost control, and you have no control beyond a certain point. This is abhorrent to decision managers; they reject that. And that's why they reject decision analysis." Instead, he observes, "emotion becomes dominant ... primarily by *what might happen,* and not so much by the probability. The more emotion there is, the less sensible people are." In other words, the worst-case scenario overwhelms the probability assessment.

It might be counterintuitive, but group-based decisions can be more extreme than individual decisions. Research with juries proves the point (individuals suppress their views to reach what they perceive to be the prevailing view of the group). In the business context, groups tend to be more optimistic and this leads to high-risk thinking. What's more, the perception of risk is distorted by incentives. Kahneman believes organizations need mechanisms to review how both individual and group decisions are made. In particular, he observes that most organizations don't learn from their own mistakes (most organizations don't even track their decisions from decision point to final outcome). As he says, "They're not investing the smallest amount in trying to actually figure out what they've done wrong. And that's not an accident: They don't want to know."

Kahneman's research confirms what most managers already know—that decisions are more subjective and irrational than we like to think. In some organizations this irrationality is reinforced by dysfunctional incentives and behavior. Indeed, some organizations have a culture of suppressing uncertainty. Sometimes it is done unwittingly, other times it is done knowingly. But it is hard to detect because it usually happens in private. Most managers believe, for example, that selling project ideas is a skill, and they cultivate it to the point of distorting the truth. Another problem is that some managers will do anything to avoid the responsibility for risks that are difficult to estimate. The temptation is to ignore it rather than deal with it explicitly.

What can we do to get people to be more realistic about the future, and more open and honest about risk and uncertainty? U.K. risk-management expert Matthew Leitch has some proposals.

- *Ensure that leaders take an ethical stance.* Leaders need to take a strong ethical stance that says concealing uncertainty is wrong. "A 'confident' presentation that conceals uncertainties is not a demonstration of a desirable social skill. It is a lie deserving a reprimand," notes Leitch.

- *Encourage early intervention.* Most business cases and high-level project plans address risk in some way. But it is often included in a subsection of the proposal marked "project risk." The problem, as Leitch points out, is that it's too little too late: "By the time we write that part of the document we are already committed to our ideas and approach. We've probably defended it verbally in more than one meeting. We identify the approval of the proposal with our personal success." His advice is that leaders should promote techniques where uncertainty gets identified early, before people are personally committed. Risk thinking needs to be part of the way ideas develop, not just part of how they are evaluated.

- *Use hard-to-fudge techniques.* Some risk-management techniques are harder to fudge than others, according to Leitch. He gives some examples: a risk analysis tool that already has the unpopular risks written down so that nobody has to volunteer them; a risk-planning tool that already has a framework of responses and the presenter's task is to tailor it, with justifications; risk ratings supported by objective risk factors, not pure subjectivity; and an unyielding requirement to state the source of all data, even if it is just to name the person whose opinion it is.

- *Focus on both downside and upside risk.* Leitch suggests that integrating upside and downside risk management makes the whole process feel less negative, more balanced, and less defensive. It encourages people to focus on being more open-minded about the future. But he warns that there are two ways to make high and low forecasts unhelpful. One problem is that we sometimes have no idea how likely the high and low forecasts are. Are they really the highest and lowest possible values? Or are they a range such that the forecaster is 80 percent sure the result will be within the high-to-low range (or some other degree of confidence)? This needs to be clear. More often people pick high and low values for each input variable and calculate the result. This means that the overall low output is the result of all your worst nightmares coming true at once, while your highest output is the result of all your wildest dreams being fulfilled. Both are very unlikely—especially if there are many input variables—so the range is unduly wide.

- *Use natural techniques.* To counter the psychology of uncertainty suppression, the risk-management toolkit needs to contain more techniques that are natural, easy, and quick to use. One example is what Leitch calls an evolving uncertainty list, and it makes sense when you are developing an idea or plan. At each iteration you simply jot down the areas of uncertainty that remain and have some relevance to what you are doing, consider their potential impact, and think about how to find out more and what you could do anyway if the uncertainty remains. Initially, the areas of uncertainty tend to drive your research and thinking in a productive direction because most of your actions are to find out or think more. Toward the end of plan development the list takes shape as the initial risk register for the project. Techniques like this that are quick and simple have a chance of becoming part of a manager's behavior even when there isn't a procedure mandating them.[45]

Provide Effective Feedback Controls

Managing risk effectively is not the whole story. It is just as important to respond rapidly when unexpected events do occur. But there are many barriers that prevent this. One is the use of annual fixed targets and short-term forecasts geared to meeting them. These invariably create a fear of failure, which in turn acts to prevent the communication of bad news immediately. No manager wants a verbal lashing every time an unexpected event happens, so managers try to find compensating good news to put in their forecasts as they finesse the bad news. These problems get worse the longer it takes to react as response options start to close down and the profit impact gets worse (see figure 6-1). If managers can see the early warning signals (e.g., market downturn, competitor actions, customer dissatisfaction) and act quickly on them, the

FIGURE 6-1

The problems of slow response

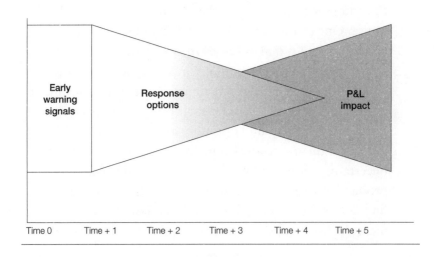

chances are that they can maximize opportunities and avoid emerging threats. The benefits to the bottom line are incalculable.

What happened at Sears Roebuck in 2002 is a good example of how bad news can be suppressed with severe adverse consequences. The credit card business was a major source of Sears's profitability—it was sometimes called a credit card company that dabbled in retail! While the recently introduced Sears MasterCard was successful, it was not achieving the planned growth levels—average user balances were well below forecasts. So, in early 2002 the company took steps to raise rates and fees to well above competitive offerings. But this move just pushed already rising delinquency rates even higher, since few Sears customers could get credit elsewhere. The big problem erupted shortly afterwards as bad debts increased by 50 percent in one quarter.

The trouble was that Sears did not write off bad debts until they were 240 days old. So even though managers could see the trend of delayed payments and the likely write-offs, they were under pressure to make their numbers and were not obliged to report them until the due dates. Sears ultimately decided that the damage caused by inadequate monitoring and reporting on the credit portfolio had surprised the company too many times. In early 2003, Sears announced that it had sold its $29 billion in receivables to Citigroup for $3 billion.[46]

Well-governed organizations assimilate bad news quickly and deal with it as a team. By doing this, local managers are not afraid of building the results of such bad news into their forecasts—the sting having already been taken out of them. Bill Gates offers some good advice: "A change in corporate attitude, encouraging and listening to bad news, has to come from the top. The CEO and the other senior executives have to insist on getting bad news, and they have to create an appetite for bad news throughout their organizations. The bearer of bad tidings should be rewarded, not punished. Business leaders have to want to listen to alerts from salespeople, product developers, and customers. You can't just turn off the alarm and go back to sleep. Not if you want your company to survive."[47] Handelsbanken managers share bad news immediately. For example, if one branch loses a customer, it needs to either try to recover the situation and gain the help of others that might have helpful knowledge, or it needs to replace the lost business, in which case it might solicit the help of regional managers.

Use a Range of Fast Feedback Controls

Most organizations manage through targets and budgets and use variances as the primary feedback loop that tells managers whether to take further action or not. But variances (typically reported monthly) are often too slow and fail to deal with the root causes of problems. That's why some leading-edge organizations use a range of feedback controls including fast financial results, key performance indicators, and near-term forecasts. Actual financial results tend to be summarized and shown as trends and moving averages (we discussed this in chapter 5). They are also compared with prior periods. The analysis and presentation of financial information needs to be fast and relevant. The objective is to have a real-time accounting system. Keeping accounting data to relevant (usually high-level) figures, together with the absence of budgets and variance analysis, lightens the reporting load. Organizations such as Slim·Fast, Tomkins, Handelsbanken, and Cognos produce results virtually online and so put their managers in control of what's happening today. This enables swift response to any abnormalities or spikes in the trends.

Key performance indicators represent the management radar screen. They provide the early warning signals that something might be going awry. They should be few in number and appropriate to the management level. When taken together, they provide a performance picture that tells managers what is happening today and likely to happen in the short-term future. Some organizations, including Handelsbanken, Borealis, and the World Bank, use measurement ranges to keep managers within agreed performance bands rather than fixed targets and budgets.

Near-term (usually rolling) forecasts are another control system that provides a fast, high-level view of future performance. But there is often a huge gap between the rhetoric and the reality when it comes to forecasting because there is often great pressure on managers to tell bosses what they want to hear and justify their conclusions with the numbers. Most organizations prepare forecasts on the basis of single-point estimates of future outcomes. These are usually simple extrapolations of existing trends. The problem is that executives often demand a number, which implies certainty in the forecast and invariably ends up being the "average" of past periods. But averages are usually wrong—and averages added to averages are even more wrong, especially if other assumptions are dependent on them.

Tomkins uses a series of short- and medium-term forecasts to anticipate future outcomes. According to CFO Ken Lever, the company is able to respond much more quickly to whatever comes up: "For example, in the third week of January 2005 we had forecasts for the first quarter. So if there are any areas where we see a weakness, we have a dialogue with those businesses about how we can address these weaknesses. Under the old system we wouldn't have got to that point until the middle of February, so we're three weeks ahead of the game. We have fortnightly management calls around the group based on current forecasts. The benefits are tangible. All the business teams are now focused on delivering their strategy and dealing with threats and opportunities as they arise. It has made us a much more dynamic organization."[48]

Cognos is another firm that uses trends, forecasts, and other feedback controls to support the compliance process and place managers in control. CFO Tom Manley notes, "the real control system is about knowing where you are right now and anticipating the near-term future rather than backward analysis and audit trails. It would be very difficult for me to have a major financial surprise in this company because we spend so much time reviewing the plan. I had a two-hour meeting this morning at 7 a.m. reviewing the plan. If risk management is defined as avoiding surprises, then I think that our continuous planning process is as good as it gets. This brings me back to the Cognos vision of performance management. I think it is essential for compliance."[49]

Despite all the money spent on updating internal control systems over recent years, there are still many ways to cheat systems if people are determined enough. The ultimate shield against excessive risk taking and poor decision making is cultural. It means setting the highest performance and ethical standards and abandoning the worst aspects of the fixed performance contract. It also means looking at the whole picture and not just focusing on a few problems that need to be fixed. Transparency and accountability are the key words.

A CHECKLIST FOR THE CFO

- ☐ Respond to the spirit rather than just the letter of the law. Governance and risk management are about much more than checking off boxes. They are more about setting the right values and walking the talk of ethical behavior.

- ☐ Influence the role of the board to constantly reinforce ethical behavior.

- ☐ Be wary about dominant CEOs. Focus the board on constantly improving profitability rather than chasing the shadows of shareholder value.

- ☐ Be uncompromising about ethical behavior. Be the guardian of ethical standards and the last line of defense against unethical reporting.

- ☐ Provide an independent internal audit function reporting directly to the board.

- ☐ Be wary of aggressive targets and incentives. They lead to high-risk strategies and the wrong behavior.

☐ Be wary of alienating employees. If senior executives are seen to be taking excessive benefits, then employees will feel they have a license to do the same.

☐ Be wary of a silo mentality toward information management. Recognize that transparency is the most powerful force for ethical behavior and reporting.

☐ Provide a framework of enterprisewide risk-management controls. Make an assessment of risk severity and frequency and plot the status of operational risks on a chart. Communicate this risk profile to the board and educate them on its meaning.

☐ Don't just make a list of risks and make notes against them. Risks are not so easily divisible. Avoid the temptation to subdivide risks to fit within acceptable risk thresholds.

☐ Maintain a constant dialogue with business-unit managers about investments and risks. Focus on risk management prior to investment commitments rather than after the event

☐ Track the outcomes of every major decision and learn from your mistakes.

☐ Encourage managers to approach uncertainty with an open mind. Deal with uncertainty at an early stage rather than allow managers to get into a position of "selling" the investment case and brushing aside key risks.

☐ Be wary of a culture of resisting bad news. If senior managers only hear what managers want them to hear, it is a disaster waiting to happen. Recognize people positively for sharing bad news immediately.

☐ Provide fast feedback controls including fast financial results, key metrics, and near-term forecasts.

CHAPTER SEVEN

THE CFO AS CHAMPION OF CHANGE

Changing *something implies not just learning something new but* unlearning *something that is already there and possibly in the way. What most learning theories and models overlook are the dynamics of unlearning, of overcoming resistance to change. They assume that if you can just get a clear enough vision of a positive future, this is motivation enough to get new learning started.*

—Edgar Schein, *The Corporate Culture Survival Guide*

THE ROLE OF transforming the finance operation and performance management practices is invariably the responsibility of the finance team led by the CFO. Though there are many books on the art of change management as well as consultants peddling panaceas, it is not an easy path to follow. Parachuting best practices from one organization into another is not easy, nor is it usually effective. How effective change is implemented varies from one organization to the next.

For instance, some want a consultant's report to rubber stamp in the boardroom while others prefer to go it alone and learn as they go. The context for change also varies significantly. For example, there are more constraints in the public than private sectors, and private companies can usually move faster than public companies (with fewer stakeholders to convince).

The change management formula we discussed briefly in the introduction serves as a reliable guide to the prospects of success. It makes the point that successful change is the outcome of three factors: $D \times V \times F > R$ (where D = dissatisfaction, V = vision, F = first steps, and R = resistance to change) and that all the first three variables must be in evidence in sufficient strength to overcome the resistance to change.

This chapter will look at this transformation journey through the prism of actual practice. It will draw on the experiences of a number of organizations, including the World Bank, Tomkins, American Express, Unilever, and others. It also sets out some milestones to look out for. It will suggest that the CFO needs to:

- Make a compelling case for change

- Set some directional goals and get started

- Gain the support of key people

- Involve operating people in the change process

- Avoid more complexity

- Show some early wins

- Be patient but maintain the momentum

Make a Compelling Case for Change

The case for transforming finance begins within the finance operation itself and extends to its business partners. Let's start with finance. How many of your team have worked overtime in the past three months? How many have worked weekends? How many have not taken all their holiday entitlements over the past year? When I ask these questions at finance seminars anywhere in the world almost every hand goes up. The work-life balance is poor *and it's getting worse.* Of course we could always do with more people. But that's not the real problem. The root cause of most problems is the way the whole performance management system works. More powerful IT systems enable more detail to be held and accessed. They allow us to set more targets and budgets at every level. They facilitate more measures and reports. In other words, despite the fine words about empowerment and accountability, our systems are taking us in the direction of more complexity and more command and control. Is that really our vision of the future? Unless we make some radical changes we will never break free from the complexity and stress that all this entails. The CFO has a duty to change direction.

Let's now turn to business partners. As we noted in the introduction, there is strong evidence to suggest that line managers are deeply dissatisfied with the service they receive from finance. They don't get the information they need when they need it. They are bound by annual targets and fiscal cycles that force them to manage the numbers instead of the business. The result is that they have little or no flexibility to respond to current reality. They are forced to play various budget games, including "negotiate the lowest target" and "spend the budget or lose it," otherwise they will be disadvantaged compared with others. They are constantly measured and appraised. They get precious little support from finance because even the best finance managers are bogged down in low-value-adding work. These problems have a negative impact on the performance of the *whole organization.* Consequently, CFOs have the opportunity to make a real difference. They just have to look at the organization and its systems in a different way.

That is easier said than done. Most performance management systems have remained unchanged for decades. Though investments in new IT systems (especially the ERP variety) have automated many time-consuming practices (while usually adding more detail), we still prepare budgets, allocate resources, and report on performance in the same old way. So how do we start the debate and get people engaged in thinking about change? Here are a few ideas:

- Find out what your people think. Do a survey. (There's a free one at the Beyond Budgeting Web site (www.bbrt.org).) The survey should cover both finance and business managers. The World Bank conducted a survey and the results helped the finance team to build momentum for change.

- Hold a conference for all your senior finance managers. Give it a name such as "Finance for the Future," "Dynamic Performance Management," or "Beyond Finance." American Express kicked off its transformation program in 2000 with a conference entitled "World-Class Finance." In 2004 it held a similar forum to check on progress and agree what more needed to be done.

- Hold a few internal workshops that include people from a range of functions to start the debate and use the survey results (which must respect the privacy of each person's views) to provoke the discussion.

- Join benchmarking or other learning groups. The Beyond Budgeting Round Table is a forum for shared learning (www.bbrt.org). It also provides an entry point into many best practices organizations. Many organizations featured in this book are members.

The case for change is usually a mix of current dissatisfaction and a future vision. Deep dissatisfaction is the CFO's best friend. Surveys and workshops will help people to articulate their feelings about current systems. They will also kick-start the process of mapping out what needs to be done and in which sequence.

The Compelling Case for Change at the World Bank

The World Bank invests around $20 billion per annum in developing countries and spends around $1.9 billion on operating expenses. The Bank is run like a cooperative, with its member countries as shareholders. It has a full-time twenty-four-person board that has traditionally micromanaged the Bank's spending through detailed budgets, which are prepared twice a year and look three years ahead. But in recent years the finance team has been challenging this process, having concluded that it takes too long, costs too much, and adds too little value. They wanted to introduce a more strategic, cost-effective process. So in 2004 they started a new project known as "budget reform." This is, however, not the first attempt at reforming the budget. The Bank had made a number of earlier attempts with mixed results. So the finance team was acutely aware of the challenges ahead. The budget reform team is led by CFO John Wilton, who explains the various pressures for change:

> There were many pressures for change, some internal and some external. From an internal perspective, there was a lot of pressure for change because the budget took too long, was too expensive, and didn't add much value. But this did not just come from our clients in other parts of the business—it was also coming from our own budget department who were concerned about the low-value-added content of some of their work. Another perspective was that the Bank was trying to strengthen its focus on results (that is, achieving its poverty-reduction objectives). But tying results on the ground directly to the work of the Bank is not easy. What national governments do has a much greater impact. So there are attribution problems. Despite this we can certainly improve how we measure and evaluate results. Another factor from the shareholder perspective is that, driven by client demand, the budget has been growing over the past four or five years at a rate that is not sustainable in the long run. And it's not clear if we're making the right strategic trade-offs in a disciplined way. Every time we're asked to do something extra it leads to a budget increase. So it requires greater scrutiny on behalf of the board to ensure that the budget is managed in a more disciplined way.

The external pressures were coming from our share-holders. The board, for example, is not like the board of a normal organization. It is a full-time board chosen by the shareholders. They come from varying backgrounds and they are asked to represent both their constituents' interests as well as the broader interests of the Bank. They began to ask searching questions about why we were increasing our budgets when their own national budgets were constrained, particularly in Europe and Japan. We were also aware of how best practice was changing elsewhere. For example, we looked at best practice evidence provided by the BBRT [Beyond Budgeting Round Table] and the APQC [American Productivity and Quality Center], and from our own knowledge of the public sector. So we had a whole range of pressures that came together to provide us with a compelling case for change.[1]

Set Some Directional Goals and Get Started

There are a number of challenging questions that the CFO should ask before embarking on the transformation journey. Here are a few:

- Are you prepared to devolve more planning, decision making, and measurement (in steps) to operating teams closer to the customer? If you are not prepared to dismantle the apparatus of top-down control based on targets and budgets, the transformation program will be a watered down version of the real thing. This means giving business managers not only the freedom to act but also the capability to act (i.e., they have the information and resources necessary to execute decisions).

- Are you willing to embrace lean thinking and encourage other leaders to see the organization as a horizontal system of processes that deliver customer value?

- Are you prepared to venture outside your comfort zone and lead a discussion about how incentives need to be revised?

- Are you willing to change your own role? This means spending less time on planning and control and more time on quarterly business reviews and providing performance insights to the board and other senior managers.

- Are you prepared to change some of your top people? It is unlikely that you can transform finance with the same people that have been associated with the current system.

- Are you prepared to fight the necessary battles with the boardroom and other senior colleagues if they stick their heads in the sand and resist your proposals? Going against the grain of conventional wisdom is never easy. When Jan Wallander suggested that Handelsbanken should abandon the annual budgeting process, he had to fight many battles. He called this the "budget bureaucratic complex . . . made up of all those within companies who feel that their position and their work is coupled to the budget system and that their job and their position might be impaired if the budget system is abandoned. To this complex also belong all the professors, management consultants, and other experts who write books, lecture, and organize conferences about budgeting and its technical complications."[2]

- Do you have the perseverance and patience to manage the change process over a number of years? This isn't a quick fix.

If you can answer "yes" to all these questions, you have a real opportunity to transform finance and deliver benefits across the whole organization. But where should you start? When asked this question, Steve Morlidge, finance change leader at Unilever, says,

There is no one right place to start or one right way to start. It depends on the culture. For example, to what extent is the vision shared by others? Where are you in the organization and what resources do you have available? It's like saying how do you win a battle? You can say there are some basic things like make sure you're carrying a sword not a butter knife or don't charge someone who is bigger than you. So there are some basic rules. You can't say that the way to win a battle is to always put your cavalry in the middle and charge the guns down the valley. Change management is rather like Sun Tzu—the art of warfare. There are some principles but no one right way of doing it.[3]

The context for change is critically important. How well does the organization deal with this type of change? Who are the key people to influence? At what stage should the CFO "break cover" and engage key influencers outside finance? Should he agree and implement a "big vision" or take a number of small steps? Can current IT systems cope with the changes? Most of the recent cases started with a limited vision (i.e., it was contained within the finance comfort zone) but as the journey progressed they realized that they needed to engage with others (particularly in human resources) to deal with thorny issues such as incentives and management roles and responsibilities.

The project team at the World Bank started with three aims. The first was to abandon the annual budgeting cycle and set medium term directional goals and guiding parameters that lead to sustainable performance improvement. The second was to give managers the flexibility to manage. The Bank wanted managers, instead of relying on annual resource allocations, to be empowered to implement agreed strategies using the resources necessary to execute them within agreed financial parameters across a multiyear framework. And the third was to focus management accountability on actual performance. Thus managers needed to be accountable not for meeting agreed targets and budgets but for executing strategy, managing resources, and improving operational effectiveness. Assessment would be with hindsight. Actual performance would be assessed continuously and transparently using trends, benchmarks, and league tables.

The project at Telecom New Zealand started in 2000 with modest ambitions. There was no grand vision that it was going to tightly implement. CFO Marko Bogoievski explains: "We took more bite-sized chunks than that. What we tried hard to do was to develop a more dynamic eighteen-month view of the business for the board so it had to understand the capability that we needed to implement rolling forecasts. We realized that the quality of forecasting was poor so we decided to provide some incentives based on forecast accuracy using key value drivers. But improving the process took us longer than we thought. In fact, it took us around two years to get forecasts as formalized as actual reporting, especially around the balance sheet components."[4]

These two case examples are typical of how many transformation projects start. They begin with changing finance-owned processes such as budgeting, forecasting, resource management, and reporting and then evolve into significant cultural changes. There is then a realization that the whole performance management system is interconnected and that you can't change one piece (such as forecasting) without affecting other pieces. For example, producing quality forecasts depends on managers taking an unbiased view of the future; but if targets and incentives remain focused on quarterly and annual results, bias is almost guaranteed. So the determined CFO is drawn into dealing with targets and measurement and, because incentives are linked to targets, he or she also needs to deal with incentives.

Articulating Problems and Visions at Unilever

Project leader Steve Morlidge is a team of one. Since 2000 he has spent his time doing missionary work across Unilever, talking to anyone who will listen to his views about transforming the traditional performance management process into something he calls "dynamic performance management." Morlidge tells us about the problems the organization was facing and how his vision for change deals with them.

> We had identified three serious problems. The first problem was the lack of flexibility within the management system. Targets were fixed and tied to rewards, and resources and plans were mapped out in great detail, restricting the scope for the business to respond to unanticipated threats and opportunities in the marketplace. Worse than that, we recognized that the people that "win"—those who are

most adept at playing the system—were those that exhibited the wrong behavior. Our system focused a disproportionate and unhealthy amount of management time internally rather than on the outside world.

A further consequence of the rigidity of our approach was the creation of contingencies. The unspoken assumption behind the traditional form of management is that the world is predictable and that the consequences of our actions are known. We all know that this is not the case but the fixed contractual management process does not allow us to recognize this uncertainty in an open fashion. The way round it, the way we deal with uncertainty, is to create contingencies. In a contractual management system a business without them would be at the mercy of events.

An additional problem was that since contingencies are not officially "allowed," they are hidden and therefore unmanageable. We simply do not know how much slack was built into our plans and where it was held. The consequences were that resources that otherwise could be deployed to generate growth were stripped away from the business, and in attempting to suppress risk by constructing a mechanistic contractual process we introduced variability elsewhere. The result was gaming. As part of target negotiation, manager A tries to hide her own contingencies and simultaneously tries to discover the contingencies of manager B. The whole budgeting process becomes infected with dishonesty and manipulation. This leads to the second major problem with the conventional fixed financial contract process—dysfunctional behavior.

In the typical process fixed targets are tied closely to rewards. Once money is involved, targets become more than a performance benchmark—they take the form of a quota. As a result, as so much now hangs on the quantum of the target, there is a need for negotiation in order to establish a fair stretch. The root of the problem is that in tying rewards in a mechanistic fashion to targets, a game is set up. As a unit head I win this game by negotiating the lowest target possible (or conversely the highest budget) and, since the target is now in the form of a quota, you must never overdeliver (or, in the case of budgets, never underspend). In order to win I therefore need to focus my attention on problems and difficulties rather than seeking out and exploiting opportunities. At a higher level in the organization, of course, the winning strategy is reversed. It is clear that the behavior encouraged by contractual performance management is completely at odds with our efforts to build an enterprise culture. As owners of this process, finance has a responsibility that goes beyond the boundaries of our function.

The final problem with the current model is its complexity and cost. It is common practice, for instance, for individual cost center managers to be asked many months in advance how much are they planning to spend on relatively trivial items such as hotels, traveling, or telephones in, say, the month of March next year. This problem is compounded by the process of negotiation; on average, budgets went through at least four iterations before the target was agreed for the following year. Each iteration required the recasting of a detailed budget and consequently generated extra work and complexity. The problem didn't stop there. Targets were changed on average three times a year, but even this was just the tip of an iceberg. For every target adjustment accepted there were many others that never saw the light of day.

The budgeting process was taking around six months to complete but as our world was becoming more dynamic and unpredictable it was rapidly out of date. We, like many other businesses, therefore now use forecasts more actively to manage our business rendering the annual planning cycle a costly irrelevance.

So what can be done? The military is generally about fifty years ahead of management thinking in industry.

Leaders of armies no longer try to plan and regulate the battlefield activities of their soldiers—they do not march around in columns or line up in squares, nor are instructions passed down the line of command like a baton. [Military leaders] are, however, obsessive about clarity of goals, creating plans but also scenarios (alternative possible outcomes) and providing themselves with the capability to respond to the most likely of them. They have plans but they are always subject to review and revision—you might recall the refusal, or in fact inability, of the military to answer questions about whether they were on plan in recent conflicts. On the ground soldiers are given maximum freedom to take decisions for themselves (including requesting extra resources (e.g., air support)), but within very clearly defined rules of engagement and the context of the "commander's intent." Training of every individual, high levels of motivation, and the free flow of information are also critical to making this model work. This creates the maximum responsiveness within the framework of tightly defined goals and strategies.

Translating these ideas into the more familiar terms of performance management means that all the functions of a performance management system still need to be performed—but if we want different results they need to be discharged in a different way. Thus we still need to set targets and goals and find ways to reward people appropriately; we still need to forecast and build plans and we still need to measure our performance so that we are able to take corrective action when (not if) things do not turn out as we have anticipated. We still need to make choices about where to allocate resources and make sure the actions of all business units are aligned and coordinated.

Our goal is to be more successful in competing for customers and for shareholders funds. If we feel we need to be more responsive and more competitively focused in order to be successful, we need to perform these functions in a different way and set them in a more flexible framework. We have to create an *adaptive system.*[5]

Getting Started at American Express

The transformation program at American Express was led by Group CFO Gary Crittenden, who quickly involved many of his senior management colleagues. Crittenden takes up the story:

It began back in 2000 when I joined the company. We got all our key finance people together and as a team we looked at what we could do to enhance the relevance and contribution of Finance to the company. At that time (remember this was before 9/11) the real driver for change was the mix of efforts between processing transactions and reporting results versus anticipating and planning for the future. I often use this analogy about a train-wreck to describe this situation. If a train-wreck happens it is important to know and report why it happened and this means doing all the forensics around it. But it's a lot more important if you can *anticipate that the train-wreck will happen* and take action to avoid it. I have always seen the role of finance as one that looks forward rather than backward. One of the outcomes from that first finance leadership meeting in 2000 was to agree to shift this balance so that we have more people influencing the direction that we want to go. In this way we could become much more useful to our business partners.

Of course, analyzing what happened in the past is helpful as well but you really add value to the organization if you can look forward and influence near-term events. Finance sits at the nexus of a lot of information, probably more than any other part of the organization. We have all of the product-line profitability information, the balance sheet information, and information about our tax strategies. There's really no one else who can analyze and interpret that information in a way that helps the business to formulate alternative decisions. We can, for example, say to our business partners "this is how things are going to play out (or could play out) and here are some alternative strategies for dealing with those potential outcomes." Our job is largely to anticipate what could happen in the future, structure the choices, and do that in a timely way so that our business partners can actually make the right decisions to move the business forward.

We had a clear direction as well as some key goals. But I wouldn't call it a grand vision. The meeting we held back in 2000 really was a seminal event for us. Our primary focus was on fixing the finance organization. But when we reconvened in 2004 we all remarked on how that had changed. Instead of the topic focusing on how to fix finance, the topic was "how do we push the business agenda forward?" And so we really did go through a phase (which isn't over, by the way) of trying to change the definition of roles and bring as many people as we could up to the front line while reducing the numbers in the back office doing the reporting (though this also has to be done and done well). We had our top seventy finance people at that event out of the six thousand or so we employ, and we committed to doing a couple of things. One was to move more people to the front lines. But we said we would pay for that by substantially improving the processes in the back-office functions. Over the next couple of years we were able to reduce the finance headcount by about a thousand people and take out around $100 million of cost in absolute terms. We were then able to take a small portion of that and plow it back into some of the more forward-thinking actions that we were trying to do. That transition has really been key for us.

I think probably the most perceptible change is that we've become a much more nimble organization. We used to have a very traditional planning process. We did the plan in September/October and it moved through various iterations till the end of the year, by which time it was often out-of-date. And then we did another forecast a few months later. What we've moved toward now is a much more flexible process. Though we still have an annual plan, this is nothing more than an update to our ongoing forecast. Our primary management tool is now a rolling twelve-month forecast process. Each month we analyze the risks and opportunities embedded within the current forecast. We also look at all of our unhedged exposures and ask, "Do we need to cut back or should we accelerate our spending in certain areas?" Then we make investment decisions as we go along. If we have more funds than we thought we'd have available then we'll decide to invest more. If we have less then we'll pull back. I think this flexible planning process is fairly unique. Many people talk about building in flexibility, but our people have really delivered on it. This happens under strong finance leaders and talented planning people in the business units who we partner with.[6]

Gain the Support of Key People

The CFO and the finance team need to gain the support of key people, especially those whom other managers respect and listen to. There are some unusual advantages to sell. For instance, unlike most major management change programs that involve more work and overtime, transforming finance is as much about what you *don't* do as about what you do differently. It is about doing less paperwork, generating fewer reports, reducing bureaucracy, attending fewer meetings, and, above all, wasting less time. These points resonate loudly with operating people. These are benefits they can immediately understand. It is not a hard sell.

John Wilton explains how he sold the transformation concept to key people at the World Bank:

I started by pulling together a reform team within the budget department. This team then prepared a case for change based on a survey that was distributed internally. We then undertook lots of internal communication early on to explain the results of the survey. Then we developed a high-level concept of how to run the budget in the future. I held many one-to-one meetings and presentations, and we received broad support across the Bank for the concepts. We then developed a set of initial proposals for implementation. This involved many individuals across the Bank in a series of working groups. Over one hundred staff participated. Since then we've maintained a regular dialogue with the board and senior management.[7]

Ken Lever, CFO of Tomkins, reckons that one key lesson to learn is that you make faster progress if you have the support of the CEO:

Another key learning for us is to ensure that what you're trying to do is clearly communicated to all the key people, especially what the benefits will be. I think it was important for us to have thought through the new incentive scheme because this certainly helps to grab people's attention. You also have to drive the changes through the senior management groups and they have to take ownership of it, otherwise you end up with an "us versus them" situation where the finance people are always at odds with the general managers. What we didn't want to happen was this attitude that general managers were doing things for head office instead of for their own benefit. We're great believers in finance people being business partners rather than being "spies in the camp," as it were.[8]

Gary Crittenden at American Express learned that you get more done with partners. As he explains:

Even when people don't have direct responsibility for an activity, they often feel that they have a stake in the outcome and therefore want to be involved. None of this was done in a vacuum. All of the thinking and execution has taken place in consultation with our business leaders. We've involved them every step of the way. We would always listen to their concerns and even when we took action that they might not agree with, they at least understood what we were trying to accomplish and why. I can't say we've had 100 percent agreement all the way through, but we've had a good understanding most of the way. That is one of the prerequisites of effective change. With that, I think the two main lessons are to deliver clear benefits and communicate continuously and effectively with all of your key people.[9]

Involve Operating People in the Change Process

If we've learned anything over the past ten or fifteen years, it's that big top-down change programs don't work that well. Leaders first need to understand their own organizations. What works for them? And how does change happen? All my experience as a management educator tells me that change has to come from within. The people affected have to be involved. Many of the best ideas for change are already in the heads of people working in the organization. They just need releasing. But to unleash the knowledge and energy within our organizations needs something else. It needs real *insights*. Just one or two fresh ideas can be the catalyst to real progress and sustainable change.

When asked if he took all the (one hundred or so) business-unit teams along the transformation journey with him, Tomkins's Ken Lever said,

Not really. The high-level messages were delivered by myself at, for example, president's meetings, annual finance conferences, and quarterly review meetings. I also met with individual management teams. That, if you like, was the town hall messaging approach. But the really hard work was making sure that each of the businesses was following what we were saying. Inevitably you'll get some people who are responsive because they want to be responsive but then you get others who push back and say we don't understand why we have to do this. But gradually they all came into line. We didn't actually come up against anyone who categorically didn't want to do this because that's not the culture of the company. People actually do things because they recognize the benefits. I think they all realized fairly quickly that what we're trying to do here is to streamline the information system and that has to be a good thing for the organization.[10]

The transformation at LaSalle Bank, the sixth-largest mortgage originator in the United States, provides a good example of involving business managers. CFO Tom Goldstein began with what he called a "circle of change"—listening to the staff describe what was going on and what they thought could be improved. It was quickly apparent that employees were overwhelmed and there were many cases of duplication of effort and inadequate systems.

Next, instead of just going out and hiring staff and purchasing new systems—as many suggested—Goldstein tried to determine what the best solution was. He realized that finance had six different systems and six different groups, so he introduced the groups to one another, merged them into one, and gave them the task of solving the duplication problem. "We gave them a small budget and very quickly we started getting results to the point where today we actually run a browser over our six systems and you can drill through the six systems, and it is seamless as you go from one system to the next because everything is completely in sync."

Another successful strategy was building teamwork. Different groups learned to work together in ways that promoted efficiency and accuracy, especially when everyone's responsibilities were clearly defined. This led to a feeling of empowerment. The organization has also become more decentralized. As a result, finance currently possesses a hybrid structure. For example, systems operations have remained centralized, whereas "things that are more analytical in nature" have not.[11]

Avoid More Complexity

It is all very well designing new processes and systems but can the company move from where it is now to where the project team wants it to be without tearing itself apart? How much IT support is needed, and when will this be available? Are the timescales realistic? Exposing plans to the people affected will give the team a reasonable guide as to whether or not the proposals are practical and feasible within the set timetable. This is a key reality check and should be done at regular intervals.

The golden rule is to make life simpler for both the finance team and their customers. Marko Bogoievski, CFO of Telecom New Zealand, makes this point:

> There is very little difference now between what the board sees and what business units use to manage the business. They get a slightly more summarized version, but essentially it's the same report that's used. So there is very limited rework needed to produce all this information. We also went away from templates and now use whatever businesses need for their own purposes. We said to ourselves, "Why are we forcing different businesses to conform to the same set of reports?" It didn't make sense. We should use whatever is optimal for managing their businesses. So we've actually eliminated a lot of work and probably improved our decision-making. We're also trying to move to a leaner corporate office. The amount of work being done at the corporate center is getting less and less, with more capability being pushed down into the business units. Inside business units themselves there's also an emphasis on simplicity, including, for example, a push toward product rationalization.[12]

Ken Lever uses a version of economic value added (EVA) that is an example of how to keep complex ideas as simple as possible: "We have adapted the concepts to suit us and not worried too much about the academic purity. To us, it is whether it is directionally correct and encourages the right behavior that really matters. Our term for EVA is 'bonusable profit.' The difference is that our managers can understand it, whereas EVA itself can be a difficult and complicated concept to understand because it requires all sorts of adjustments, such as the capitalization of training, R&D, and so forth. We didn't want to do all that."[13]

Gary Crittenden also makes a few strong points about simplicity: "The first is that if you don't do too much detailed planning then you don't have to do too much detailed reporting! We learned that the amount of detail in no way improves the quality of a plan or forecast. In fact, I'd say that less detail improves the quality of the numbers. The second point is to reduce the number of hand-offs in our systems. Each hand-off is a potential control problem so if we can automate them then we can improve our control system even more."[14]

Show Some Early Wins

Demonstrating short-term wins is important to keep the resisters at bay. There will always be people looking for the first signs of failure, so there is nothing better than to show them hard evidence of success. Short-term wins should have three characteristics: they should be visible (people can see the results for themselves); they should be unambiguous; and they should be clearly related to the changes. Some early wins include:

- More time for value-adding work. By reducing detail and complexity, you will enable managers to focus their time and energy on improving the business rather than managing numbers.

- Cost savings from not producing (often irrelevant) management reports and pursuing nonstrategic projects. The costs of producing reports can be much greater than managers think.

- Less dysfunctional behavior. There will likely be less gaming-type behavior. With no fixed target to meet, people have no reason to play the numbers game.

- Faster and better decisions based on improved management information. Organizations that provide their frontline people with fast information are in a stronger position to act quickly and grab the profit making opportunities.

At the World Bank, short-term benefits included clearer strategic guidance (and certainty) from above including resource availability, less micro-management, more trust, more transparent relationships with senior management, a clearer link between strategy and resource decisions, more emphasis on value-adding activities and a more appropriate accountability framework. At the corporate level they included a more efficient and effective use of Bank resources in pursuit of its mission, a clearer direction and understanding of resource availability over the medium term, a greater strategic focus on planning and monitoring, much greater accountability of units for actual performance, and more scope for the Bank to demonstrate leadership in public sector thinking. There are a lot of big prizes on offer if only the CFO can grasp them.

When asked about the quick wins at American Express, Gary Crittenden gave this reply: "Early wins are really important because they help to build credibility in the organization. Delivering significant cost savings and better information sent clear messages to all the businesses that these changes meant something."[15]

At Tomkins, the early wins were connected to the improved quality of information, which in turn led to more effective control. Notes Ken Lever:

All the information comes into our group consolidation system. We then represent the information back to the business group levels so they can see what their overall performance looks like. The consolidation system has improved the efficiency of that process enormously. For example, it has reduced the time it takes to collate and present information. Remember, while all of this has been going on, we have been dealing with other issues, such as moving towards international financial reporting standards. We now produce information quarterly for U.K. and U.S. GAAP. Although there has been a very marginal increase in resource capacity in the corporate centre we've been able to make all these improvements without significant increase in headcount. We just couldn't have done all this without the work we did on systems improvement. So all our work has focused on speeding up the process, improving the quality of the information and improving the efficiency with which it is produced.[16]

Be Patient but Maintain the Momentum

It is vitally important to set realistic time expectations for completing the change but equally important to maintain the momentum. Periodic reviews are essential to give people a chance to assess their achievements and deal with any outstanding problems. One certainty is that there will be problems. Leaving them unattended will sow the seeds of discontent and potentially ruin what otherwise could be a significant change in people's attitudes. It may be that more training and education is needed, so project leaders shouldn't hesitate to provide it.

The World Bank's John Wilton speaks for all transformation leaders when he says, "this process is exhausting and you have to keep the momentum going. So periodically you have to revisit it from my level and ask is it going in the right direction? What can I do to reenergize it? Luckily I have staff that will tell me if we've hit a roadblock and we need help to get over it."[17]

Most transformation leaders quickly realize that in the first phase of the project you can't alter everything, owing to constraints on time, energy, and/or money. Barriers associated with the organization's culture, for example, are extremely difficult to remove completely until after the performance improvements are clear. Systems are easier to move, but if you tried to iron out every little inconsistency between the new vision and the current systems, you'd simply fail. Most transformational projects accept a "directional" approach rather than a predefined path. In other words, they know that they will learn as they go.

So are you up for the challenge? Can you articulate and sell the case for change? Can you generate some real excitement and rally enough support? There is a growing band of high-profile organizations that are either on the journey or ready to go, and they are listening to and learning from each other's experiences. CFOs are also beginning to realize that the scope of the changes is potentially greater than they first thought. It's not a familiar role for the CFO and the finance team. But they really can make a huge difference. The result will be a fitter, stronger, and more value-adding finance team and a more adaptive, lean, and ethical organization.

A CHECKLIST FOR THE CFO

- [ ] Start a debate around the performance of finance. Talk to both finance and business managers. Organize a survey and hold some workshops.

- [ ] Ask yourself some challenging questions. Are you prepared to devolve planning and decision making to teams closer to the customer? Are you prepared to change your own role and bring in some new people? Are you prepared for the long haul? Answering these questions will tell you a lot about your vision for improvement.

- [ ] Don't waste too much time on grand visions. Set some directional goals and get started. Learn as you go.

- [ ] Share your ideas with key people and gain their support.

☐ Don't alienate the managers most impacted by the changes. Involve them in the change process. They often have the best (and most practical) ideas for improvement.

☐ Whatever you do, don't make management life more complex! Avoid complex systems. Aim to simplify everything at every level.

☐ Build confidence by showing some early wins. Don't assume they will be self-evident. Point them out and celebrate your success.

☐ Recognize at the outset that this is a long-term journey. You need perseverance and patience. So take your time but maintain the momentum.

NOTES

INTRODUCTION

1. Claudia H. Deutsch, "Where Have All the Chief Financial Officers Gone?" *New York Times*, November 28, 2004, www.nytimes.com/2004/11/28/business/yourmoney/28cfos.html.

2. Ibid.

3. "Finance Under Pressure: How Innovative CFOs Do More with Less," *CFO Magazine* Research Series, January 2004, www.cfoenterprises.com/research.shtml.

4. Kris Frieswick, "Hard Times," *CFO Magazine*, November 1, 2004, www.cfo.com/article.cfm/3329236.

5. Ibid.

6. Deutsch, "Where Have All the Chief Financial Officers Gone?"

7. Francis J. Aguilar and Thomas W. Malnight, "General Electric Co.: Preparing for the 1990s," Harvard Business School Case 9-390-091, October 1990.

8. Quoted in David A. J. Axson, *Best Practices in Planning and Management Reporting* (Hoboken, NJ: John Wiley & Sons, 2003), 89.

9. John Goff, "Who's the Boss?" *CFO Magazine*, September 1, 2004, www.cfo.com/article.cfm/3127506.

10. Price Waterhouse Financial & Cost Management Team, *CFO: Architect of the Corporation's Future* (New York: John Wiley & Sons, 1997), 3–4.

11. John Goff, "Drowning in Data," *CFO Magazine*, November 1, 2003, www.cfo.com/printable/article.cfm/3010723.

12. Ibid.

13. Axson, *Best Practices in Planning and Management Reporting*, 64.

14. Tom Hoblitzell, "Best Practices in Planning and Budgeting," Answerthink white paper, 2004, 4.

15. Axson, *Best Practices in Planning and Management Reporting*, 60.

16. Hoblitzell, "Best Practices in Planning and Budgeting," 2.

17. According to the Hackett Group there are three types of finance processes: (1) transaction processes (accounts payable/receivable, travel and expense, fixed assets, credit, collections, customer billing, general accounting, external reporting, project accounting, cost accounting, cash management, tax accounting/reporting, and payroll); (2) control and risk management processes (budgeting, forecasting, business performance reporting, treasury management, tax planning, and internal auditing; and (3) decision support processes (cost analysis, business performance analysis, new business/pricing analysis, and strategic planning support). Hackett Group, *Best Practices 2002 Book of Numbers—Finance*, 1.

18. Patrick Slattery, "Apply Best Practices to External Financial Reporting," Answerthink paper, 2003, 5.

19. Ibid.

20. David M. Katz, "Is Finance Strategically Challenged?" *CFO Magazine*, May 19, 2004, www.cfo.com/article.cfm/3013927.

21. "CFOs: Driving Finance Transformation for the 21st Century," *CFO Magazine* Research Series, August 2002. www.cfoenterprises.com/research.shtml.

22. John Goff, "In the Fast Lane," *CFO Magazine*, December 1, 2004, www.cfo.com/printable/article.cfm/3419652.

23. Ibid.

24. Katz, "Is Finance Strategically Challenged?"

25. Answerthink press release, March 20, 2002, www.answerthink.com/news_and_events/press_release.

26. Mark Krueger, "Best Practices in Cost Rationalization," Answerthink report, 2004, 6.

27. Answerthink press release, October 22, 2004, www.answerthink.com/04_news/01_press/pr_2004_printfriendly/prpf_10222004_0.

28. A balanced scorecard is a management and measurement framework that views a business unit's performance from four perspectives: financial, customer, internal business process, and learning and growth. It enables managers to "map" and describe a business unit's strategy. See Robert S. Kaplan and David P. Norton, *The Strategy-Focused Organization: How Balanced Scorecard Companies Thrive in the New Business Environment* (Boston: Harvard Business School Press, 2001), 375.

29. Answerthink press release, October 22, 2004.

30. See Axson, *Best Practices in Planning and Management Reporting*.

31. Ibid., 59.

32. Hoblitzell, "Best Practices in Planning and Budgeting," 3.

33. Ibid., 8.

34. Katz, "Is Finance Strategically Challenged?"

35. Tom Buerkle, "Europe's Best CFOs," *Institutional Investor*, May 2005, 33–41.

36. W. Edwards Deming, *The New Economics for Industry, Government, Education* (Cambridge, MA: MIT Press, 2000), 31–33.

37. "CFOs: Driving Finance Transformation for the 21st Century," 8.

38. Taiichi Ohno, *Toyota Production System: Beyond Large-Scale Production* (Cambridge, MA: Productivity Press, 1988), ix.

CHAPTER 1

1. Larry D. Rosen, "Help! I'm Drowning in Information," *The National Psychologist* (January–February 2004), www.technostress.com/tnp44.html.

2. As quoted in David Adams, "Spinning Around," *Sydney Morning Herald,* May 20, 2003, www.smh.com.au/articles/2003/05/19/1053196515705.html.

3. Ibid.

4. Steve Morlidge, interview with author, January 26, 2005.

5. Chris Argyris, "Empowerment: The Emperor's New Clothes," *Harvard Business Review* (May–June 1998): 98–105.

6. Mark Krueger, "Best Practices in Cost Rationalization," Answerthink report, 2004, 4.

7. "CFOs: Driving Finance Transformation for the 21st Century," *CFO Magazine* Research Series, August 2002, www.cfoenterprises.com/research.shtml.

8. Krueger, "Best Practices in Cost Rationalization."

9. "CFOs: Driving Finance Transformation for the 21st Century."

10. Ken Lever, interview with author, February 11, 2005.

11. Hackett Benchmarking Solutions, http://www.thgi.com/pprfax.htm (accessed April 14, 2002).

12. David A. J. Axson, *Best Practices in Planning and Management Reporting* (Hoboken, NJ: John Wiley & Sons, 2003), 160.

13. Vinay Couto, Mark J. Moran, and Irmgard Heinz, "Not Your Father's CFO," *Strategy+Business* (Spring 2005): 1–10.

14. Brian Maskell and Bruce Baggaley, *Practical Lean Accounting* (New York: Productivity Press, 2004), 218–219.

15. Axson, *Best Practices in Planning and Management Reporting*, 59.

16. "Finance Under Pressure: How Innovative CFOs Do More with Less," *CFO Magazine* Research Series, January 2004, www.cfoenterprises.com/research.shtml.

17. Ibid.

18. H. Thomas Johnson and Anders Bröms, *Profit Beyond Measure: Extraordinary Results through Attention to Work and People* (London: Nicholas Brealey Publishing, 2000), 104.

19. John Goff, "Drowning in Data," *CFO Magazine,* November 1, 2003, www.cfo.com/printable/article.cfm/3010723.

20. Roy Harris, "What Works: Building a Strong Finance Team," *CFO Magazine.* November 1, 2002, www.cfo.com/printable/article.cfm/3007050.

21. Bill Gates, *Business @ The Speed of Thought* (London: Penguin Books, 1999), 18.

22. Lennart Francke, interview with author, January 24, 2005.

23. Answerthink press release, October 22, 2004, www.answerthink.com/04_news/01_press/pr_2004_printfriendly/prpf_10222004_0.

24. Robert S. Kaplan and David. P. Norton, *The Strategy-Focused Organization* (Boston: Harvard Business School Press, 2001), 14.

25. Jeffrey K. Liker, *The Toyota Way: 14 Management Principles from the World's Greatest Manufacturer* (London: McGraw-Hill, 2004), 5.

26. Robert Maluhan, "How CRM Impacts on the Bottom Line," *Marketing,* May 9, 2002, 25.

27. Liker, *The Toyota Way,* 162.

28. Adams, "Spinning Around."

29. Dr. Jan Wallander, *Decentralization: When and How to Make It Work* (Stockholm: SNS Förlag, 2003), 49.

30. Francke, interview.

CHAPTER 2

1. Gary Siegel, James E. Sorensen, and Sandra B. Richtermeyer, "Are You a Business Partner?" *Strategic Finance* (September 2003): 1–5.

2. Tom Buerkle, "Europe's Best CFOs," *Institutional Investor* (May 2005), 33–41.

3. Jim Parke, interview with author, January 25, 2005.

4. Abe De Ramos, "The Future of Outsourcing," *CFO Magazine,* June 15, 2005, www.cfo.com/printable/article.cfm/3860276.

5. Ibid.

6. Jim Bramante, Gregor Pillen, and Doug Simpson, *CFO Survey: Current State and Future Direction,* IBM Business Consulting Services, 2003, 18.

7. David A. J. Axson, *Best Practices in Planning and Management Reporting* (Hoboken, NJ: John Wiley & Sons, New Jersey, 2003), 65.

8. Ibid.

9. "Finance Transformed: How Leading Companies Are Succeeding," *CFO Magazine* Research Series, September 2003, www.cfoenterprises.com/research.shtml.

10. "CFOs: Driving Finance Transformation for the 21st Century," *CFO Magazine* Research Series, 2002, www.cfoenterprises.com/research.shtml.

11. Ulla K. Bunz and Jeanne D. Maes, "Learning Excellence: Southwest Airlines' Approach," *Managing Service Quality* 8, no. 3 (1998): 165.

12. "Finance Under Pressure: How Innovative CFOs Do More with Less," January 2004, www.cfoenterprises.com/research.shtml.

13. Ibid.

14. Ibid.

15. Thierry Moulonguet, interview with author, February 23, 2005.

16. Vinay Couto, Mark J. Moran, and Irmgard Heinz, "Not Your Father's CFO," *Strategy+Business* (Spring 2005): 1–10.

17. Clifton Leaf, "Temptation Is All Around Us," *Fortune*, November 18, 2002, 69.

18. Buerkle, "Europe's Best CFOs."

19. Ibid.

20. Siegel, Sorensen, and Richtermeyer, "Are You a Business Partner?"

21. Roy Harris, "Are You Ready for Your Close-up?" *CFO Magazine*, March 1, 2005, www.cfo.com/article.cfm/3709814.

22. "CFOs: Driving Finance Transformation for the 21st Century."

23. Couto, Moran, and Heinz, "Not Your Father's CFO."

24. Jim Parke, interview with author, January 25, 2005.

25. "Finance Seeks a Seat at the Strategy Table," *CFO Magazine* Research Series, July 2004, www.cfoenterprises.com/research.shtml.

26. John A. Byrne, "Visionary vs. Visionary," *BusinessWeek*, August 28, 2000, 122.

27. Alix Nyberg Stuart, "Keeping Secrets," *CFO Magazine*, June 1, 2005, www.cfo.com/printable/article.cfm/4007474.

28. Ken Lever, interview with author, February 11, 2005.

29. Jim Parke, interview with author, January 25, 2005.

30. Bramante, Pillen, and Simpson, *CFO Survey*, 8.

31. Gary Crittenden, interview with author, February 14, 2005.

32. Tim Reason, "Budgeting in the Real World," *CFO Magazine*, July 1, 2005, www.cfo.com/printable/article.cfm/4124788.

33. Tom Manley, interview with author, March 23, 2005.

34. Ibid.

35. W. A. Dimma, "Competitive Strategic Planning," *Business Quarterly* 50, no. 1 (Spring 1985), 25.

36. Quoted in *Enterprise Governance*, IFAC Report, 2003.

37. Andrew Campbell and Michael Goold, *Synergy* (Oxford: Capstone, 1998), 12.

38. Gary Hamel, *Leading the Revolution* (Boston: Harvard Business School Press, 2000), 47–48.

39. Steven E. Prokesch, "Unlearning the Power of Learning: An Interview with British Petroleum's John Browne," *Harvard Business Review* (September–October 1997), 147–168.

40. Robin Cooper and Robert S. Kaplan, *The Design of Cost Management Systems* (Englewood Cliffs, NJ: Prentice-Hall, 1991), 472.

41. Frederick F. Reichheld and W. Earl Sasser Jr., "Zero Defections: Quality Comes to Services," *Harvard Business Review* (September–October 1990): 105–111.

42. Gary Crittenden, interview with author, February 14, 2005.

CHAPTER 3

1. Tim Reason, "Budgeting in the Real World," *CFO Magazine*, July 1, 2005, www.cfo.com/printable/article.cfm/4124788.

2. Simon Caulkin, "Business Schools for Scandal," *Observer*, March 28, 2004, Management Section, 9.

3. Mitchel Resnick, "Changing the Centralized Mind," *Technology Review*, July 1994, http://llk.media.mit.edu/papers/archive/CentralizedMind.html.

4. Theodore Levitt, "Marketing Myopia," *Harvard Business Review Business Classics: Fifteen Key Concepts for Managerial Success* (September–October 1975): 1–12.

5. Howard W. Biederman, letter to the editor, *Financial Times*, April 7, 2001, 10.

6. John Seddon, *Freedom from Command & Control: A Better Way to Make the Work Work* (Buckingham, England: Vanguard Education Limited, 2003), 13.

7. Kevin Freiberg and Jackie Freiberg, *Nuts! Southwest Airlines' Crazy Recipe for Business and Personal Success* (Austin, TX: Bard Press Inc., 1996), 85–86.

8. Michael E. Porter, "Creating Tomorrow's Advantages," in *Rethinking the Future: Rethinking Business, Principles, Competition, Control & Complexity, Leadership, Markets and the World*, ed. Rowan Gibson (London: Nicholas Brealey Publishing, 1997), 53.

9. Ibid.

10. Jim Parke, interview with author, January 25, 2005.

11. Adapted from Deming's model. Deming was talking about a manufacturing system or subsystem, whereas we are referring to a business planning system. For example, when Deming talked about "plan" he meant have an idea for improving the system; check was "see if the idea works," "do" was "put it in the line," and "act" was "go live." See W. Edwards Deming, *Out of the Crisis,* 26th edition (Cambridge, MA: MIT Press, 1998).

12. Marko Bogoievski, interview with author, February 5, 2005.

13. Daniel Bogler and Adrian Michaels, "Attempting to Shift the Stretch-Goal Posts," *Financial Times,* January 2000.

14. Ken Lever, interview with author, February 11, 2005.

15. Gary Crittenden, interview with author, February 14, 2005.

16. Bogoievski, interview.

17. BBRT case study on Tomkins.

18. Joan Warner, "Chief Executives Can't Win at the Numbers Game," *Financial Times,* June 13, 2005, 12.

19. See C. C. Pinder, *Work Motivation in Organizational Behavior* (Upper Saddle River, NJ: Prentice Hall, 1998).

20. Warner, "Chief Executives Can't Win at the Numbers Game."

21. Steve Morlidge, interview with author, January 26, 2005.

22. Steve Morlidge, *Dynamic Performance Management,* program designed for MTP and Unilever 2004, 99.

23. Jeffrey Pfeffer, "Six Dangerous Myths About Pay," *Harvard Business Review* (May–June 1998): 109–119.

CHAPTER 4

1. Peter F. Drucker, "Managing for Business Effectiveness," *Harvard Business Review* (May–June 1963): 53–60.

2. Jeffrey K. Liker, *The Toyota Way* (London: McGraw-Hill, 2004), 192–193.

3. Quoted in ibid., 87.

4. I used a version of this example in my first book, *Transforming the Bottom Line* (Boston: Harvard Business School Press, 1995).

5. James P. Womack, Daniel T. Jones, and Daniel Roos, *The Machine That Changed the World* (New York: Rawson Associates, 1990), 13.

6. Ibid.

7. Simon Caulkin, "The Model That Really Computes," *Observer,* January 23, 2005, Business Section, 10.

8. Miles Brignall, "Gas Pressure Hits Danger Level," *Guardian Money,* September 17, 2005.

9. W. Edwards Deming, *Out of the Crisis,* 26th edition (Cambridge, MA: MIT Press, 1998), 315.

10. Simon Caulkin, "The Quality of Mersey," *Observer,* April 17, 2005, Business Section, 9.

11. "Catching Up with Uncle Sam," Engineering Employers Federation research report, December 2001.

12. Liker, *The Toyota Way,* 198.

13. John Wilton, interview with author, March 1, 2005.

14. Lennart Francke, interview with author, January 24, 2005.

15. Joan Magretta, "The Power of Virtual Integration: An Interview with Dell Computer's Michael Dell," *Harvard Business Review* (March–April 1998): 72–79.

16. Brian Maskell and Bruce Baggaley, *Practical Lean Accounting* (New York: Productivity Press, 2004), 191–192.

17. Stuart F. Brown, "Toyota's Global Body Shop," *Fortune,* February 9, 2004, 68–70.

18. Gary Hamel, "Bringing Silicon Valley Inside," *Harvard Business Review* (September–October 1999): 76.

19. Robert S. Kaplan and David P. Norton, *The Strategy-Focused Organization* (Boston: Harvard Business School Press, 2001), 296.

20. BBRT case study, 10 May 1999.

21. Wilton, interview.

22. Nicole Tempest, "Wells Fargo Online Financial Services (B)," Harvard Business School Case 9-199-019, 1998.

23. Liker, *The Toyota Way,* 237.

24. Ibid., 238.

25. Ibid.

26. Taiichi Ohno, *Toyota Production System: Beyond Large-Scale Production* (Cambridge, MA: Productivity Press, 1988), 17.

27. Ibid.

28. Liker, *The Toyota Way,* 244.

29. Ibid., 5.

CHAPTER 5

1. Margaret Wheatley and Myron Kellner-Rogers, "What Do We Measure and Why? Questions About the Uses of Measurement," The Berkana Institute, http://www.berkana.org/articles/whymeasure.html.

2. H. Thomas Johnson and Anders Bröms, *Profit Beyond Measure* (London: Nicholas Brealey Publishing, 2000), 69.

3. http://www.solonline.org/com/AR98/index.html.

4. The law was named after Charles Goodhart, a chief economic adviser to the Bank of England. The law was first stated in the 1980s in the context of the attempt by the government of Margaret Thatcher to conduct monetary policy on the basis of targets for broad and narrow money.

5. Wheatley and Kellner-Rogers, "What Do We Measure and Why?"

6. The Editors of *BusinessWeek* with Cynthia Green, *A BusinessWeek Guide: The Quality Imperative* (New York: McGraw-Hill Inc., 1994), 11.

7. http://www.solonline.org/com/AR98/index.html.

8. Robert Simons, *Levers of Organizational Design* (Boston: Harvard Business School Press, 2005), 104.

9. Lori Calabro, "On Balance: An Interview with Robert Kaplan and David Norton," *CFO Magazine*, February 2001.

10. David P. Norton, "Beware: The Unbalanced Scorecard," *Balanced Scorecard Report* 2, no. 2 (March–April 2000): 13–14.

11. Ibid.

12. Gary Hamel, *Strategy Decay and the Challenge of Creating New Wealth,* Strategos Institute Report, March 1999).

13. Ibid.

14. W. Edwards Deming, *Out of the Crisis*, 26th edition (Cambridge, MA: MIT Press, 1998), 309.

15. John Seddon, "Measurement and Management," www.lean-service .com/measurement.asp.

16. Gary Crittenden, interview with author, February 14, 2005.

17. Ken Lever, interview with author, February 11, 2005.

18. Simon Caulkin, "The Scary World of Mr. Mintzberg," *Observer*, January 26, 2003, Business Section, 10.

19. See Simons, *Levers of Organizational Design*, 89.

20. Jeremy Hope and Robin Fraser, *Beyond Budgeting* (Boston: Harvard Business School Press, 2003), 126.

CHAPTER 6

1. Jim Bramante, Gregor Pillen, and Doug Simpson, *CFO Survey: Current State and Future Direction*, IBM Business Consulting Services, 2003, 11.

2. Dan Durfee, "It's Better (and Worse) Than You Think," *CFO Magazine*, May 3, 2004, www.cfo.com/printable/article.cfm/3013527.

3. "Enterprise Governance—Getting the Balance Right," IFAC report, 2003.

4. Carol J. Loomis, "The 15% Delusion," *Fortune*, February 5, 2001, 48–53.

5. Ibid.

6. Ibid.

7. Carol J. Loomis, "Citigroup's CEO Chuck Prince Talks with Carol Loomis About Scandals, Profits, and the Company's Stock," *Fortune*, November 29, 2004, 45–51.

8. David S. Hilzenrath and Carrie Johnson, "SEC Tells Fannie Mae to Restate Earnings," *Washington Post*, December 16, 2004, A1 and A13.

9. "One-Third of Publicly-Traded Companies Do Not Accurately Portray Their True Financial Condition," *Businesswire*, June 18, 2004.

10. Jim Collins, "Good to Great," Fast Company (October 2001): 90–104.

11. Bill Gates, "What I Learned from Warren Buffett," *Harvard Business Review* (January–February 1996): 148–153.

12. Henry Mintzberg, "Musings on Management," *Harvard Business Review* (July–August 1998): 61–67.

13. W. Edwards Deming, *Out of the Crisis*, 26th edition (Cambridge, MA: MIT Press, 1998), 98.

14. Scott Leibs, "New Terrain," *CFO Magazine*, February 2004, www.cfo.com/printable/article.cfm/3011491.

15. Robert Simons, "Control in an Age of Empowerment," *Harvard Business Review* (March–April 1995), 80–88.

16. Leibs, "New Terrain."

17. Robert Simons, "How Risky Is Your Company?" *Harvard Business Review* (May–June 1999): 85–94.

18. Loomis, "The 15% Delusion."

19. Ibid.

20. Lori Calabro, "Above Board," *CFO Magazine*, October 1, 2003: 43–46.

21. Quoted in Simon Caulkin, "Keep It Simple—Not Stupid," *Observer*, February 27, 2003, 8.

22. Paul Y. Mang, Ansgar Richter, Jonathan D. Day, and John Roberts, "Has Pay for Performance Had Its Day?" *McKinsey Quarterly* 21, no. 4 (Fall 2002), http://www.mckinseyquarterly.com/article_page.aspx?ar=1233&L2=18&L3=31&srid=8&gp=1.

23. Kate Burgess and Norma Cohen, "Sainsbury Investors Urged to Vote Against Directors' Pay," *Financial Times*, July 6, 2005, 44.

24. Calabro, "Above Board."

25. Hilzenrath and Johnson, "SEC Tells Fannie Mae to Restate Earnings."

26. Louise O'Brien, "How to Restore the Fiduciary Relationship: An Interview with Eliot Spitzer," *Harvard Business Review* (May 2004): 71–77.

27. John W. Hunt, "Reward Systems and Disincentives," *Financial Times*, April 21, 1999, 21.

28. Robert Simons, *Levers of Organizational Design* (Boston, MA: Harvard Business School Press, 2005), 111.

29. Margaret J. Wheatley, *Leadership and the New Science* (San Francisco: Berrett-Koehler, 1999), 67–68.

30. Lennart Francke, interview with author, January 24, 2005.

31. Handelsbanken, *Annual Report*, 2000, 39.

32. Ibid.

33. Russ Banham, "Fear Factor," *CFO Magazine*, June 1, 2003, www.cfo.com/printable/article.cfm/3009436.

34. Ibid.

35. "Strategic Risk Management (2002)," *CFO Magazine* Research Series, Report, March 2002, www.cfoenterprises.com/research.shtml.

36. "The Future of Business Risk Management," conference sponsored by CFO Research Services, New York, March 26, 2002.

37. Ibid.

38. Ibid.

39. Ibid.

40. "Strategic Risk Management (2002)."

41. Ken Lever, interview with author, February 11, 2005.

42. "The Future of Business Risk Management."

43. Stephan Haeckel, *Adaptive Enterprise: Creating and Leading Sense-and-Respond Organizations* (Boston: Harvard Business School Press, 1999), 40.

44. Michael Schrage, "Daniel Kahneman: The Thought Leader Interview," *Strategy/Business* 33 (2003).

45. Matthew Leitch, "Open and Honest About Risk and Uncertainty," speech, IIR Risk Management Congress, London. July, 7, 2004, www.internalcontrolsdesign.co.uk/honest/index.html.

46. Kenneth G. McGee, *Heads Up: How to Anticipate Business Surprises and Seize Opportunities First* (Boston: Harvard Business School Press, 2004), 101–103.

47. Bill Gates, *Business @ The Speed of Thought* (London: Penguin Books, 1999), 179.

48. Lever, interview.

49. Tom Manley, interview with author, March 23, 2005.

CHAPTER 7

1. John Wilton, interview with author, March 1, 2005.

2. Jeremy Hope and Robin Fraser, *BBRT Case Report on Svenska Handelsbanken*, May 6, 1998.

3. Steve Morlidge, interview with author, January 26, 2005.

4. Marko Bogoievski, interview with author, February 5, 2005.

5. Morlidge, interview.

6. Gary Crittenden, interview with author, February 14, 2005.

7. Wilton, interview.

8. Ken Lever, interview with author, February 11, 2005.

9. Crittenden, interview.

10. Lever, interview.

11. "Corporate Performance Management: What Finance Must Do to Move the Needle," *CFO Magazine* Research Series, August 2004, www.cfoenterprises.com/research.shtml.

12. Bogoievski, interview.

13. Lever, interview.

14. Crittenden, interview.

15. Ibid.

16. Lever, interview.

17. Wilton, interview.

INDEX

ABOUT THE AUTHOR

JEREMY HOPE is cofounder of the Beyond Budgeting Round Table (BBRT), a members' collaborative dedicated to helping firms improve their performance management processes. He is coauthor (with Robin Fraser) of the book *Beyond Budgeting: How Managers Can Break Free from the Annual Performance Trap*, published by Harvard Business School Press, and the *Harvard Business Review* article "Who Needs Budgets?" He is also coauthor (with his brother Tony Hope) of *Transforming the Bottom Line* (1995) and *Competing in the Third Wave* (1997), both published by Harvard Business School Press. He can be reached at jeremyhope@bbrt.org.